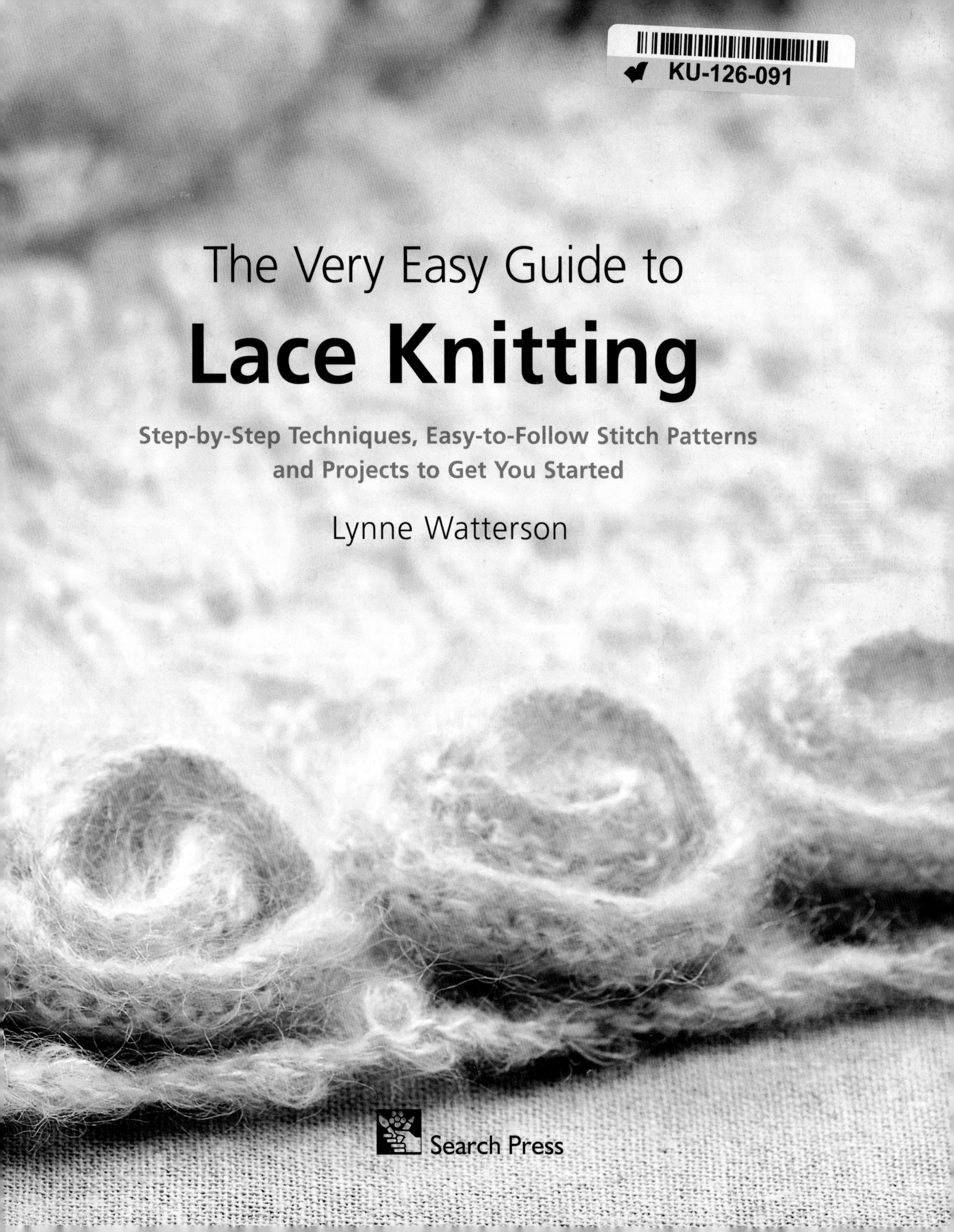

The Very Easy Guide to

Lace Knitting

Step-by-Step Techniques, Easy-to-Follow Stitch Patterns and Projects to Get You Started

Lynne Watterson

Search Press

A QUARTO BOOK

Published in 2011 by Search Press Ltd
Wellwood
North Farm Rd
Tunbridge Wells
Kent TN2 3DR

Reprinted 2011

ISBN: 978-1-84448-651-9

Conceived, designed and produced by
Quarto Publishing plc
The Old Brewery
6 Blundell Street
London
N7 9BH

QUAR.GLK

Senior editor: Katie Crous
Copy editor: Liz Jones
Proofreader: Diana Chambers
Art editor: Joanna Bettles
Photographers: Lizzie Orme,
Phil Wilkins
Illustrator: Neal Monk Stevens
Art director: Caroline Guest
Creative director: Moira Clinch
Publisher: Paul Carslake

Colour separation by PICA Digital Pte Ltd, Singapore
Printed in Singapore by Star Standard Pte Ltd

10 9 8 7 6 5 4 3 2

contents

introduction

I have lost count of the number of knitters I've met who have expressed a fear of lace knitting. Knitting lace doesn't have to be daunting and I hope this book will banish those fears once and for all.

The simple-to-follow lessons in this book take you through the process of knitting, from the wide variety of beautiful yarns available and the basic tools required to knit them, the knitting basics – cast on, cast off, knit and purl – to perfect seaming and finishing touches that add that all-important finish.

The lace knits are divided into four lessons: Eyelet patterns, Lace panels, Lace patterns and Lace edgings. Each lesson opens with an essential lace technique in a simple step-by-step format – featuring both written instructions and clear photographs.

The techniques are followed by a selection of stunning stitch patterns worked in a soft pastel colour palette.

To complete each lesson, a collection of simple stylish projects has been designed using a selection of the stitch patterns – from a child's hat and scarf – ideal for beginners – to a sumptuous wrap, for the more experienced.

The patterns use little or no shaping, making it easier to keep patterns correct, so go on, give lace knitting a try and enjoy!

This book is dedicated to my beautiful daughter Lauren. Thank you for your endless love and support. I love you.

about this book

This book guides you through the entire process of lace knitting, from the very basics of knitting, through the different stitches and patterns, to making projects with the perfect finish.

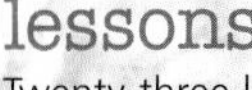

lessons

Twenty-three lessons teach you all you need to know, with step-by-step artworks and photography to ensure clarity.

Written patterns provide clear instruction

Charts provide a quick visual reference

Perfectly knitted examples show the individual stitches and the overall pattern

Pattern rows are highlighted with markers for additional clarity

Step-by-step photography breaks down the instructions into easy-to-follow parts, showing close-ups of essential detail

Understanding the patterns and charts

For a key to the abbreviations used in the patterns and the symbols used in the charts, turn to page 140.

Yarn information

The details of the specific yarn used in each project are supplied on page 144, but you can choose your own yarns, following the yarn type given next to the symbol on the sample pages.

the lace knits

Large swatches of the different stitches feature throughout, with all the information you need to emulate the design.

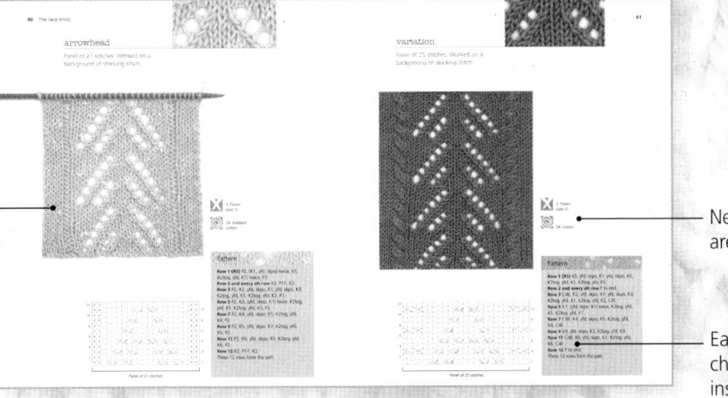

Good-sized examples show clearly individual stitches and the overall pattern

Needle size and yarn information are given throughout

Easy-to-follow patterns and charts provide the essential instructions

projects

Put everything you've learnt into practice and make beautiful items for you and your home.

Patterns, materials lists and size and tension details provide the essential information you need to make your chosen item

Concise instructions guide you through the finishing process/ additional elements

Photographs show the end product and suggest uses/ placements

Finishing

To find out how to add a professional and decorative finish to your projects, and how to care for them once they're in use, turn to pages 126–139.

lesson 1 yarns

Knitting yarns are usually produced by spinning fibres together. There are two main categories of fibre – natural and synthetic. Natural fibres are divided into two categories: animal and vegetable. Animal fibres include wool, angora, cashmere and silk; vegetable fibres include cotton, linen and ramie.

The stitch samples and projects in this book have been made using natural fibres to show the stitch patterns off to their best advantage and to enhance the texture and durability of the projects.

Mohair is spun from the hair of the angora goat. It is both soft and fluffy, as well as being very warm due to its great insulating properties.

Wool is the yarn most commonly associated with knitting. Spun from the fleece of sheep, it has many excellent qualities – durability, elasticity and warmth. It is available in a wide range of colours, as well as 100 per cent undyed virgin wool.

Cotton is a soft, natural plant fibre that grows around the seeds of the cotton plant. The yarn produced by spinning the fibres is ideal for all seasons – warm in the winter and cool in the summer. Cotton gives a special crispness to patterns, making the detail stand out well, but it tends to lack resilience. Mercerised cotton is chemically treated to make it more lustrous and less liable to shrink.

understanding yarn labels

The band or label attached to yarn gives you important information about the yarn, helping you to make the right choice for your project. In a prominent position on the band you will find the company logo followed by the yarn name and its knitted weight. The band also tells you what the yarn is made from, the length and weight of yarn in the ball, the shade and dye lot numbers, the recommended knitting needle sizes and in some cases the recommended knitted tension (see page 24). Aftercare and washing instructions are shown by a list of symbols (see page 139).

It is important to use yarn from the same dye lot for a project, as slight differences in colour could be noticeable in the finished piece.

Tip

Keep one label as a reference with the tension swatch in a safe place, together with any leftover yarn and spare buttons. The label can be referred to when washing the item and spare yarn and buttons can be used for repairs.

50 g – 1.75 oz
102 m – 110 yds

55% Cotton • Coton
45% Nylon • Nylon

Purchase sufficient yarn of this dye lot as the next lot may differ slightly in shade.

Alpaca is a soft, luxurious yarn spun from the fleece of the alpaca – an animal related to the llama. It is a strong yarn with excellent thermal properties and is valued highly for its silky feel, weightlessness and warmth.

Synthetic fibres such as acrylic, polyester and polyamide are derived from coal and petroleum products and are spun in various ways to resemble natural fibre yarns. These yarns are usually machine washable; however, care should be taken when blocking and pressing – too much heat will cause the knitting to lose its shape and the stitch pattern its crispness.

Silk is spun from the cocoons of silkworms. It is a smooth, luxurious yarn with a soft sheen, cool to the touch and very strong.

yarn weights

Yarns are available in many different weights or thicknesses – from very fine to extra-chunky. Your chosen pattern will tell you which weight of yarn is required and the needle sizes used to achieve the designer's recommended tension (number of stitches and rows over a given measurement, see page 24).

lesson 2 knitting kit

Before you begin any knitting project, read the materials section to see what size knitting needles are required and what other equipment, if any, is needed. Here you will find details of the equipment that will form the basis of your knitting workbox and a selection of other equipment that isn't essential but could be useful as you move onto more complicated projects.

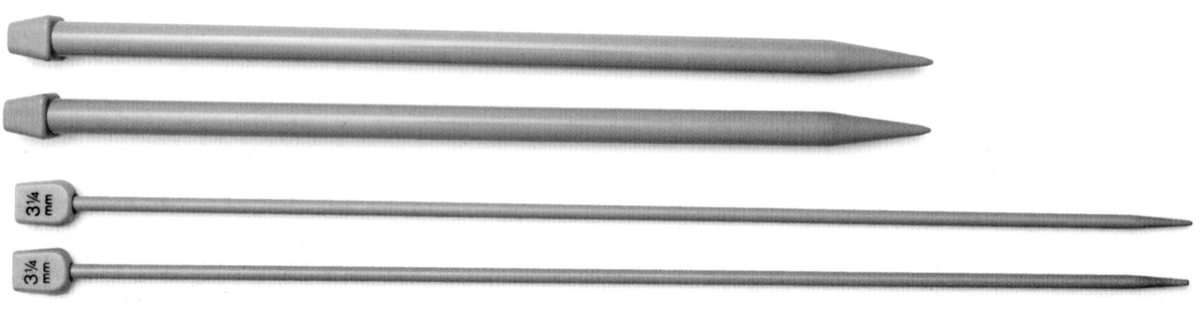

the essentials

Pairs of knitting needles

Knitting needles come in a wide range of sizes to suit different weights of yarn and a variety of lengths to suit the number of stitches required for a particular project – from 20cm (8in) to 40cm (16in). They are available in various materials from rigid aluminium to flexible bamboo. Metal needles are made mostly from aluminium, though some are made from steel. These strong materials are particularly suited to small needle sizes. Plastic needles are lightweight and flexible, but can become sticky in humid conditions. Larger-sized needles are made of plastic to reduce their weight. Wood and bamboo needles are lightweight and flexible and virtually silent when knitting. Some knitters find them less tiring to the hands than either plastic or metal.

Pins

Long glass-headed pins or knitting pins with a large head are best suited to knitted fabrics – they are easy to see on the knitting and will not get lost in the fabric.

Tapestry needles

A blunt-tipped needle with a large eye is required for sewing seams and sewing in ends. These are available in different sizes to suit different weights of yarn; tapestry needles may be used for fine yarns.

Scissors

Use small, sharp scissors to cut yarn. Don't attempt to break the yarn with your fingers as this may result in you cutting your skin.

Stitch holders

These long pins are used for holding groups of stitches until they are required – such as the centre of a neckline.

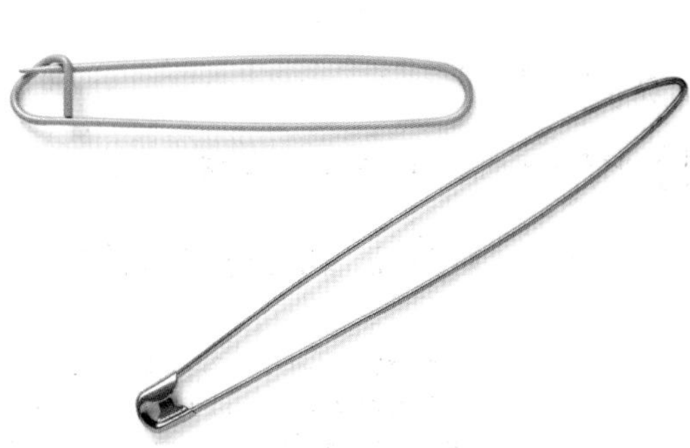

Tape measure

These come in various materials, colours and casings – choose one that has clear numbers and is easy to read. A tape measure stretches with use so buy a new one from time to time to ensure accurate measurements.

the extras

Graph paper, pencil and eraser

If you want to design your own lace patterns you'll find it easy to plan and see your design if you chart on graph paper. Graph paper with eight or 10 squares to 2.5cm (1in) is a useful size, or you can use a larger-scale graph paper with 5mm (¼in) squares.

Row counters

A row counter can be very useful when working lace patterns to help you keep track of the pattern and the repeats. The barrel type is slipped onto a straight needle and pushed up to the knob. If using large-sized straight needles you will need the clutch type.

Ring markers

These small plastic rings are used to mark a particular place along a row and are slipped from row to row. They are available in various sizes – choose a size that fits loosely over the needles so it is easy to slip from one needle tip to the other.

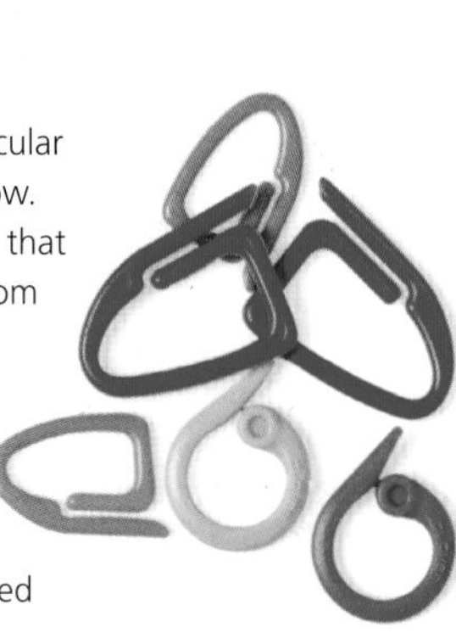

Split markers

Made from plastic, these split-ring markers are used to mark a particular stitch. They can be added and removed at any time.

Teasel brush

This is a very useful tool when working with fluffy yarns such as mohair. Use it to brush up the surface to enhance the hair.

lesson 3 circular needles

Consisting of two short conventional knitting needles joined by a thin flexible cord, circular needles can be used to knit in the round – enabling items such as bags or sweaters to be worked in a tubular fashion without seams – or to work backwards and forwards in rows, particularly useful when working on a large number of stitches.

Circular needles can be used to knit in rows in the same way as conventional knitting needles, and they are becoming increasingly popular, especially for working big projects such as throws or wraps. The long linking cord enables large numbers of working stitches to be stored safely without the risk of dropped stitches. In addition, the weight of the work is distributed evenly along the cord, making heavy pieces easier to handle.

They are available in the same diverse range of materials as ordinary knitting needles. Stainless steel, aluminium, nickel-plated brass and resin are all popular options, while bamboo needles are lightweight and warmer to the touch. The pliable cables are generally thin hollow plastic tubes that meet the needles in a smooth joint over which yarns can slide easily without snagging.

Working in the round

Cast on the number of stitches required. Mark the beginning of the round by placing a ring marker or a loop of thread in a contrasting colour onto the tip of the right-hand needle. Bring the needle ends together making sure the stitches are not twisted around the needle. Work the stitches from the left-hand needle onto the right-hand needle, pushing the stitches to be worked along the left-hand needle and the worked stitches down the right-hand needle, so all the stitches slip around the cord.

When you reach the marker you will have completed one round. Slip the marker from the left-hand needle onto the right-hand needle and work the next round. The right side of the knitting is always facing you.

Working in rows

Work as for 'Working in the round', but turn the work when you reach the marker and work back across the stitches for the second row and each subsequent row. The right and wrong side will be facing you on alternate rows.

use the right circular needle

Circular needles come in a range of sizes that correspond with standard knitting needles, and in various cord lengths. The choice depends on the yarn and the number of stitches – the pattern you work from will state the size required. Special circular needles for lace knitting are generally made of lightweight, smooth metal with extra-long tapered tips and a completely smooth transition from needle to cord to protect fine yarns. Most circular needles are permanently fixed to the cord. However, there are circular needle systems now on the market, including some for lace knitting. These provide a range of different sized needle tips together with alternative lengths of pliable cord that are easily interchangeable.

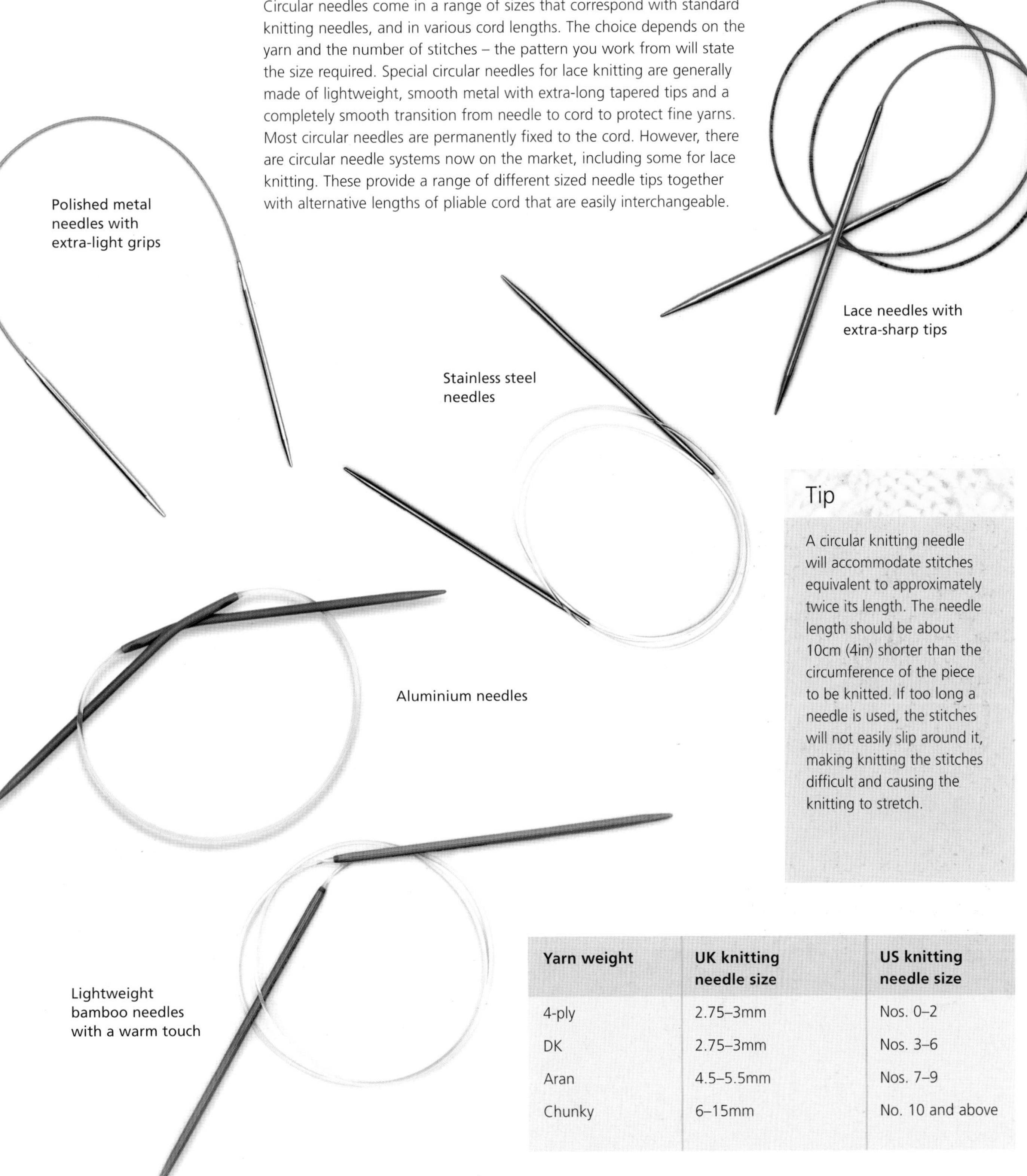

Polished metal needles with extra-light grips

Lace needles with extra-sharp tips

Stainless steel needles

Aluminium needles

Lightweight bamboo needles with a warm touch

Tip

A circular knitting needle will accommodate stitches equivalent to approximately twice its length. The needle length should be about 10cm (4in) shorter than the circumference of the piece to be knitted. If too long a needle is used, the stitches will not easily slip around it, making knitting the stitches difficult and causing the knitting to stretch.

Yarn weight	UK knitting needle size	US knitting needle size
4-ply	2.75–3mm	Nos. 0–2
DK	2.75–3mm	Nos. 3–6
Aran	4.5–5.5mm	Nos. 7–9
Chunky	6–15mm	No. 10 and above

knitting basics

Cast on, cast off, knit, purl, stocking stitch, reverse stocking stitch, garter stitch, moss stitch, tension and reading charts – simple steps for perfect results.

lesson 4 casting on

There are several methods of casting on – here we show the thumb method, both English and Continental, and the cable method. These are the most frequently used methods. Unless a pattern states a particular cast on, choose the one you are most comfortable with.

Tip

When you make your slip knot loop, ensure you leave a long enough end of yarn to cast on the number of stitches required. You need 1m (1yd) of yarn to cast on around 100 stitches in standard weight yarn.

making a slip knot loop

Before you begin your cast on, you first need to make a slip knot loop. This is placed on one needle and is counted as the first stitch.

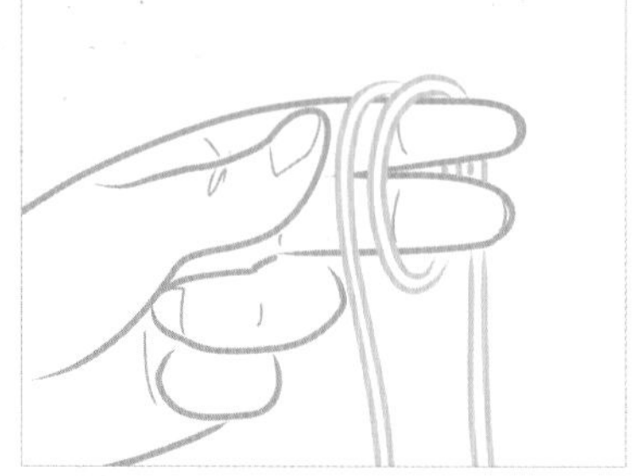

1 Leaving a long end, wind the yarn from the ball around two fingers of your left hand to form a circle.

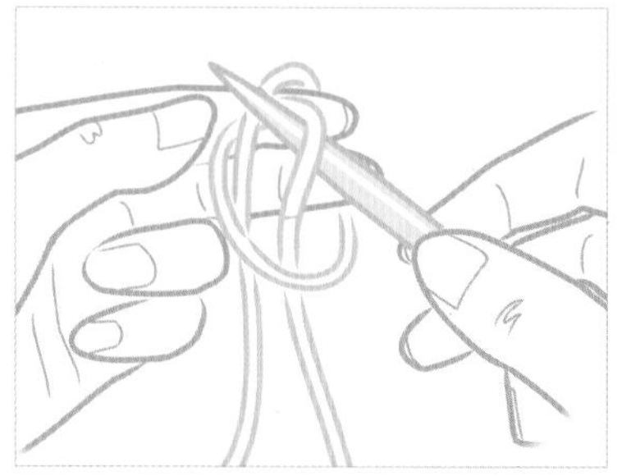

2 Use one of your knitting needles to pull a loop of yarn from the ball through the circle.

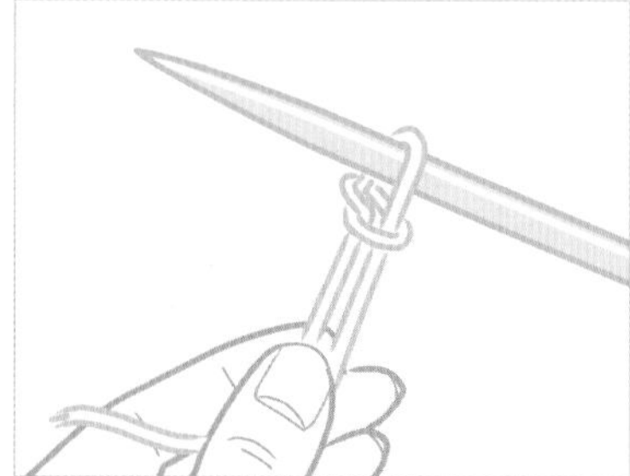

3 Pull the end from the ball of yarn to tighten the loop on the knitting needle. This loop forms your first stitch.

casting on – thumb method (English)

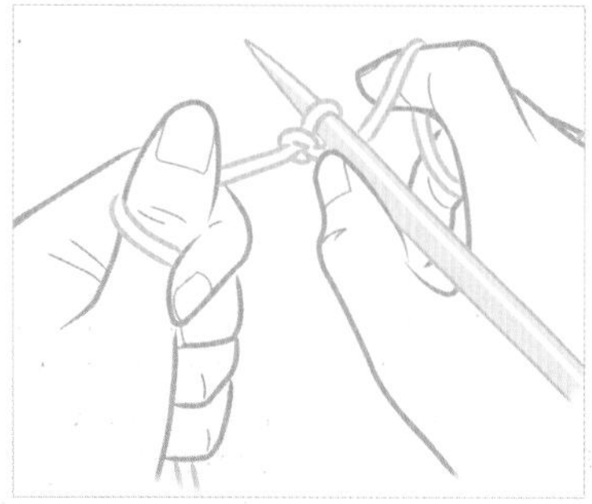

1 Make a slip knot loop on one needle. Hold the needle with the slip knot loop in your right hand. Gripping the loose end of the yarn in the palm of your left hand, wind the yarn clockwise around your thumb.

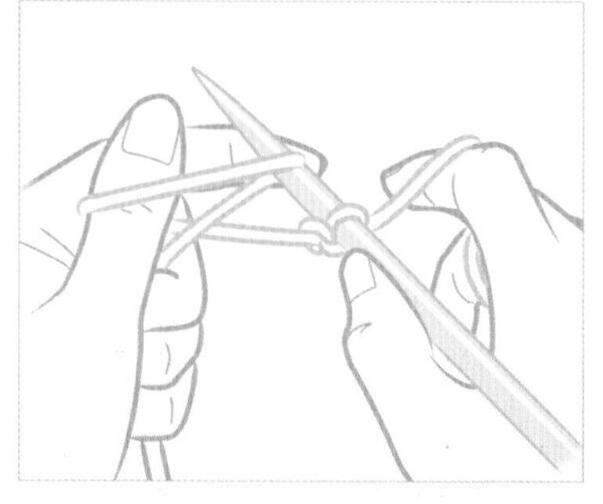

2 Insert the needle into the loop on your thumb from front to back ready to make the next stitch.

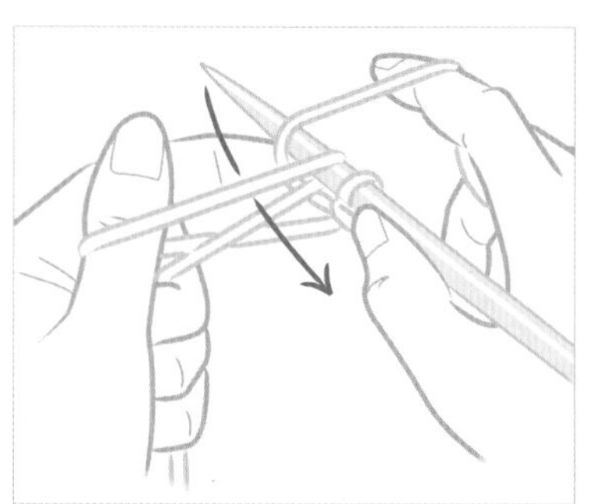

3 Now take the yarn from the ball under the needle and between the needle and your thumb. Draw the needle through the loop and remove your thumb. Pull the end of yarn to tighten the stitch. Continue to cast on stitches in this way.

casting on – thumb method (Continental)

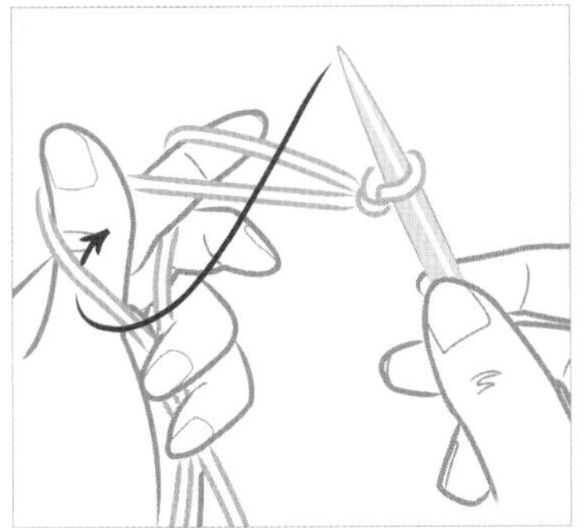

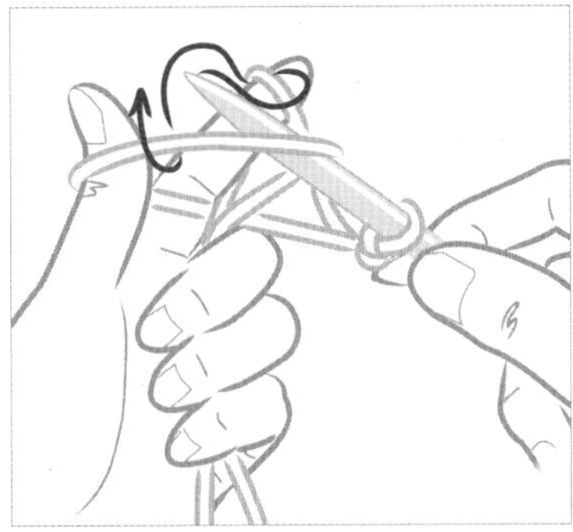

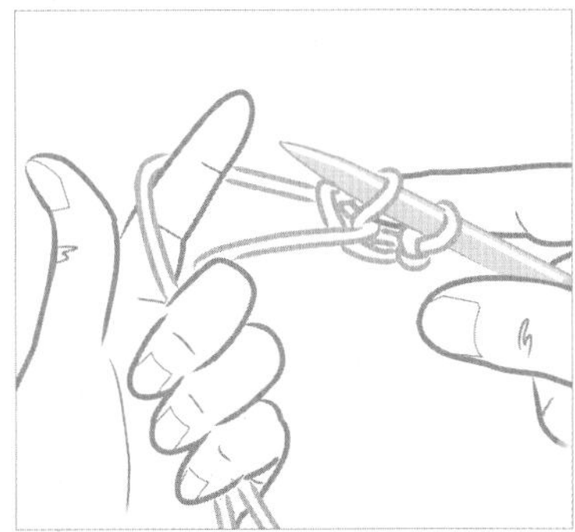

1 Make a slip knot loop on one needle. Hold the needle with the slip knot loop in your right hand. Take the yarn from the ball over the index finger of your left hand and grip both ends of the yarn in the palm of your left hand, then wind the yarn clockwise around your thumb.

2 Insert the needle under the yarn across the front of your thumb, then under the yarn across your index finger, and pull a loop through the loop on your thumb.

3 Remove your thumb and pull the ends of the yarn to tighten the stitch. Continue to cast on stitches in this way, making sure the stitches are even and move freely on the needle.

casting on – two-needle method or cable cast on

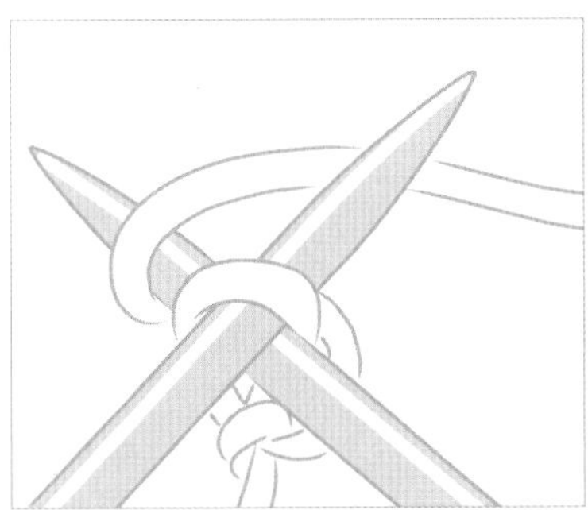

1 Make a slip knot loop, about 12cm (5in) from the end of the yarn. Hold the needle with the slip knot loop in your left hand and insert the right-hand needle into the front of the loop from front to back. Take the yarn from the ball under the right-hand needle and up between the two needles.

2 Draw the right-hand needle back and towards you, pulling the yarn through the slip knot loop to make a new stitch, then transfer the stitch to the left-hand needle.

3 Now insert the right-hand needle between the two stitches on the left-hand needle and take the yarn under the right-hand needle and up between the needles. Draw a loop through and transfer the new stitch to the left-hand needle. Continue to cast on stitches in this way.

lesson 5

knit and purl

Knit and purl stitch are the two basic knitting stitches and are used in various combinations to make up most stitch patterns. Knit stitch, when used alone, creates a reversible fabric called garter stitch (see page 20). Alternate rows of knit stitch and purl stitch create a stocking stitch fabric.

The fabric is knitted in rows with each row knitted from right to left, transferring the stitches from the left-hand needle to the right-hand needle. At the end of each row the work is turned, ready to work the next row.

knit stitch

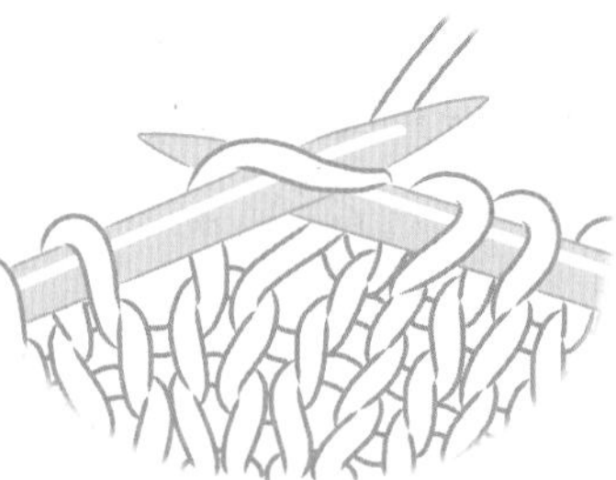

1 Hold the needle with the stitches in your left hand and the yarn from the ball in your right hand. Insert the right-hand needle into the first stitch on the left-hand needle from front to back.

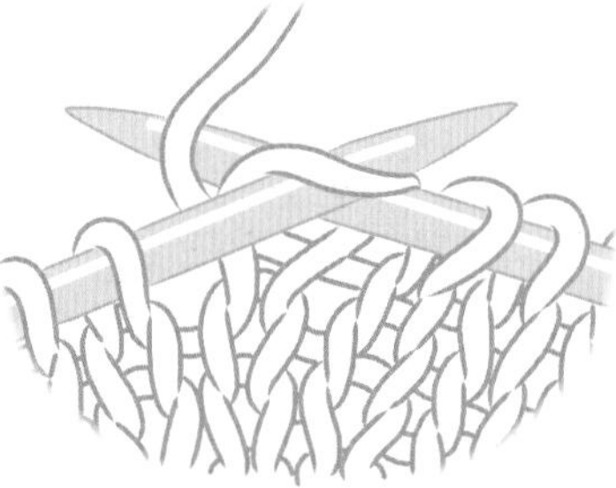

2 Take the yarn under the right-hand needle, between the two needles and over the right-hand needle.

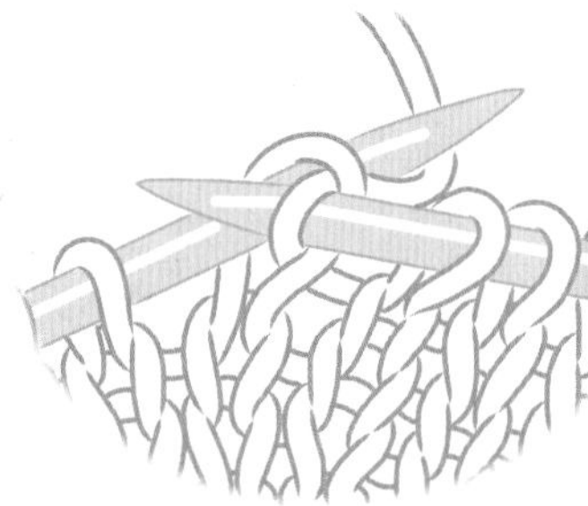

3 With the right-hand needle draw the yarn through the stitch, so forming a new stitch on the right-hand needle. Slip the original stitch off the left-hand needle to complete the first knit stitch. Knit into each stitch in this way until all stitches have been knitted from the left-hand needle onto the right-hand needle.

purl stitch

1 Hold the needle with the stitches in your left hand and the yarn from the ball in your right hand. Insert the right-hand needle into the first stitch on the left-hand needle from back to front.

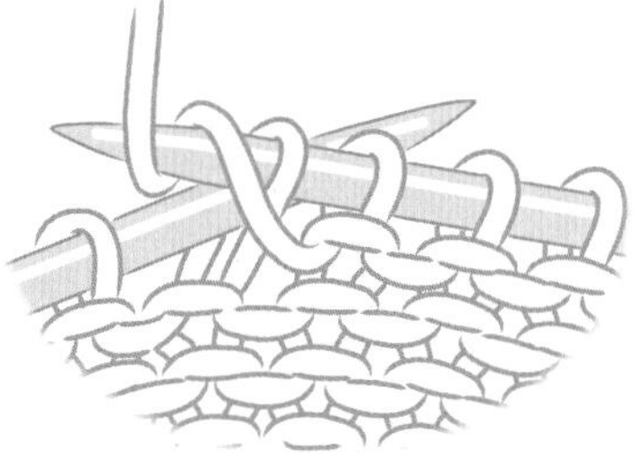

2 Take the yarn over the right-hand needle, between the two needles and under the right-hand needle.

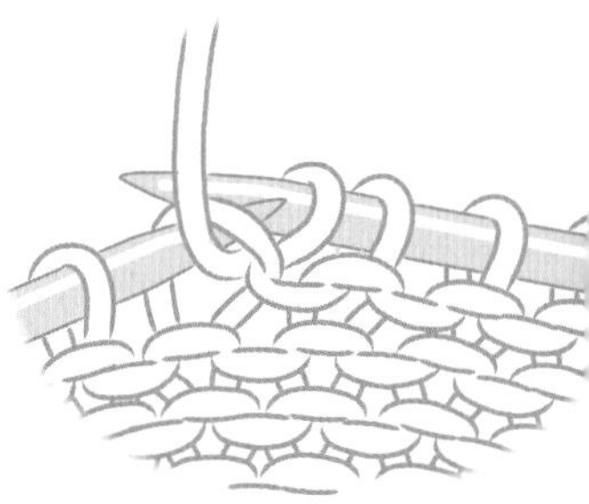

3 With the right-hand needle draw the yarn through the stitch, so forming a new stitch on the right-hand needle. Slip the original stitch off the left-hand needle to complete the first purl stitch. Purl into each stitch in this way until all stitches have been knitted from the left-hand needle onto the right-hand needle.

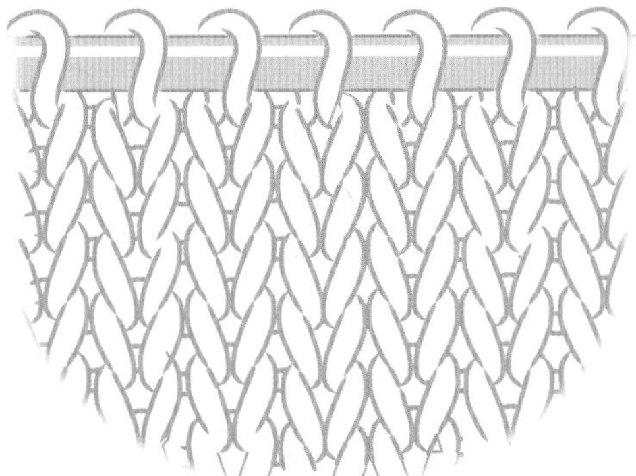

Stocking stitch

By knitting every right-side row and purling every wrong-side row a stocking stitch fabric is produced.

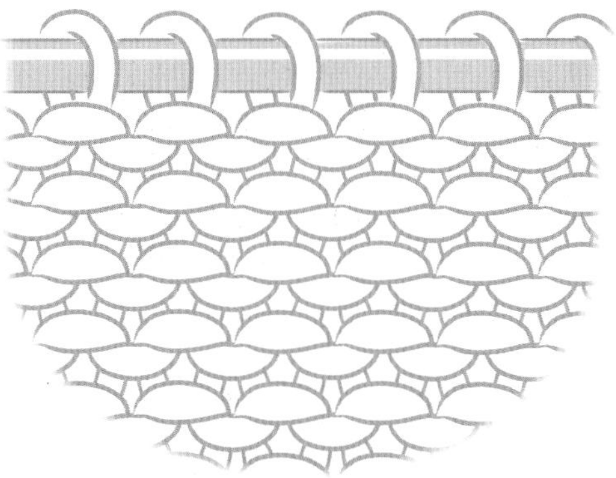

Reverse stocking stitch

By purling every right-side row and knitting every wrong-side row a reverse stocking stitch is produced.

knit and purl through the back of the loop

To give a stitch a twisted appearance and make it firmer you can work into the back of the loop.

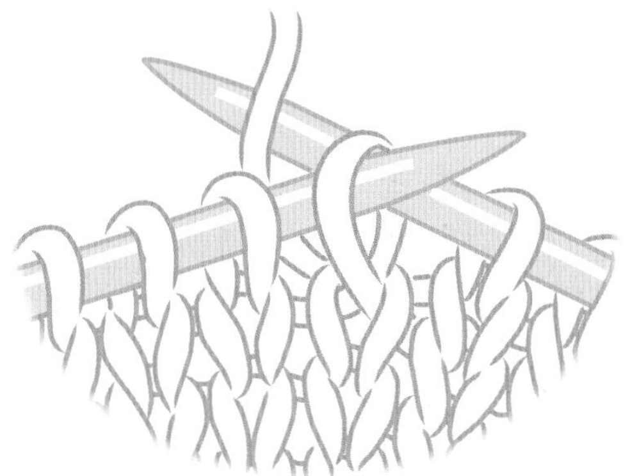

1 To knit through the back of the loop, insert the right-hand needle into the back of the next stitch on the left-hand needle from front to back and knit it in the usual way.

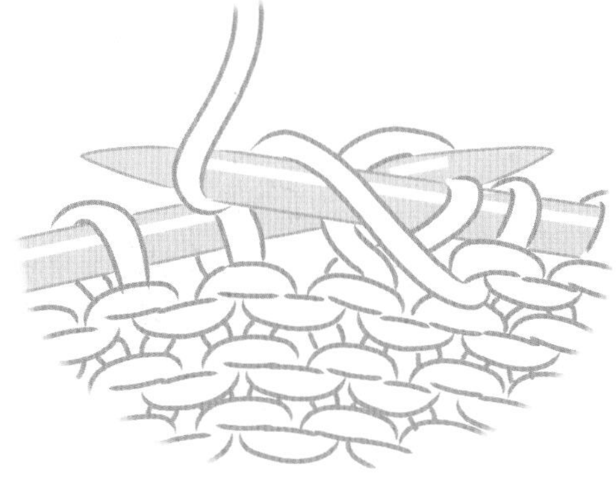

2 To purl through the back of the loop, insert the right-hand needle into the back of the next stitch on the left-hand needle from back to front and purl it in the usual way.

lesson 6 reversible fabrics

Reversible knitted fabrics include those worked in garter stitch and moss stitch. Both of these stitches can be worked as a simple panel between decorative lace panels.

garter stitch

Garter stitch is a simple, reversible fabric that is formed by working every row in knit stitch. It takes a little longer to 'grow' than stocking stitch because two rows show as only one row.

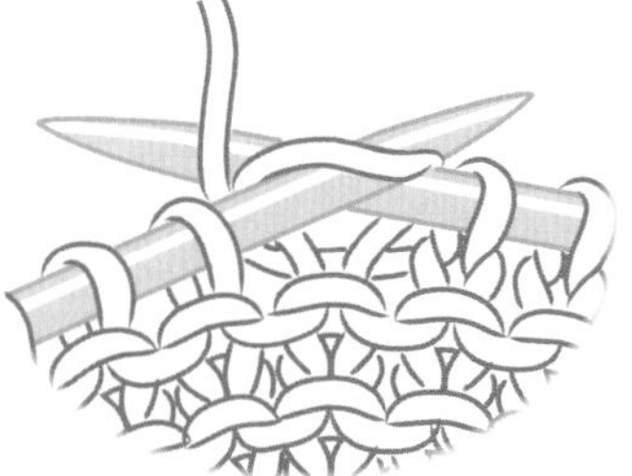

1 Hold the needle with the stitches in your left hand. Use the right-hand needle to knit the first row – 'V' stitches are formed on the front of the knitting and ridges on the back.

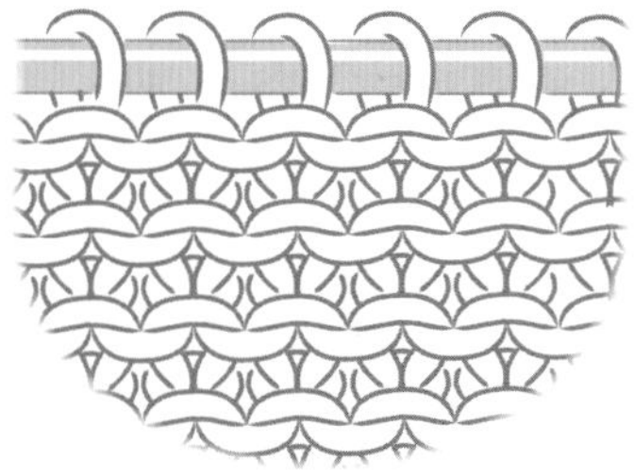

2 Continue to knit every row in this way to produce a garter stitch fabric.

Tip

When using garter stitch in conjunction with lace panels you will need to block the fabric carefully to open out the length of the garter stitch sections.

moss stitch

Moss stitch is another simple stitch to work and is an ideal fabric to team with lace. It is produced by knitting and purling alternate stitches across a row and knitting purl stitches and purling knit stitches on subsequent rows.

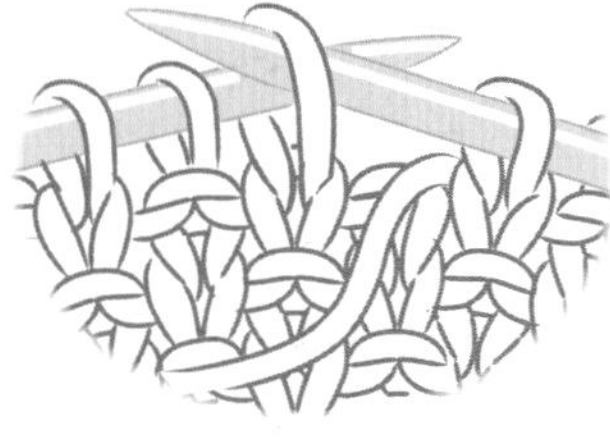

1 Cast on an odd number of stitches and hold the needle with the stitches in your left hand. Use the right-hand needle to knit the first stitch, bring the yarn to the front between the needles and purl the next stitch.

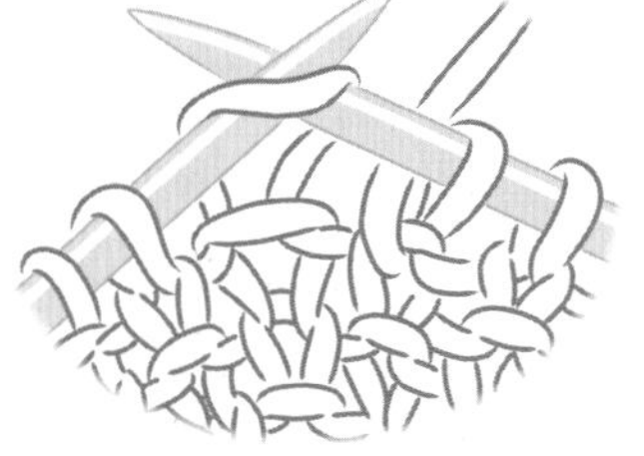

2 Take the yarn to the back and knit the next stitch. Now purl one stitch then knit one stitch all the way across the row. Each knit stitch will produce a 'V' on the front of the fabric and each purl stitch a ridge.

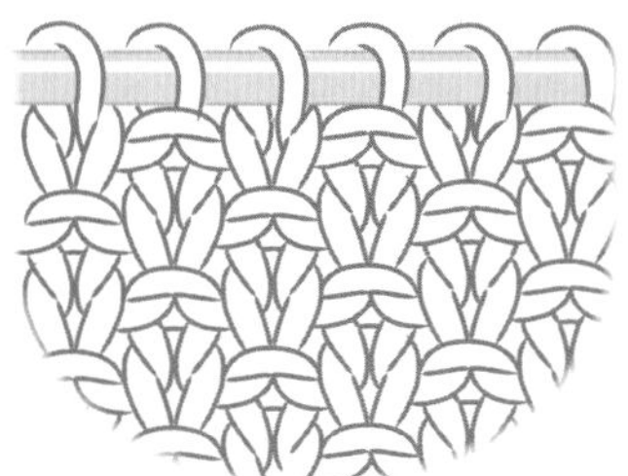

3 On the next row a 'V' (knit stitch) is worked over each ridge and a ridge (purl stitch) over each 'V'. Knit one stitch, then purl one stitch across the row. Continue to work every row in this way to produce a moss stitch fabric.

lesson 7 casting off

Stitches are cast off to complete your knitting and when a group of stitches is to be decreased – for a buttonhole, an armhole or a neckline. When casting off stitches it is important that an even tension is maintained – neither too tight nor too loose – and that it is elastic. Cast off in the stitch pattern being used, unless stated otherwise.

casting off technique

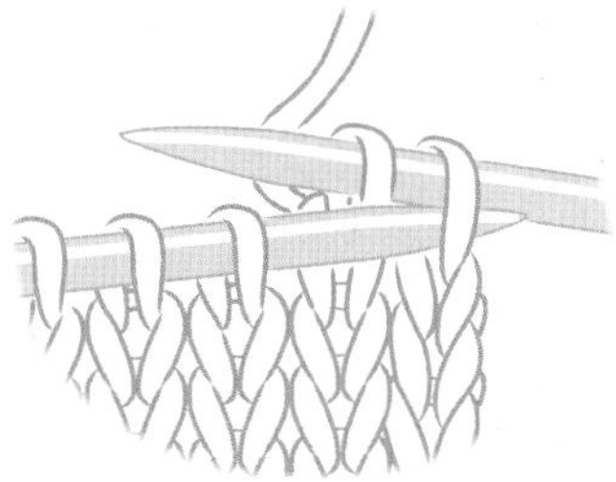

1 When casting off on a knit row, knit the first two stitches so that they are transferred onto the right-hand needle. Insert the left-hand needle, from left to right, into the front of the first stitch on the right-hand needle.

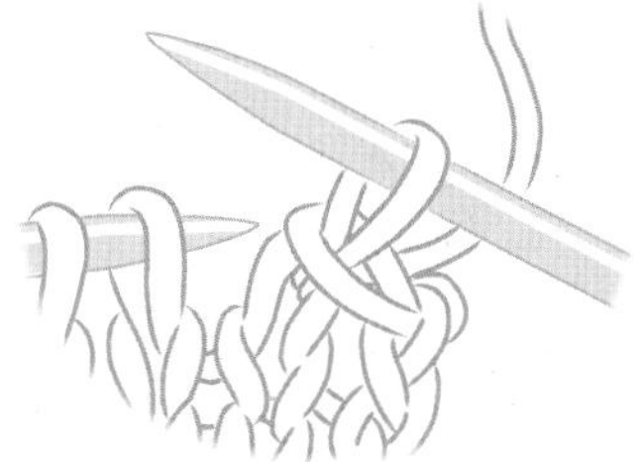

2 Use the left-hand needle to lift the first stitch over the second stitch and off the needle. The first stitch has been cast off and the second stitch remains on the right-hand needle.

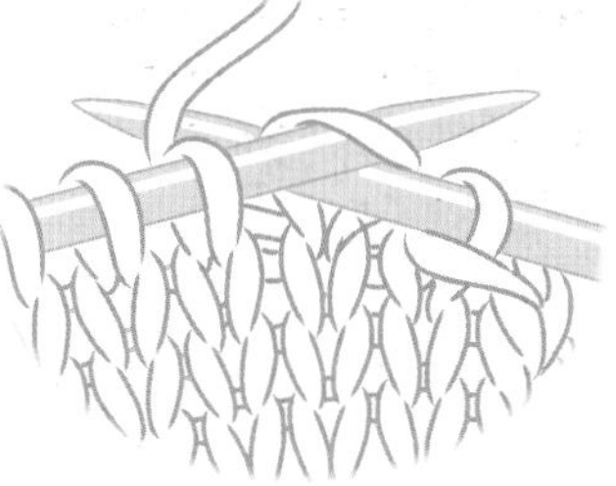

3 Knit the next stitch and repeat Step 2 to cast off one stitch. Continue to cast off stitches in this way until one stitch remains on the right-hand needle.

4 To secure the last stitch, cut off the yarn about 10cm (4in) from the knitting and draw the end through the last stitch. Pull the end to tighten.

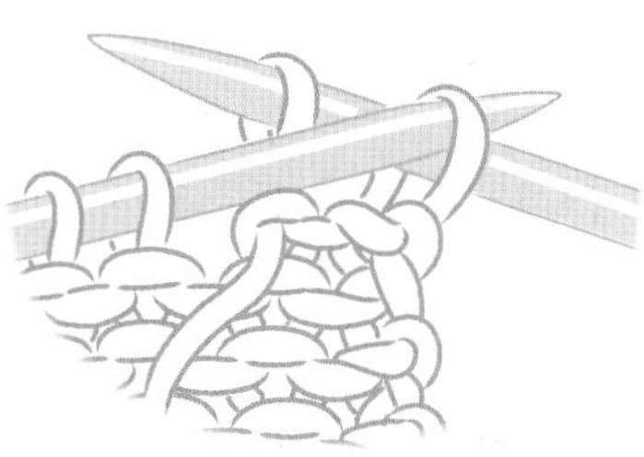

5 When casting off on a purl row, purl the first two stitches so that they are transferred onto the right-hand needle. Insert the left-hand needle, from left to right, into the front of the first stitch on the right-hand needle.

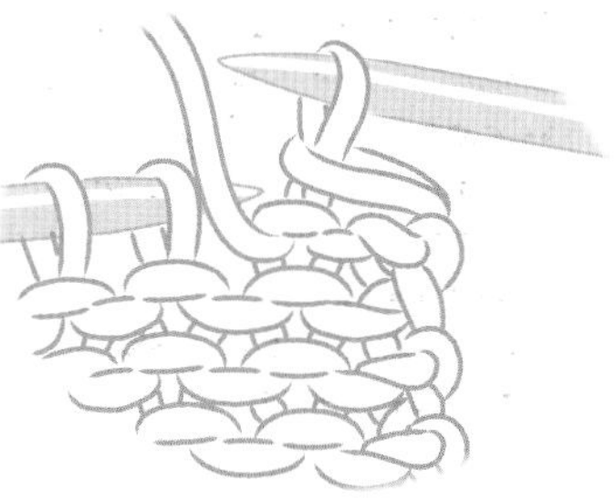

6 Use the left-hand needle to lift the first stitch over the second stitch and off the needle. Continue to cast off stitches in this way and secure the last stitch, as before.

lesson 8 decorative increases

Holes in lace knitting are formed by working a decorative increase – the type of increase used depends on the size of the hole required and the stitch being worked.

Yarn forward is worked between two knit stitches. Yarn round needle is worked between two purl stitches. Yarn over needle is worked between a purl and a knit stitch.

yarn forward (yfd)

Bring the yarn to the front of the work between the needles. Knit the next stitch, so taking the yarn across the needle and making one stitch.

yarn round needle (yrn)

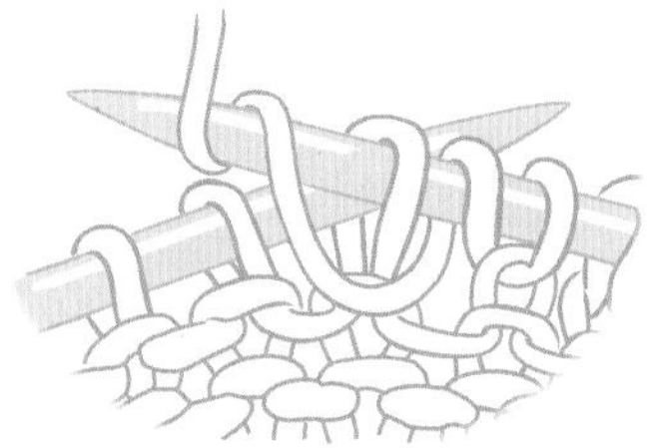

Take the yarn over the needle from front to back, around the needle and to the front. Purl the next stitch. The yarn has been wrapped around the needle, so making a stitch.

yarn over needle (yon)

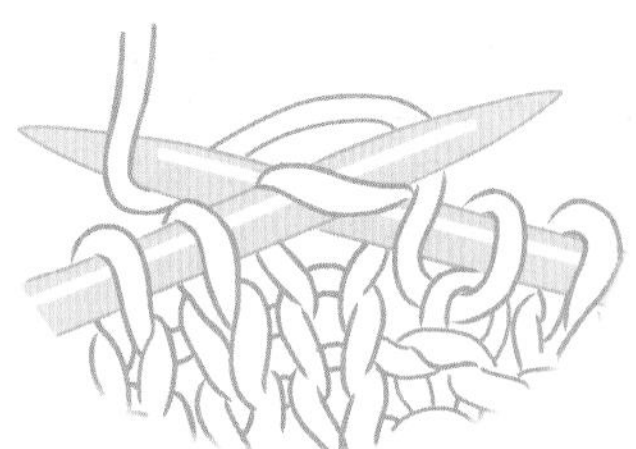

Take the yarn over the needle from front to back and knit the next stitch. The yarn lays across the right-hand needle, so making a stitch.

Yarn forward and round needle is worked between a knit and a purl stitch.

Yarn twice round needle is worked between two knit stitches to form a double increase.

yarn forward and round needle (yfrn)

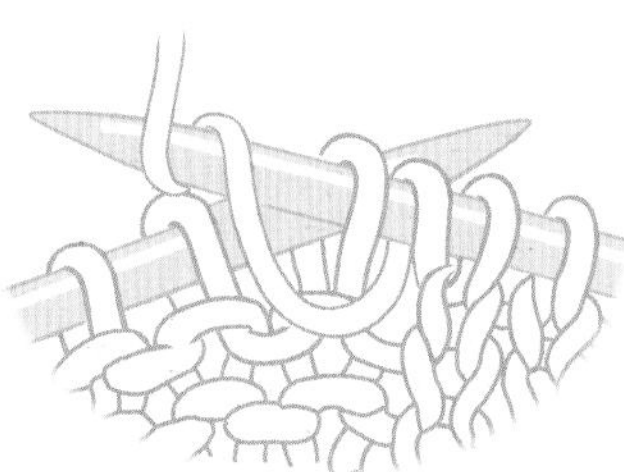

Bring yarn to the front between the needles, then take it over and around the needle and purl the next stitch. The yarn has been wrapped around the needle, so making a stitch.

yarn twice round needle (ytrn)

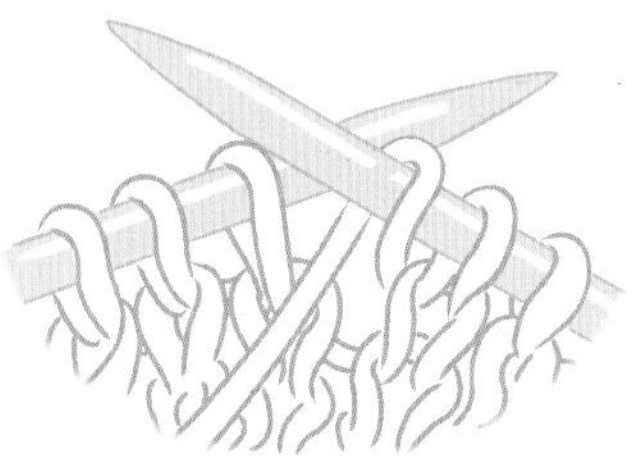

1 Bring the yarn to the front between the needles, then take it over and around the needle so that the yarn is at the front.

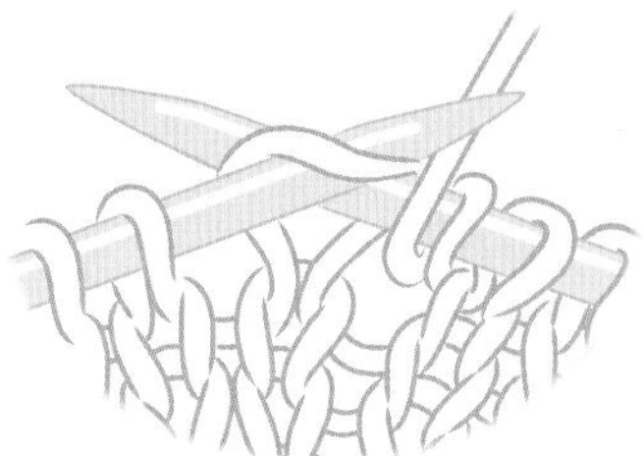

2 Knit the next stitch, so taking the yarn across the needle. The yarn wraps around the needle and lays over the needle, so making two stitches.

lesson 9

decorative decreases

To keep the number of stitches consistent within a row of knitting, decreases are worked before or after increases. There are different styles of decreases, depending on the number of stitches to be decreased and the way the stitches are to 'sit'.

Single decreases are worked over two stitches – knit two together, purl two together and slip one, knit one, pass slipped stitch over.

knit 2 together (K2tog)

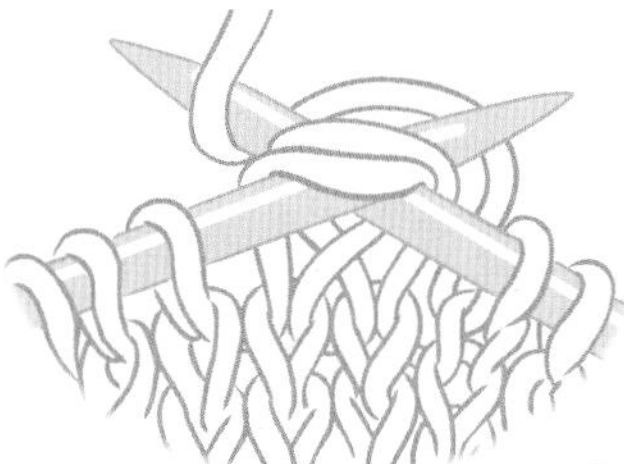

On a knit row, insert the right-hand needle into the next two stitches on the left-hand needle and knit the two stitches together. The decrease slopes to the right on the right side.

purl 2 together (P2tog)

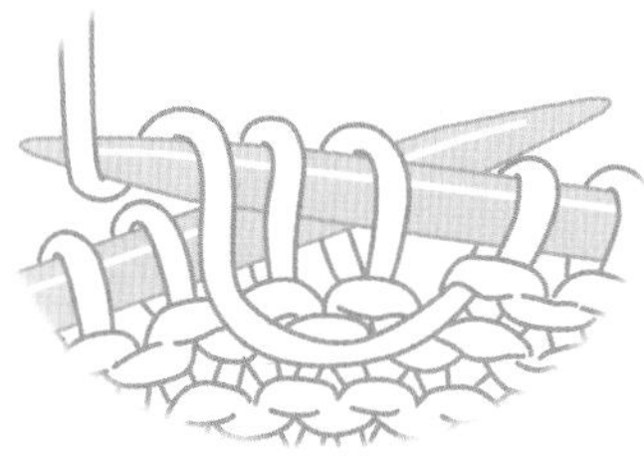

On a purl row, insert the right-hand needle into the next two stitches on the left-hand needle and purl the two stitches together. The decrease slopes to the right on the right side.

slip 1, knit 1, pass slipped stitch over (skpo)

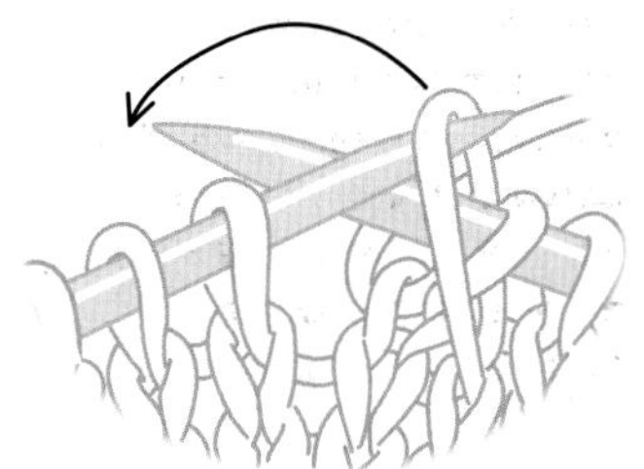

On a knit row, slip the next stitch, then knit the next stitch. Use the point of the left-hand needle to lift the slipped stitch and pass it over the knit stitch and off the needle. The decrease slopes to the left on the right side.

Double decreases are worked over three stitches – slip one, knit two together, pass slipped stitch over and slip two, knit one, pass two slipped stitches over.

slip 1, knit 2 together, pass slipped stitch over (sl 1, K2tog, psso)

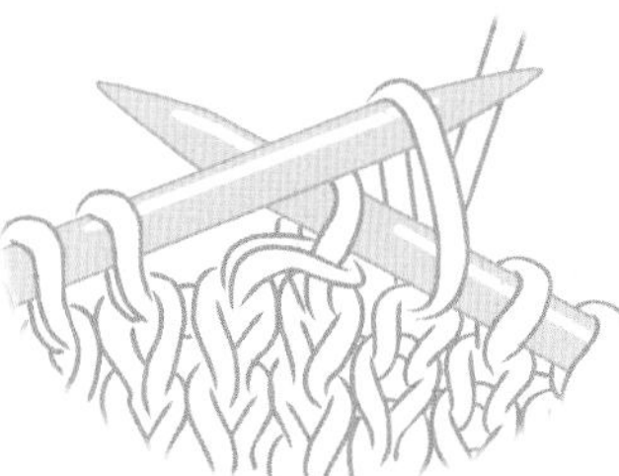

Slip the next stitch, then knit the next two stitches together to decrease a stitch. Use the point of the left-hand needle to lift the slipped stitch and pass it over the knit stitch and off the needle to work the second decrease, which slopes to the left on the right side.

slip 2, knit 1, pass 2 slipped stitches over (sl 2, K1, p2sso)

1 Slip the next two stitches on the left-hand needle onto the right-hand needle as if working knit two together.

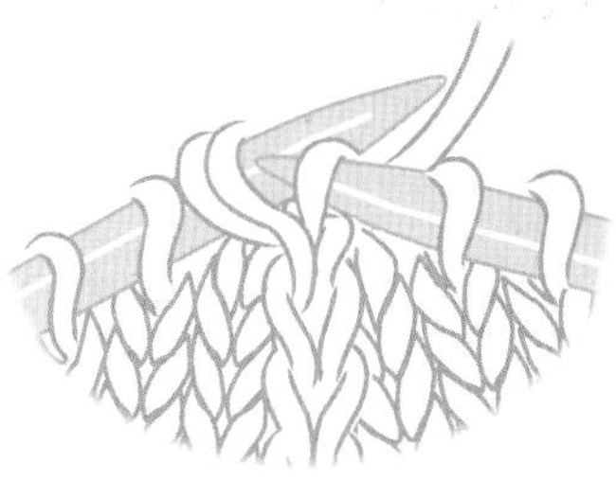

2 Knit the next stitch, then use the point of the left-hand needle to lift the slipped stitches and pass them over the knit stitch and off the needle to work the double decrease. The decrease sits upright on the right side.

lesson 10 tension

Before starting any knitting project it is important that you check your tension – the number of stitches and rows to a centimetre (or inch). The tension achieved by the designer needs to be matched as it determines the measurements of your knitting and ensures you produce an item that is the correct size and shape.

To knit your tension swatch, check the number of stitches and rows required under the heading 'Tension' at the start of each pattern. The tension recommended is chosen to give a correct 'handle' to the work – too tight, and the work will be firm and heavy; too loose, and it will be floppy and open, and will tend to lose its shape.

knitting a tension swatch

Stocking stitch has been used in the following steps for clarity.

1 Using the correct yarn and needle size for your project, cast on a few more stitches than the number quoted to suit the stitch repeat stated in the tension instructions. Knit the number of rows required plus about 5cm (2in) – this enables you to measure within the cast-on and top edge. Cast off the stitches and block your knitting (see page 128). Lay the knitting, with right side facing, on a flat surface and calculate the number of stitches. Insert a pin centrally on the fabric, a few stitches from the left-hand edge.

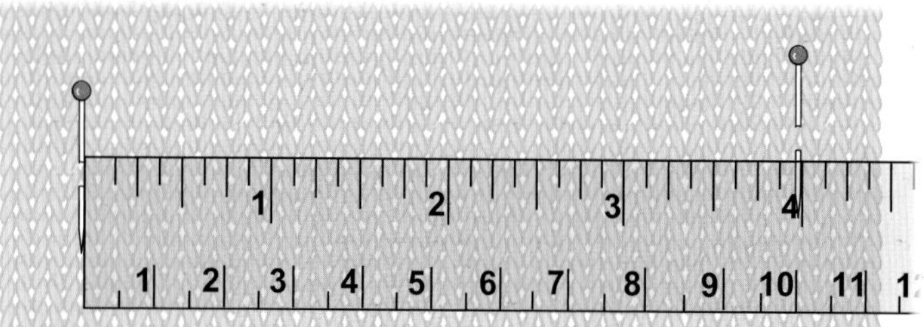

2 Place the end of a tape measure in line with the pin and measure across 10cm (4in) and insert another pin. Remove the tape measure and count the number of stitches (including any half stitches). This is the number of stitches to 10cm (4in).

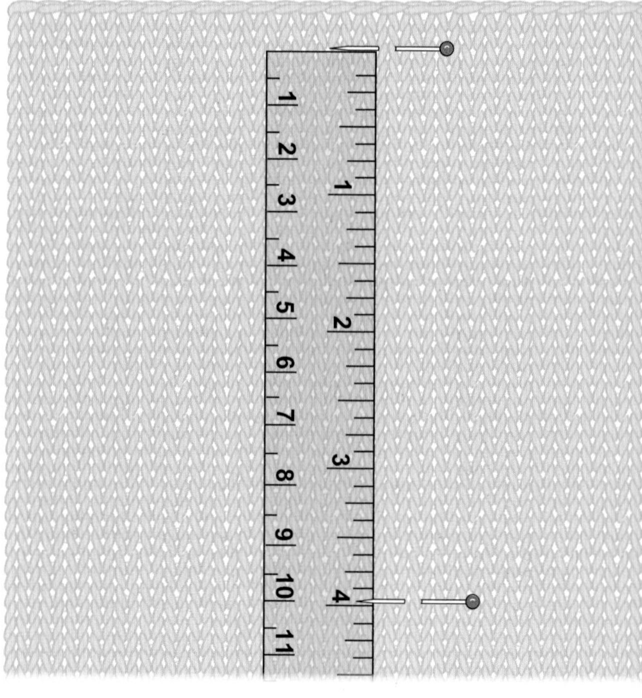

3 To calculate the number of rows, measure 10cm (4in) vertically on a straight line in the centre of the fabric and insert two pins exactly 10cm (4in) apart. Remove the tape measure and count the number of rows between the pins. If your tension matches the recommended tension exactly, you are ready to start your project. If not, you will need to adjust your tension (see right).

adjusting your tension

If your knitting has too many stitches or rows to 10cm (4in), your work is too tight and you need to work on larger needles; too few stitches or rows to 10cm (4in) means your work is too loose and you need to work on smaller needles. Change your needle size accordingly and work another tension swatch. Block the knitting as before and measure the tension (see left). Repeat this process until your tension is exactly right. Remember that a small difference over 10cm (4in) can add up to a big difference over the complete project.

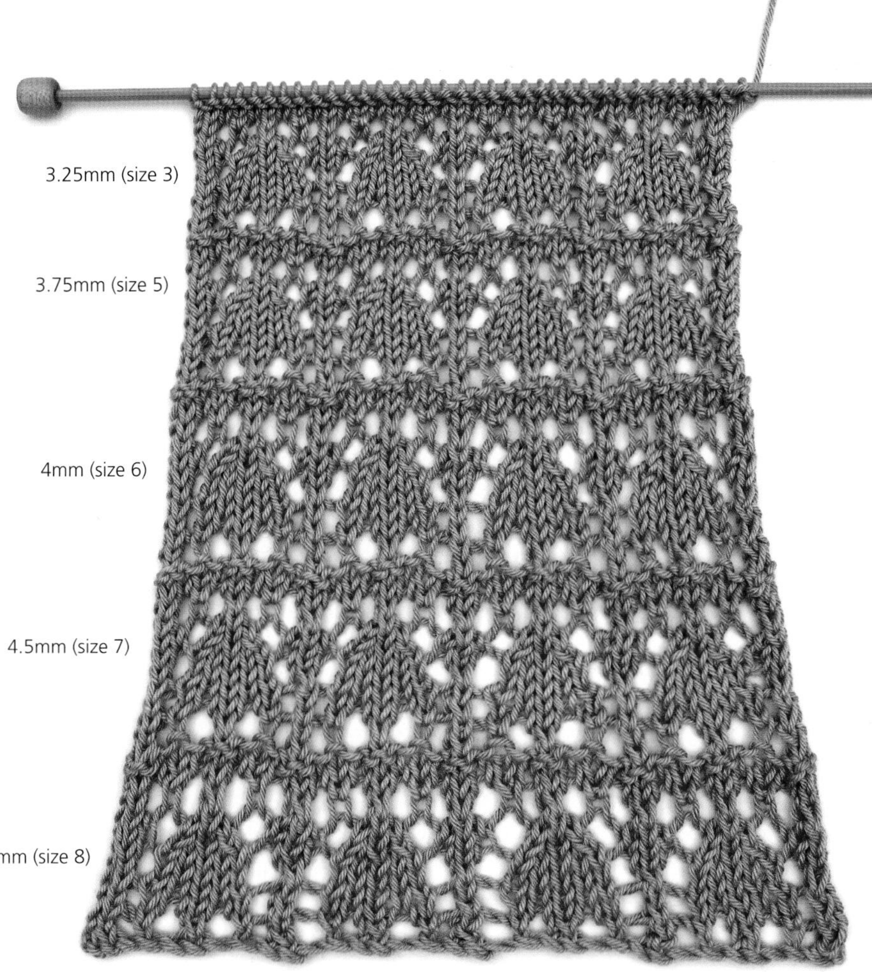

Size difference
With just a needle change you can alter the appearance and tension of your knitting. The knitted sample shows how the lace pattern is tighter when knitted on smaller needles, 3.25mm (size 3); and more open when knitted on larger needles, 5mm (size 8).

Knitting needle conversion chart

METRIC SIZES (mm)	US SIZES
2.0	0
2.25	1
2.75	2
3.0	–
3.25	3
3.5	4
3.75	5
4.0	6
4.5	7
5.0	8
5.5	9
6.0	10
6.5	10½
7.0	–
7.5	–
8.0	11
9.0	13
10.0	15
12.0	17
16.0	19
19.0	35
25.0	50

lesson 11 charts

The patterns in this book have been both written and charted. A chart gives a clear visual impression of how the pattern will appear – this can be very useful when placing panels together in a pattern and altering the number of rows in a repeat to make panels work together.

reading charts

Charts are read from the bottom to the top following the direction of the knitting. Each square on the chart represents a stitch and each horizontal line of squares a row of knitting. The symbols represent an instruction and have been designed to resemble the appearance of the knitting.

Before you start knitting familiarise yourself with the symbols on the chart you are going to knit and the techniques involved, making a note of them for quick reference if desired. The symbols and their descriptions can be found on page 140.

rows and repeats

The numbers on each side of the chart indicate the row number, the right- and wrong-side rows and the pattern repeat. The numbers on the right of the chart indicate the right-side rows and the numbers on the left the wrong-side rows. Check the position of row 1 before you start to knit so that you know whether this is a right- or wrong-side row.

Right-side rows are always read from right to left and wrong-side rows from left to right. Therefore, the symbols on the charts appear from the right side of the work just as they will on the knitting – a knit stitch worked on the wrong side will appear as a ridge on the right side and is shown as a dot (•) on the chart. A blank square represents knit on a right-side row and purl on a wrong-side row.

To keep the pattern repeat correct, not all charts are repeated from row 1. The rows that are to be worked only once to set the pattern, and not repeated, are shaded.

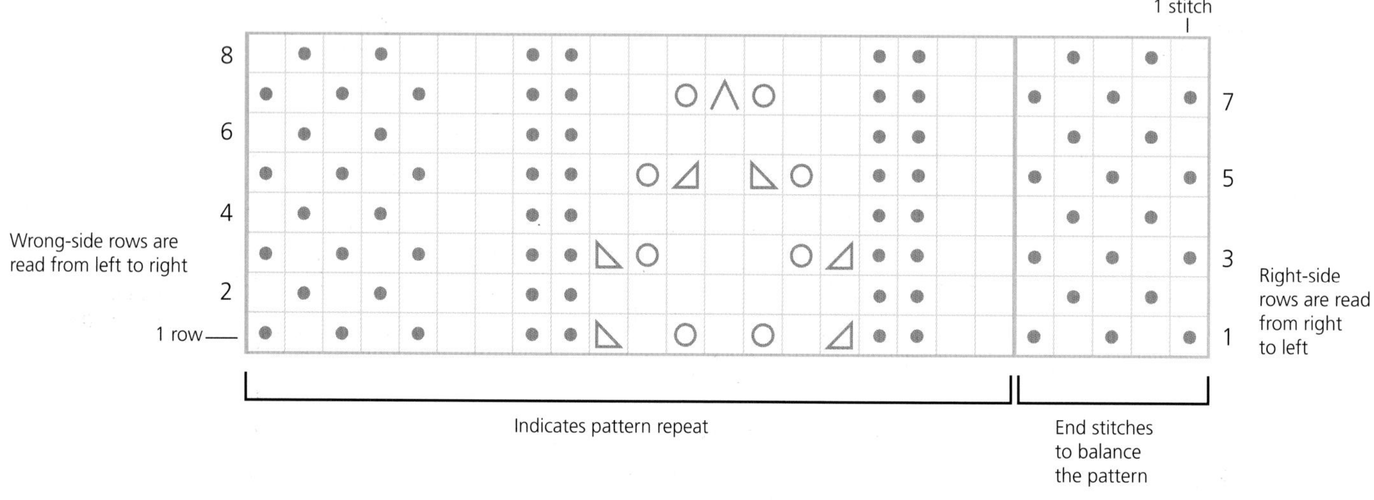

symbols for lace

The main techniques used in lace knitting to decrease stitches are knit two together (K2tog), purl two together (P2tog), slip one, knit one, pass slipped stitch over (skpo) and slip two, knit one, pass two slipped stitches over (sl 2, K1, p2sso). The triangular and line symbols used for these decreases show the direction in which the stitch will slant on the right side of the work. For example, K2tog will slant to the right, the symbol representing this is a triangle slanting to the right (◿). For skpo, where the decrease slopes to the left, a triangle with a left slant (◺) is used. An eyelet or 'hole' in the pattern is symbolised with an open circle (○).

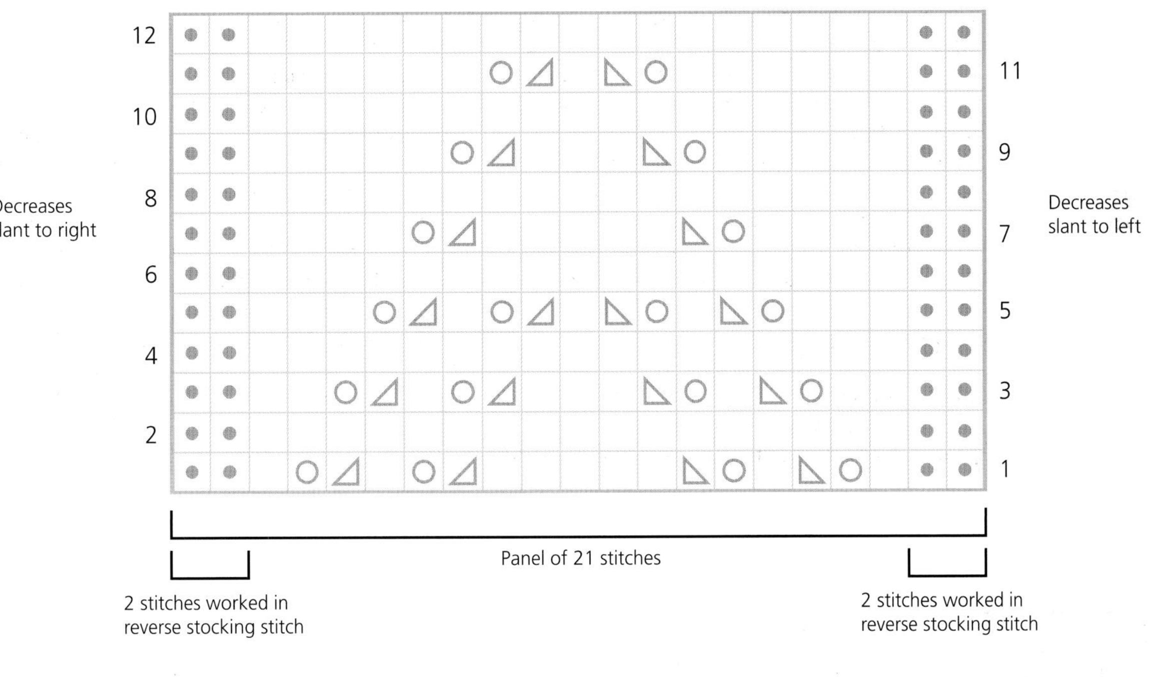

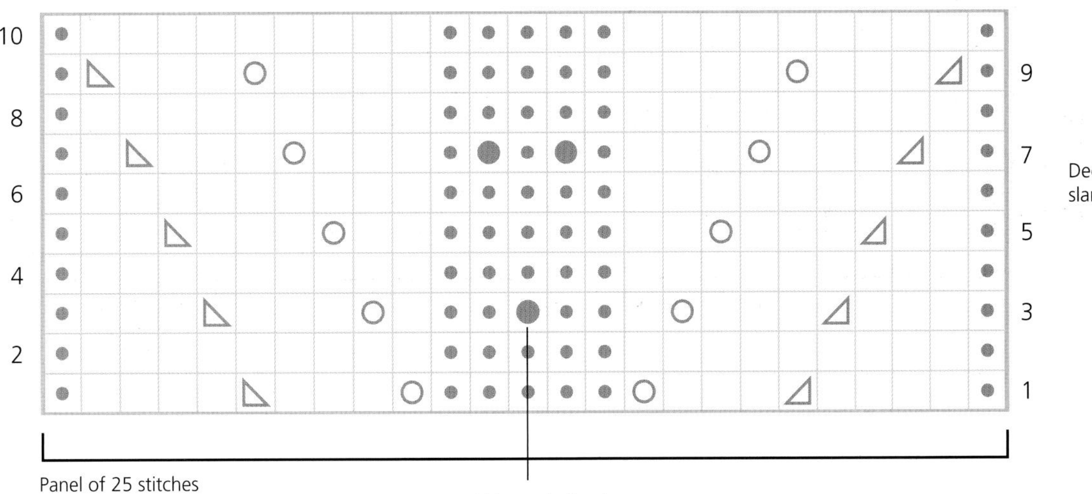

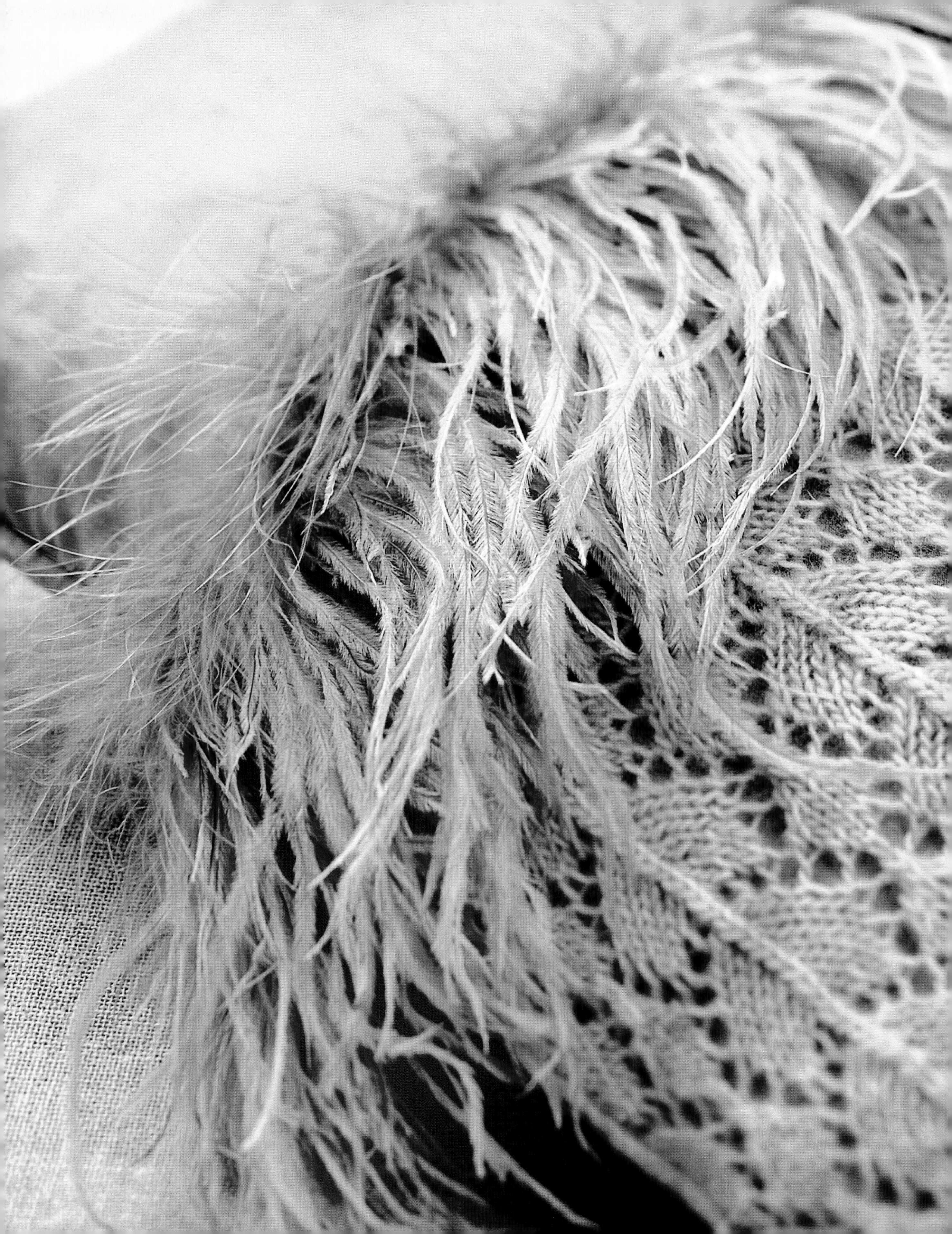

the lace knits

Eyelet lace and lace panels, patterns and edgings – easy-to-follow stitch guides and beautiful openwork designs in an appealing colour palette.

lesson 12 eyelet patterns

The difference between eyelet patterns and lace patterns lies in the relative laciness of the fabrics they create. Lace knitting creates a very open fabric that is mostly holes supported by little or no background knitted fabric. An eyelet pattern, on the other hand, is the reverse, featuring a more solid background that is punctuated with holes.

Eyelets are created with a basic increase and decrease. They are easy to work, charming in their simplicity and suitable for most types of yarn from 4-ply to DK, aran and even mohair and bouclé. Simple eyelet patterns make pretty border details as well as attractive all-over patterns.

The holes can be arranged singly at regular intervals, scattered randomly or worked in clusters to form designs such as leaf or rosette patterns. As with more open lace patterns, you can combine several eyelet patterns for a decorative knitted patchwork effect. In addition, the regular, firm holes make a perfect vehicle for accenting with threaded ribbon or narrow strips of fabric, while the solid spaces between the groups of holes invite embellishment with buttons and beads.

Practice pattern
Use this pattern to work through the step-by-step exercise overleaf to make the sample shown.

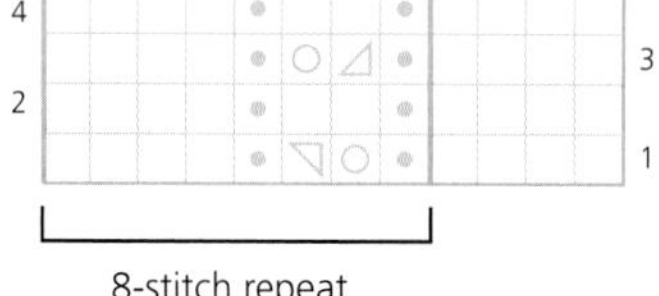

8-stitch repeat

Pattern

Row 1 (RS) K4, *P1, yon, K2tog tbl, P1, K4, rep from * to end.
Row 2 P4, *K1, P2, K1, P4, rep from * to end.
Row 3 K4, *P1, K2tog, yfrn, P1, K4, rep from * to end.
Row 4 As row 2.
These 4 rows form the patt.

eyelet rib

This sample shows four pattern repeats. Worked on a multiple of 8 stitches plus 4.

3.25mm (size 3)

4-ply wool

simple eyelets

1 Eyelets are worked on rows 1 and 3 of the eyelet rib pattern (see page 30). On row 1 the eyelet is formed between a purl and a knit stitch – the method used to create the eyelet is yarn over needle (abbreviated as yon). The yarn is at the front of the knitting after working the purl stitch before the position for the eyelet.

2 By keeping the yarn at the front and knitting the next two stitches together, the yarn is automatically taken over the needle, so making a stitch – this shows as an eyelet in the pattern once the next row is worked.

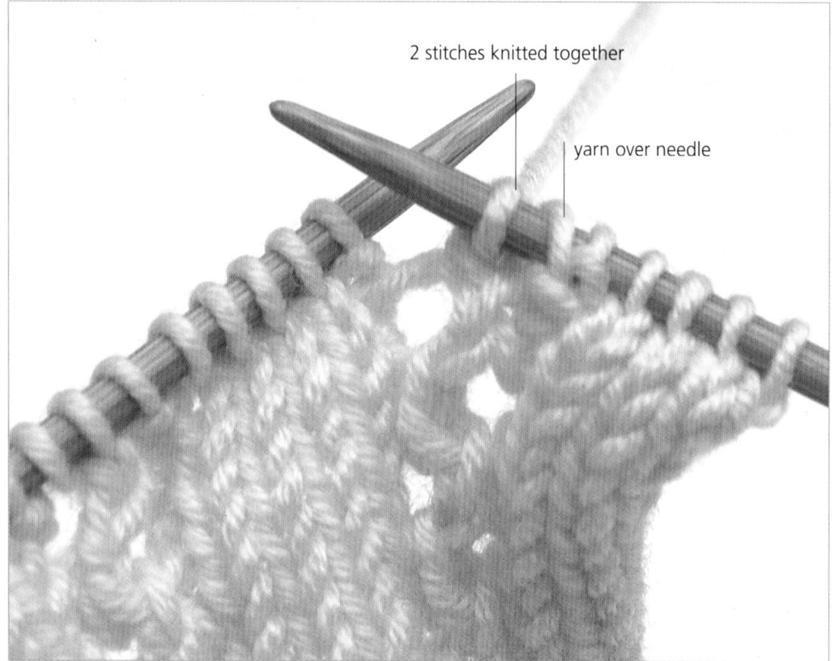

3 The next two stitches are knitted together through the back of the loop (abbreviated as K2togtbl). The number of stitches remains consistent by making a stitch, then working a decrease.

4 On row 3 the eyelet is formed between a knit and a purl stitch. To stagger the eyelets the extra stitch is made after the decrease – on row 1 it was worked before the decrease. Knit the next two stitches together (abbreviated as K2tog); the yarn will be at the back of the knitting.

5 To form the eyelet, the yarn is taken forward and around the needle (abbreviated as yfrn) ready to work the purl stitch. Take the yarn to the front of the knitting, then around the needle from front to back and to the front again.

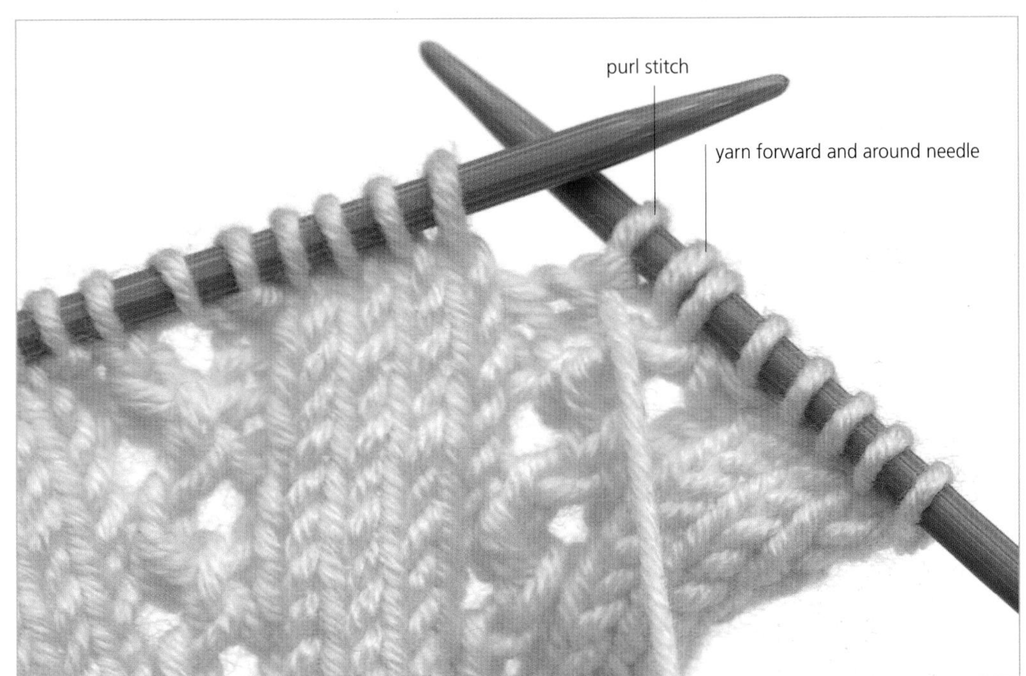

6 Now purl the next stitch. A decrease is followed by a make stitch, so keeping the number of stitches consistent.

staggered eyelets

This sample shows five pattern repeats. Worked on a multiple of 6 stitches plus 3.

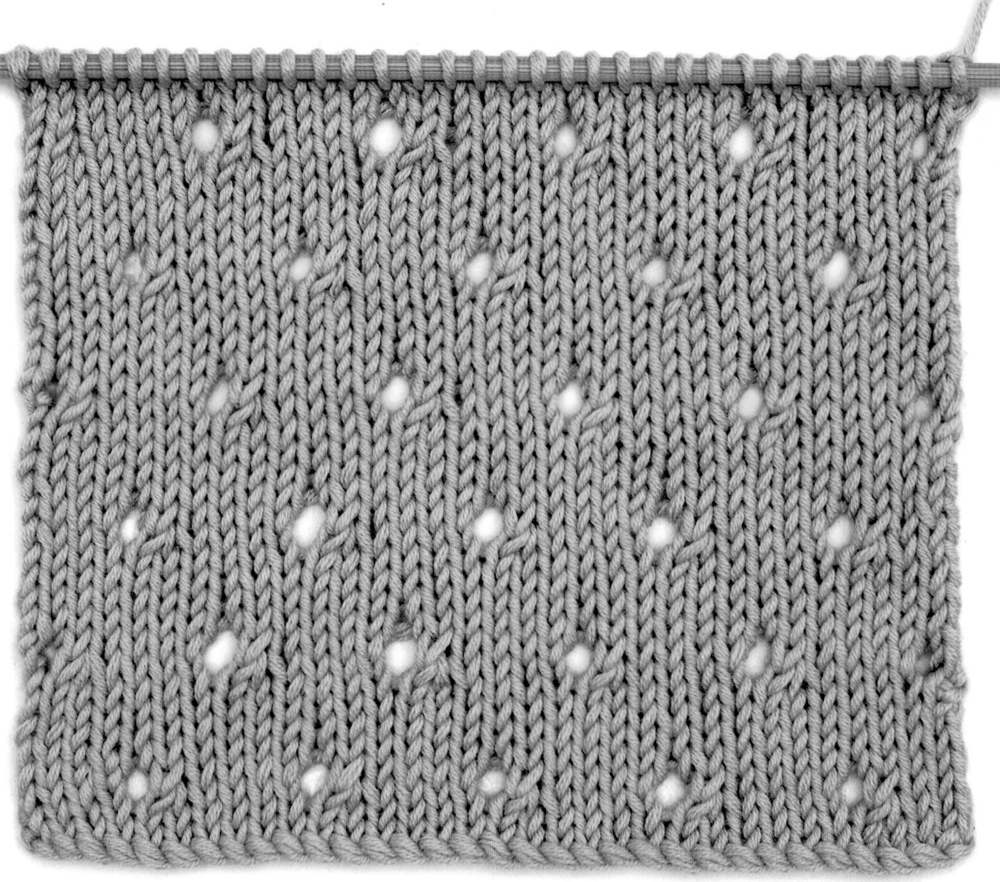

3.25mm (size 3)

4-ply cotton

Pattern

Row 1 (RS) K to end.
Row 2 P to end.
Row 3 K3, *K2tog, yfd, K4, rep from * to end.
Rows 4 to 8 Beg with a P row, work 5 rows st st.
Row 9 K2tog, *yfd, K4, K2tog, rep from * to last st, yfd, K1.
Rows 10 to 12 Beg with a P row, work 3 rows st st.
These 12 rows form the patt.

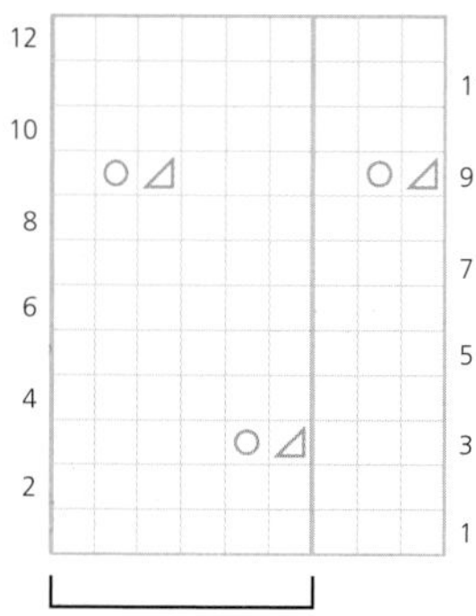

variation

Worked on a multiple of 6 stitches plus 3.

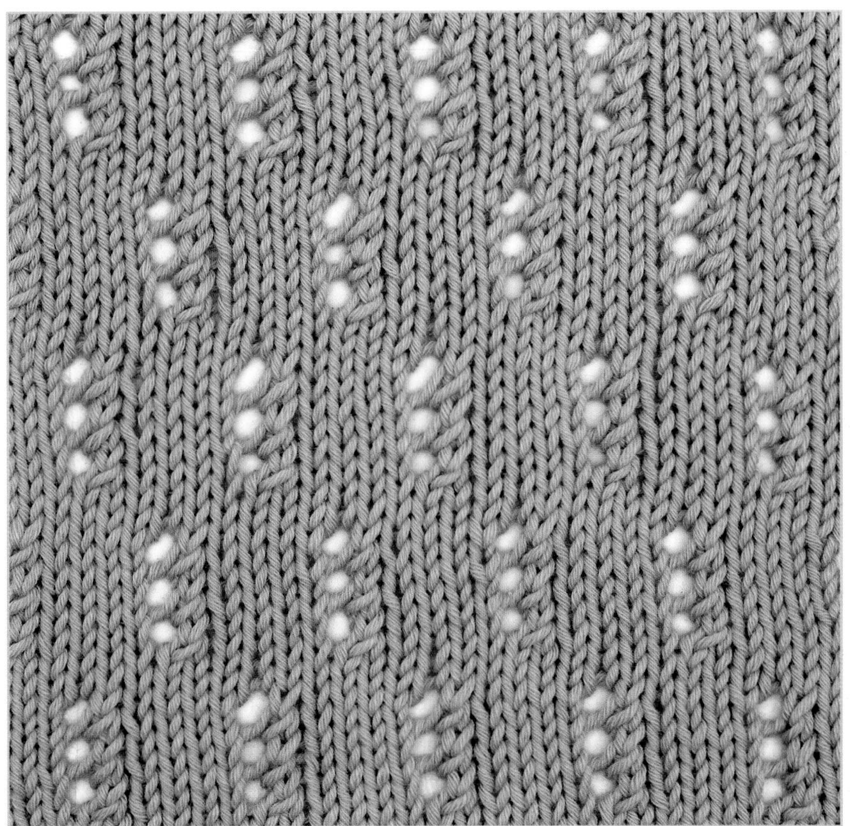

3.75mm (size 5)

DK cotton

Pattern

Row 1 (RS) K to end.
Row 2 P to end.
Row 3 K3, *K2tog, yfd, K4, rep from * to end.
Row 4 P to end.
Rows 5 to 8 Work rows 3 and 4 twice.
Row 9 K to end.
Row 10 P to end.
Row 11 K2tog, *yfd, K4, K2tog, rep from * to last st, yfd, K1.
Row 12 P to end.
Rows 13 to 16 Work rows 11 and 12 twice.
These 16 rows form the patt.

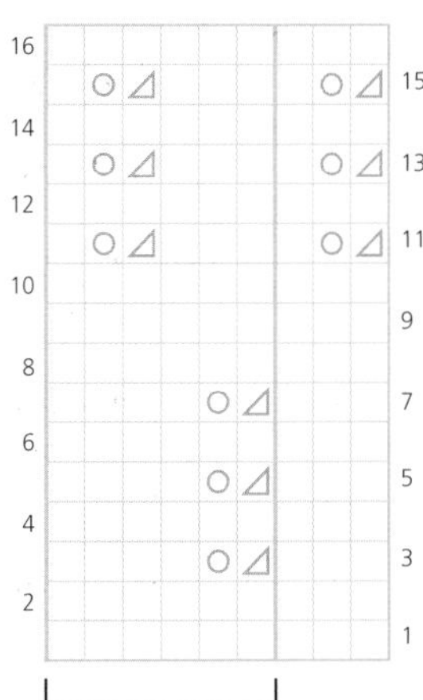

diagonal eyelets

This sample shows four pattern repeats. Worked on a multiple of 9 stitches.

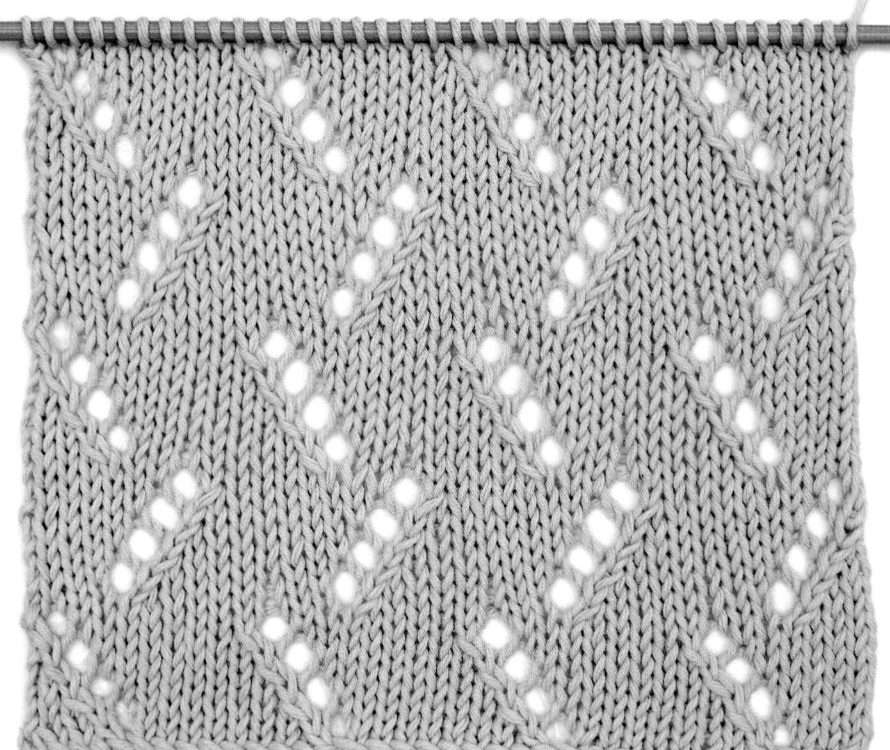

3.25mm (size 3)

4-ply cotton

Pattern

Row 1 (RS) *K4, yfd, skpo, K3, rep from * to end.
Row 2 and every alt row P to end.
Row 3 *K5, yfd, skpo, K2, rep from * to end.
Row 5 *K6, yfd, skpo, K1, rep from * to end.
Row 7 *K7, yfd, skpo, rep from * to end.
Row 9 *K3, K2tog, yfd, K4, rep from * to end.
Row 11 *K2, K2tog, yfd, K5, rep from * to end.
Row 13 *K1, K2tog, yfd, K6, rep from * to end.
Row 15 *K2tog, yfd, K7, rep from * to end.
Row 16 P to end.
These 16 rows form the patt.

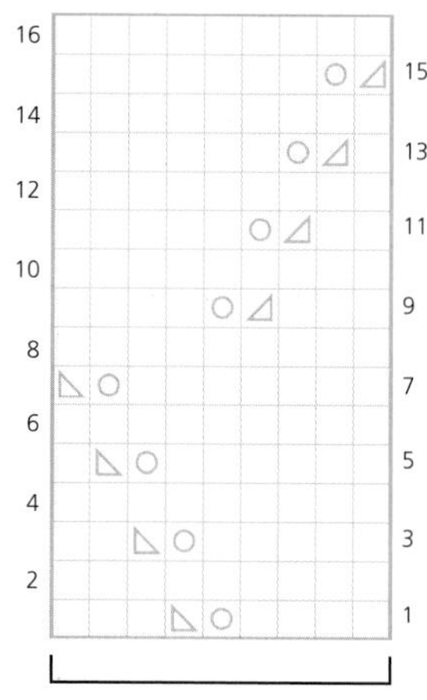

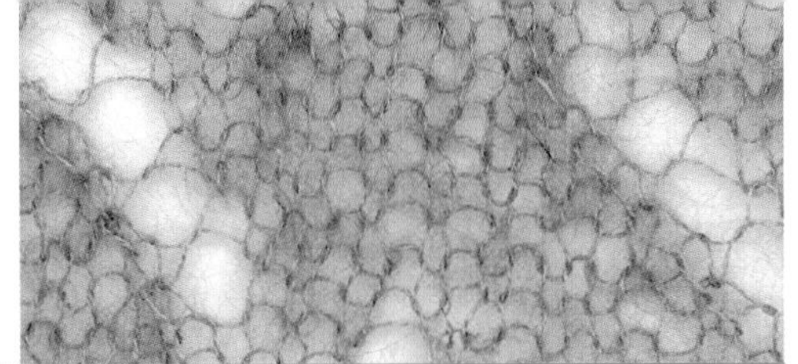

variation

Worked on a multiple of
9 stitches.

4mm
(size 6)

Fine mohair

Filigree
Worked in a fine mohair yarn on 4mm (size 6) knitting needles, the eyelet pattern has a delicate appearance. The pattern looks equally good on the knit side and the purl side.

triangles

This sample shows two pattern repeats. Worked on a multiple of 14 stitches plus 5.

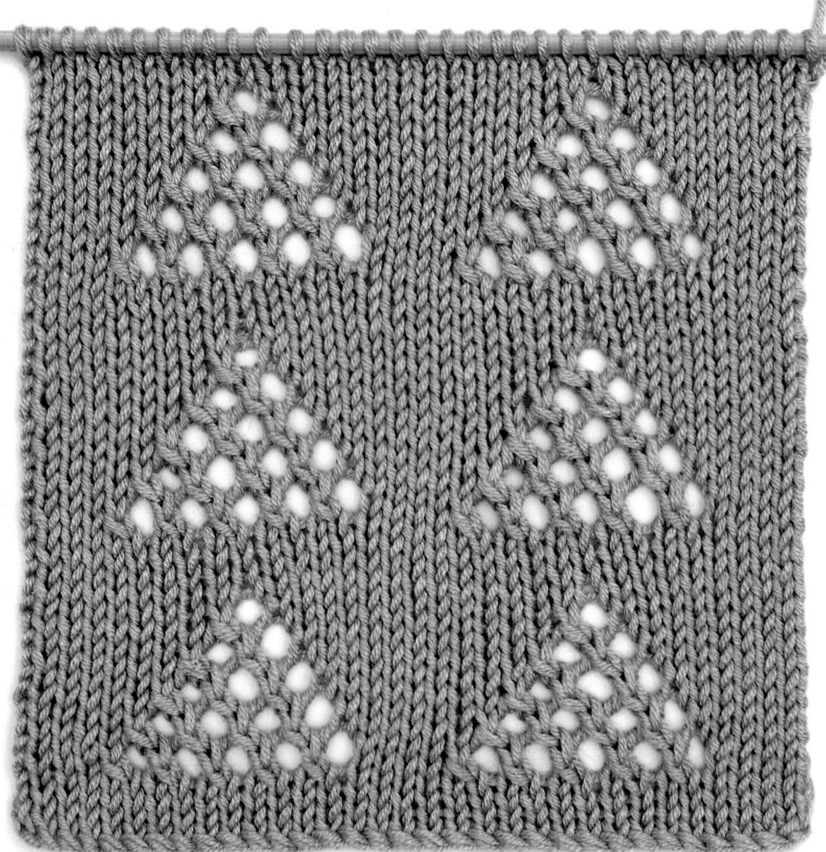

3.75mm (size 5)

DK cotton

Pattern

Row 1 (RS) K to end.
Row 2 and every alt row P to end.
Row 3 K to end.
Row 5 K5, *(yfd, skpo) 5 times, K4, rep from * to end.
Row 7 K6, *(yfd, skpo) 4 times, K5, rep from * to end.
Row 9 K7, *(yfd, skpo) 3 times, K6, rep from * to end.
Row 11 K8, *(yfd, skpo) twice, K7, rep from * to end.
Row 13 K9, *yfd, skpo, K8, rep from * to end.
Row 14 P to end.
These 14 rows form the patt.

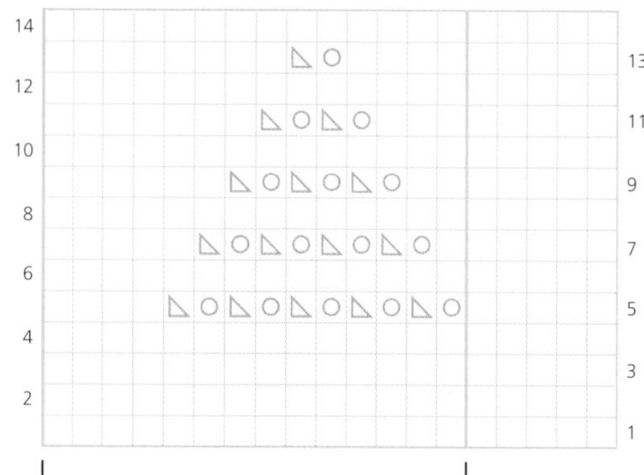

variation

Worked on a multiple of 14 stitches plus 15.

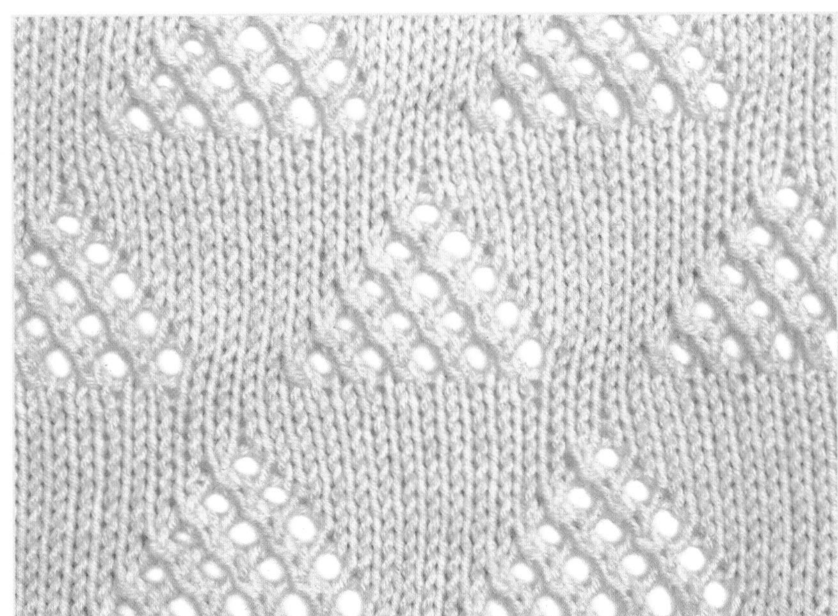

Pattern

Row 1 (RS) K to end.
Row 2 and every alt row P to end.
Row 3 K to end.
Row 5 K3, *(yfd, skpo) 5 times, K4, rep from * to end, finishing last rep K2.
Row 7 K4, *(yfd, skpo) 4 times, K6, rep from * to end, finishing last rep K3.
Row 9 K5, *(yfd, skpo) 3 times, K8, rep from * to end, finishing last rep K4.
Row 11 K6, *(yfd, skpo) twice, K10, rep from * to end, finishing last rep K5.
Row 13 K7, *yfd, skpo, K12, rep from * to end, finishing last rep K6.
Row 15 K to end.
Row 17 K to end.
Row 19 K10, *(yfd, skpo) 5 times, K4, rep from * to end, finishing last rep K9.
Row 21 K11, *(yfd, skpo) 4 times, K6, rep from * to end, finishing last rep K10.
Row 23 K12, *(yfd, skpo) 3 times, K8, rep from * to end, finishing last rep K11.
Row 25 K13, *(yfd, skpo) twice, K10, rep from * to end, finishing last rep K12.
Row 27 K14, *yfd, skpo, K12, rep from * to end, finishing last rep K13.
Row 28 P to end.
These 28 rows form the patt.

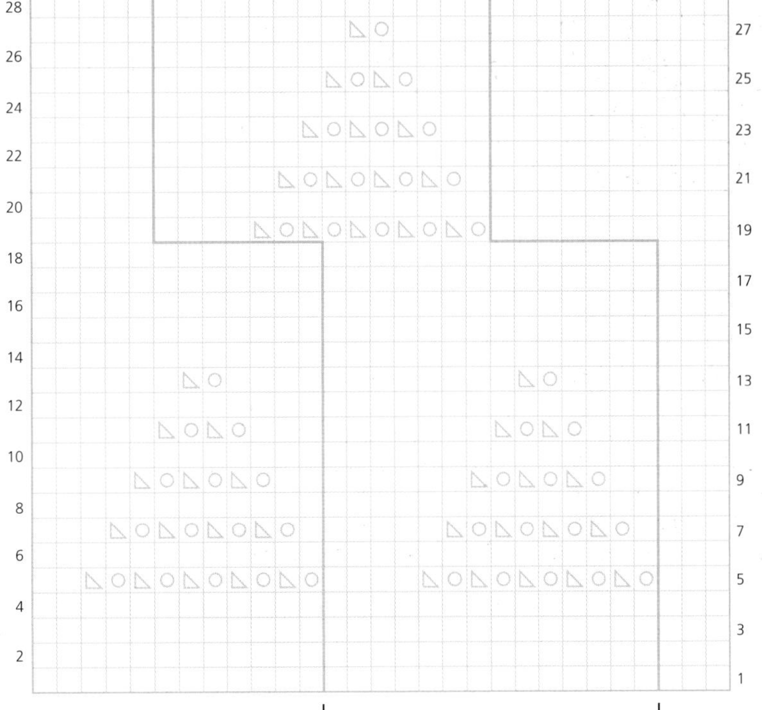

3.25mm (size 3)

4-ply wool

eyelet blocks

This sample shows one pattern repeat. Worked on a multiple of 16 stitches plus 9.

3.75mm (size 5)

DK perlé cotton

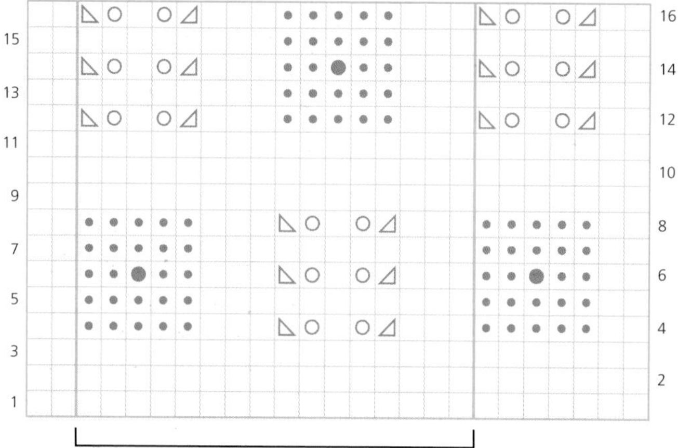

Pattern

Row 1 (WS) P to end.
Row 2 K to end.
Row 3 P to end.
Row 4 K2, P5, *K3, K2tog, yfd, K1, yfd, skpo, K3, P5, rep from * to last 2 sts, K2.
Row 5 P2, K5, *P11, K5, rep from * to last 2 sts, P2.
Row 6 K2, P2, MB-1, P2, *K3, K2tog, yfd, K1, yfd, skpo, K3, P2, MB-1, P2, rep from * to last 2 sts, K2.
Row 7 As row 5.
Row 8 As row 4.
Rows 9 to 11 Beg with a P row, work 3 rows st st.
Row 12 K2, K2tog, yfd, K1, yfd, skpo, *K3, P5, K3, K2tog, yfd, K1, yfd, skpo, rep from * to last 2 sts, K2.
Row 13 P10, *K5, P11, rep from * to end, finishing last rep P10.
Row 14 K2, K2tog, yfd, K1, yfd, skpo, *K3, P2, MB-1, P2, K3, K2tog, yfd, K1, yfd, skpo, rep from * to last 2 sts, K2.
Row 15 As row 13.
Row 16 As row 12.
These 16 rows form the patt.

variation

Worked on a multiple of 16 stitches plus 9.

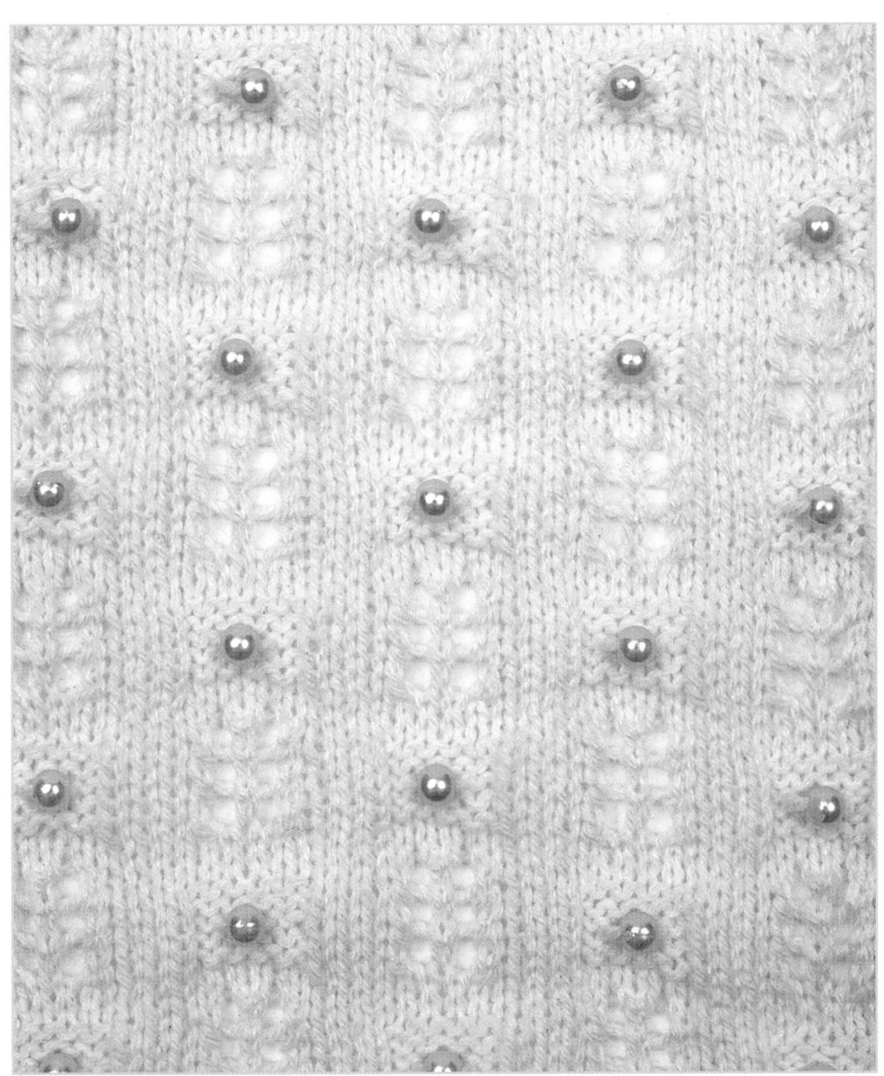

3.25mm (size 3)

3-ply wool

Beads instead of bobbles

Thread beads onto a ball of yarn, pushing them along until you need them.

Work the 16 rows of eyelet blocks pattern, but knit a bead (B1) into the pattern on rows 6 and 14 instead of a bobble.

Special abbreviation

B1 (bead 1) = With yarn at front, slip the next stitch purlwise and push the bead against the right-hand needle, ready to work the next stitch.

small heart

Worked over 13 stitches on a background of stocking stitch.

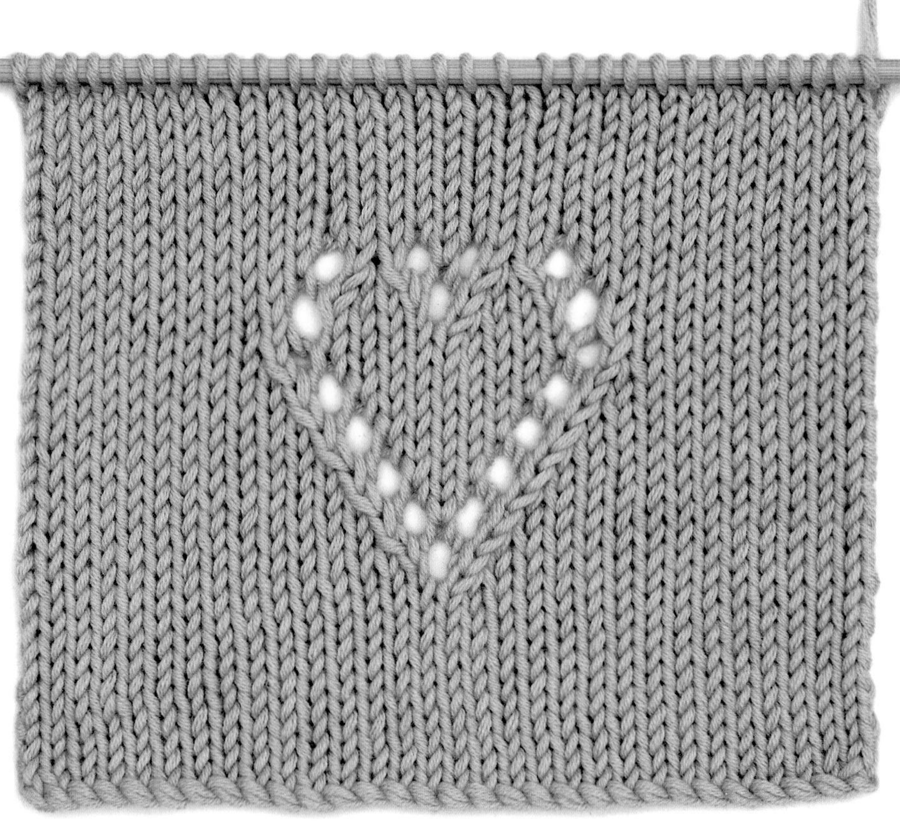

3.25mm (size 3)

4-ply cotton

Pattern

Row 1 (RS) K5, K2tog, yfd, K6.
Row 2 and every alt row P to end.
Row 3 K4, K2tog, yfd, K1, yfd, skpo, K4.
Row 5 K3, K2tog, yfd, K3, yfd, skpo, K3.
Row 7 K2, K2tog, yfd, K5, yfd, skpo, K2.
Row 9 K1, K2tog, yfd, K7, yfd, skpo, K1.
Row 11 K2tog, yfd, K9, yfd, skpo.
Row 13 Skpo, yfd, K3, K2tog, yfd, K4, yfd, K2tog.
Row 15 K2, yfd, skpo, K2tog, yfd, K1, yfd, skpo, K2tog, yfd, K2.
Row 16 P to end.
These 16 rows form the patt.

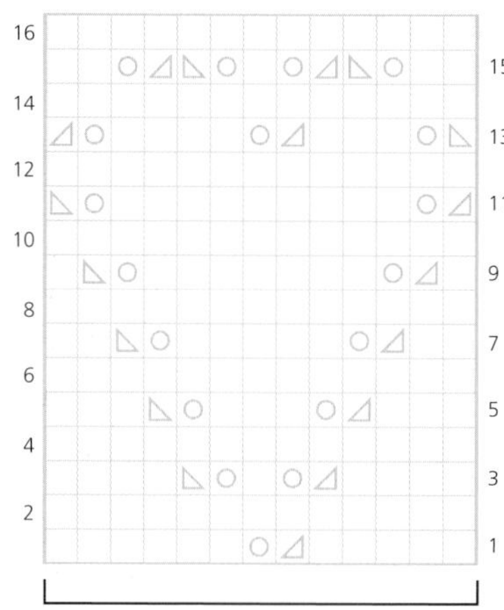

variation

Worked over 21 stitches on a background of stocking stitch.

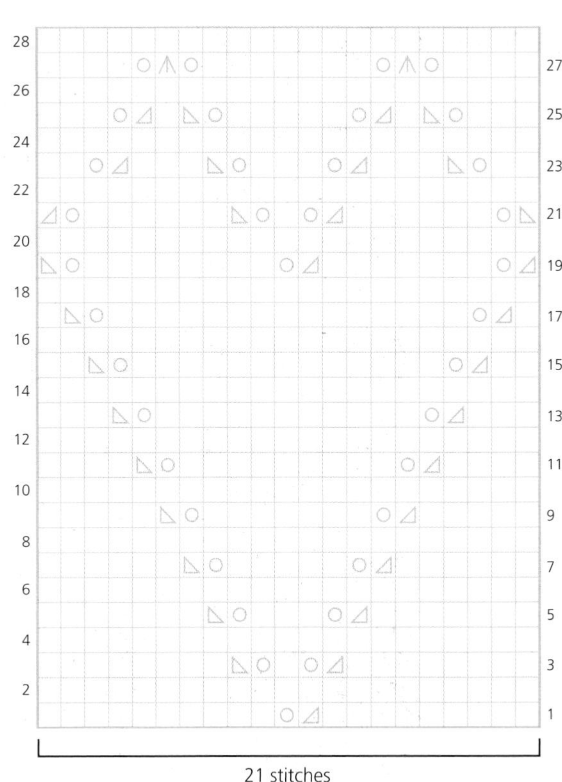

3.25mm (size 3)

4-ply wool

Pattern

Row 1 (RS) K9, K2tog, yfd, K10.
Row 2 and every alt row P to end.
Row 3 K8, K2tog, yfd, K1, yfd, skpo, K8.
Row 5 K7, K2tog, yfd, K3, yfd, skpo, K7.
Row 7 K6, K2tog, yfd, K5, yfd, skpo, K6.
Row 9 K5, K2tog, yfd, K7, yfd, skpo, K5.
Row 11 K4, K2tog, yfd, K9, yfd, skpo, K4.
Row 13 K3, K2tog, yfd, K11, yfd, skpo, K3.
Row 15 K2, K2tog, yfd, K13, yfd, skpo, K2.
Row 17 K1, K2tog, yfd, K15, yfd, skpo, K1.
Row 19 K2tog, yfd, K7, K2tog, yfd, K8, yfd, skpo.
Row 21 Skpo, yfd, K6, K2tog, yfd, K1, yfd, skpo, K6, yfd, K2tog.
Row 23 K2, yfd, skpo, K3, K2tog, yfd, K3, yfd, skpo, K3, K2tog, yfd, K2.
Row 25 K3, yfd, skpo, K1, K2tog, yfd, K5, yfd, skpo, K1, K2tog, yfd, K3.
Row 27 K4, yfd, sl 2 as if to K2tog, K1, then p2sso, yfd, K7, yfd, sl 2 as if to K2tog, K1, then p2sso, yfd, K4.
Row 28 P to end.
These 28 rows form the patt.

project 1: baby blanket and slippers

This cosy blanket and slipper set is sure to keep baby warm from head to toe. The blanket is trimmed with blanket stitch and the slippers with a pretty flower.

YOU WILL NEED

For blanket:

- 200g (7oz) aran yarn in cream
- 50g (1¾oz) DK yarn in duck-egg blue
- 5mm (size 8) knitting needles
- Tapestry needle

For slippers:

- 50g (1¾oz) 4-ply cotton in duck-egg blue
- 3.25mm (size 3) knitting needles
- 2 small buttons

SIZE

Blanket: 47 x 50.5cm (18½ x 20in)
Slippers: length of foot 8cm (3in)

TENSION

20 sts and 30 rows to 10cm (4in) over moss st on 5mm (size 8) needles
26 sts to 10cm (4in) over g st on 3.25mm (size 3) needles

Blanket pattern

TO MAKE

Using 5mm (size 8) needles, cast on 101 sts.

Moss st row K1, (P1, K1) to end.

Rep this row 5 times more.

Cont in Eyelet Blocks patt and moss st as follows:

Row 1 (WS) K1, (P1, K1) twice, *P27, (K1, P1) twice, K1, rep from * to end.

Row 2 K1, (P1, K1) twice, *K27, (K1, P1) twice, K1, rep from * to end.

Row 3 Rep row 1.

Row 4 K1, (P1, K1) twice, *K3, P5, K3, K2tog, yfd, K1, yfd, skpo, K3, P5, K3, (K1, P1) twice, K1, rep from * to end.

Row 5 K1, (P1, K1) twice, *P3, K5, P11, K5, P3, (K1, P1) twice, K1, rep from * to end.

Row 6 K1, (P1, K1) twice, *K3, P2, MB-1, P2, K3, K2tog, yfd, K1, yfd, skpo, K3, P2, MB-1, P2, K3, (K1, P1) twice, K1, rep from * to end.

Row 7 As row 5.

Row 8 As row 4.

Rows 9 to 11 As rows 1 to 3.

Row 12 K1, (P1, K1) twice, *K3, K2tog, yfd, K1, yfd, skpo, K3, P5, K3, K2tog, yfd, K1, yfd, skpo, K3, (K1, P1) twice, K1, rep from * to end.

Row 13 K1, (P1, K1) twice, *P11, K5, P11, (K1, P1) twice, K1, rep from * to end.

Row 14 K1, (P1, K1) twice, *K3, K2tog, yfd, K1, yfd, skpo, K3, P2, MB-1, P2, K3, K2tog, yfd, K1, yfd, skpo, K3, (K1, P1) twice, K1, rep from * to end.

Row 15 As row 13.

Row 16 As row 12.

Rows 17 to 27 Work rows 1 to 11.

Rows 28 to 34 K1, (P1, K1) to end.

These 34 rows form the patt.

Rep them twice more, then work rows 1 to 33 again.

Cast off.

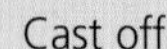

TO FINISH BLANKET

Block knitting to size. Sew in the ends. Using a long length of duck-egg blue yarn, work blanket stitch (see designer's tip) evenly around outer edge, making stitches about 1cm (⅜in) long and spacing them 1cm (⅜in) apart.

TO FINISH SLIPPERS

Join back and sole seam. Join ends of flowers to form a circle, then sew to top of slippers. Sew a button to the centre of each flower.

designer's tip

To blanket stitch, working from left to right with the edge you are working on towards you, bring the needle through the knitting from back to front 1cm (3/8in) from the edge. Now take the needle to the back, 1cm (3/8in) to the right and level with the first stitch, bring the point of the needle towards you and over the loop of yarn, and pull through so that the loop lies on the edge. Continue in this way.

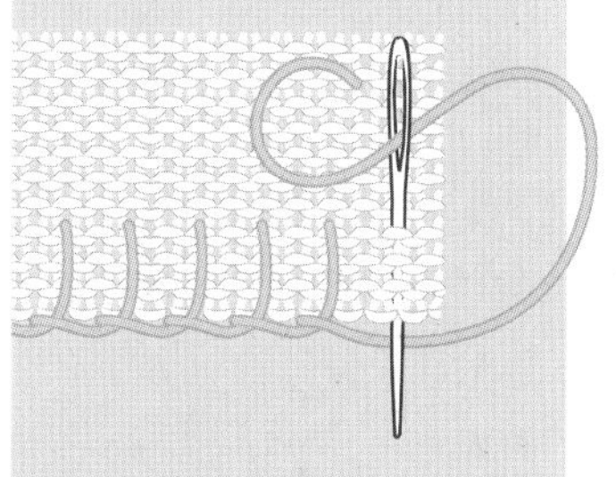

Slipper pattern

TO MAKE (Both alike)
Using 3.25mm (size 3) needles, cast on 33 sts. Working in g st throughout, cont as follows:
Row 1 K to end.
Row 2 K1, puk, K15, puk, K1, puk, K15, puk, K1. 37 sts.
Row 3 K to end.
Row 4 K2, puk, K15, puk, K3, puk, K15, puk, K2. 41 sts.
Row 5 K to end.
Row 6 K3, puk, K15, puk, K5, puk, K15, puk, K3. 45 sts.
Row 7 K to end.
Row 8 K4, puk, K15, puk, K7, puk, K15, puk, K4. 49 sts.
Rows 9 to 19 K to end.
Row 20 K16, (skpo) 4 times, K1, (K2tog) 4 times, K16. 41 sts.
Row 21 K to end.
Cast off.

FLOWER
Using 3mm (size 3) needles, cast on 5 sts.
Row 1 P to end.
Row 2 K1, (yfd, K1) to end. 9 sts.
Row 3 P to end.
Row 4 K1, (ytrn, K1) to end.
Row 5 P to end, working P1 and K1 into each double loop. 25 sts.
Row 6 K to end.
Cast off knitwise.

project 2: hat and scarf

Keep a little one wrapped up warm with this adorable hat and scarf set. The hat has a band of heart motifs and the scarf a single heart at each end.

Hat pattern

TO MAKE
(made in one piece)
Using 4mm (size 6) needles, cast on 87 sts.
Moss st row K1, *P1, K1, rep from * to end.
Rep this row 6 times more.
Beg with a K row, work 4 rows st st.
Now work heart motifs as follows:
Row 1 (RS) K8, *K2tog, yfd, K15, rep from * to end, finishing last rep K9.
Row 2 and every alt row P to end.
Row 3 K7, *K2tog, yfd, K1, yfd, skpo, K12, rep from * to end, finishing last rep K7.
Row 5 K6, *K2tog, yfd, K3, yfd, skpo, K10, rep from * to end, finishing last rep K6.
Row 7 K5, *K2tog, yfd, K5, yfd, skpo, K8, rep from * to end, finishing last rep K5.
Row 9 K4, *K2tog, yfd, K7, yfd, skpo, K6, rep from * to end, finishing last rep K4.
Row 11 K3, *K2tog, yfd, K9, yfd, skpo, K4, rep from * to end, finishing last rep K3.
Row 13 K3, *skpo, yfd, K3, K2tog, yfd, K4, yfd, K2tog, K4, rep from * to end, finishing last rep K3.
Row 15 K5, *yfd, skpo, K2tog, yfd, K1, yfd, skpo, K2tog, yfd, K8, rep from * to end, finishing last rep K5.
Row 16 P to end.
Inc row Inc in first st, K to last st, inc in last st. 89 sts.
Beg with a P row, cont in st st until work measures 11cm (4½in) from beg, ending with a P row.
Shape top
Dec row 1 K1, (K2tog, K9) to end. 81 sts.
P 1 row.
Dec row 2 K1, (K2tog, K8) to end. 73 sts.
P 1 row.
Dec row 3 K1, (K2tog, K7) to end. 65 sts.
P 1 row.
Cont to dec in this way, working 1 st less between decreases on next and every foll alt row until 17 sts rem, ending with a P row.
Next row K1, (K2tog) to end. 9 sts.
Cut off yarn, leaving a long end.

YOU WILL NEED
- 200g (7oz) DK yarn in cream
- 4mm (size 6) knitting needles
- Tapestry needle
- Thin card
- Pair of compasses and pencil
- Scissors

SIZE
Hat: circumference 38cm (15in)
Length 16cm (6½in)
Scarf: 13.5 x 66cm (5½ x 26in)

TENSION
23 sts and 35 rows to 10cm (4in) over st st

TO FINISH HAT

Block knitting to size. Thread end of yarn onto a tapestry needle, then thread through remaining stitches at top of hat. Draw up tightly and secure the end. Join centre back seam. Press seam.

TO FINISH SCARF

Block knitting to size. Join the cast-off edges of both pieces with backstitch. Fold the scarf across the join to gather. Wrap the centre band around the gathers and join the ends. Using 2cm (¾in) diameter circles of card, make six pompoms (see page 138). Sew a pompom at each corner and one in the centre of each end.

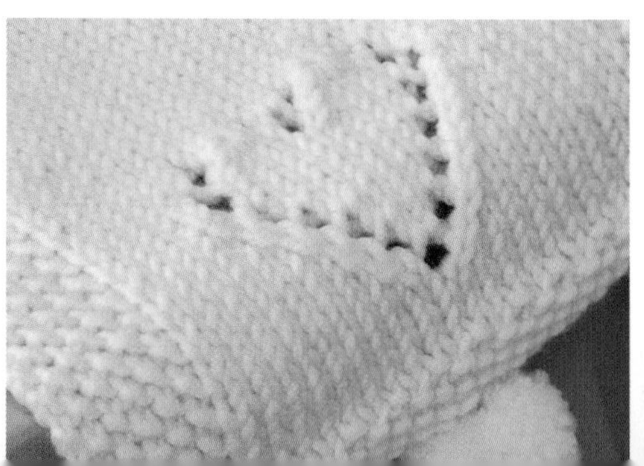

Scarf pattern

TO MAKE (2 pieces alike)
Using 4mm (size 6) needles cast on 33 sts.
Moss st row K1, *P1, K1, rep from * to end.
Rep this row 6 times more.
Next row (RS) (K1, P1) 3 times, K21, (P1, K1) 3 times.
Next row K1, (P1, K1) twice, P23, K1, (P1, K1) twice.
Rep last 2 rows once more.
Now work heart panel as follows:
Row 1 (K1, P1) 3 times, K9, K2tog, yfd, K10, (P1, K1) 3 times.
Row 2 and every alt row K1, (P1, K1) twice, P23, K1, (P1, K1) twice.
Row 3 (K1, P1) 3 times, K8, K2tog, yfd, K1, yfd, skpo, K8, (P1, K1) 3 times.
Row 5 (K1, P1) 3 times, K7, K2tog, yfd, K3, yfd, skpo, K7, (P1, K1) 3 times.
Row 7 (K1, P1) 3 times, K6, K2tog, yfd, K5, yfd, skpo, K6, (P1, K1) 3 times.
Row 9 (K1, P1) 3 times, K5, K2tog, yfd, K7, yfd, skpo, K5, (P1, K1) 3 times.
Row 11 (K1, P1) 3 times, K4, K2tog, yfd, K9, yfd, skpo, K4, (P1, K1) 3 times.
Row 13 (K1, P1) 3 times, K4, skpo, yfd, K3, K2tog, yfd, K4, yfd, K2tog, K4, (P1, K1) 3 times.
Row 15 (K1, P1) 3 times, K6, (yfd, skpo, K2tog, yfd, K1) twice, K5, (P1, K1) 3 times.
Cont in st st with moss st borders as set until work measures 33cm (13in), ending with a WS row. Cast off.

CENTRE BAND
Using 4mm (size 6) needles, cast on 5 sts.
Work the moss st row for 13cm (5in).
Cast off.

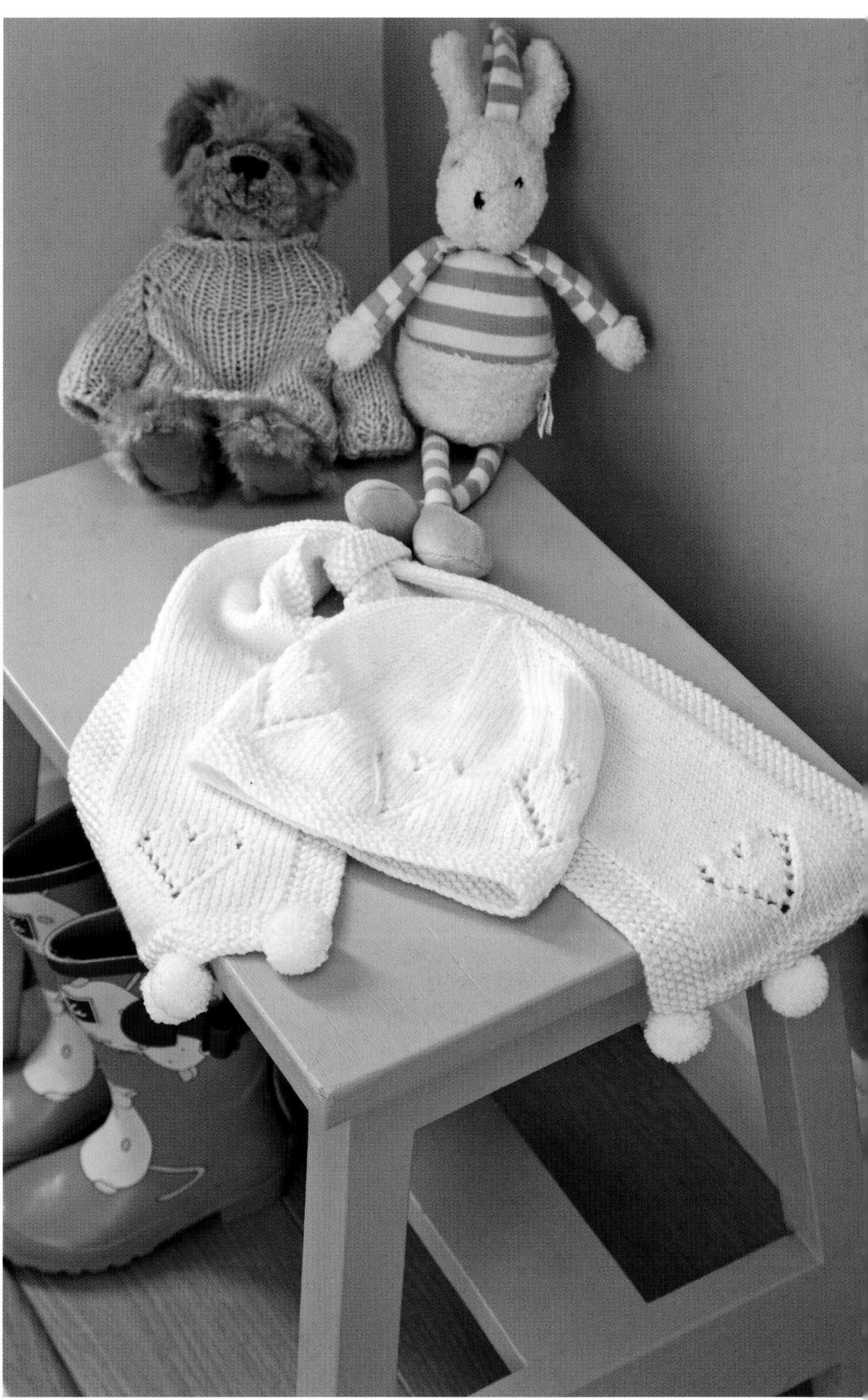

project 3: child's cardigan

A pretty cardigan every little girl will love to wear. Knitted in a simple eyelet pattern and bordered with a cute flounce in a contrasting colour.

YOU WILL NEED

- 150g (5¼oz) 4-ply cotton in green (A)
- 50g (1¾oz) 4-ply cotton in duck-egg blue (B)
- 2.75mm (size 2) and 3.25mm (size 3) knitting needles
- 1 button

SIZE

To fit chest 61–66cm (24–26in)
Actual measurement 67cm (26½in)
Length 25cm (10in)
Sleeve seam 10cm (4in)

TENSION

26 sts and 34 rows to 10cm (4in) over Staggered Eyelets patt

TO FINISH

Press work lightly on WS using a warm iron over a damp cloth, omitting ribbing. Mark depth of armholes 13cm (5in) from shoulder seams on back and fronts. Sew sleeves to armholes between markers, then join side and sleeve seams. Sew on button to correspond with buttonhole.

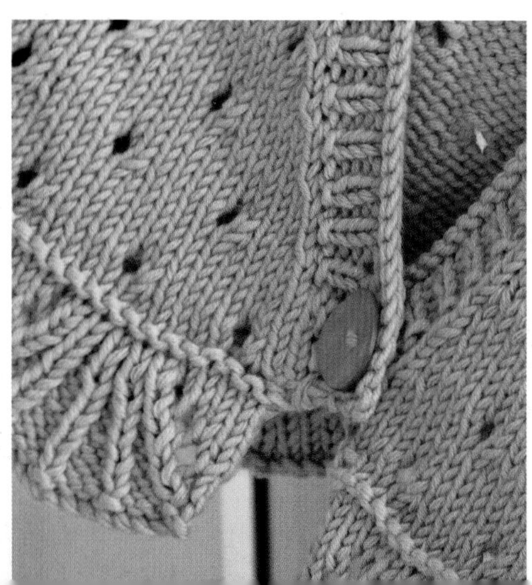

Pattern

BACK

Using 3.25mm (size 3) needles and B, cast on 109 sts.
**Work in Ribbed Flounce patt as follows:
Row 1 (RS) P to end.
Row 2 P2, *K3, (P1, K3) 3 times, P3, rep from * to end, finishing last rep P2.
Row 3 K1, *yfd, K1, P2tog, P1, (K1, P3) twice, K1, P1, P2tog, K1, yfd, K1, rep from * to end.
Row 4 P3, *K2, P1, (K3, P1) twice, K2, P5, rep from * to end, finishing last rep P3.
Row 5 K2, *yfd, K1, P2, (K1, P1, P2tog) twice, K1, P2, K1, yfd, K3, rep from * to end, finishing last rep K2.
Row 6 P4, *K2, (P1, K2) 3 times, P7, rep from * to end, finishing last rep P4.
Row 7 K3, *yfd, K1, P2tog, (K1, P2) twice, K1, P2tog, K1, yfd, K5, rep from * to end, finishing last rep K3.
Row 8 P5, *K1, (P1, K2) twice, P1, K1, P9, rep from * to end, finishing last rep P5.
Row 9 K4, *yfd, K1, P1, (K1, P2tog) twice, K1, P1, K1, yfd, K7, rep from * to end, finishing last rep K4.
Row 10 P6, *K1, (P1, K1) 3 times, P11, rep from * to end, finishing last rep P6.
Row 11 K5, *(skpo) twice, K1, (K2tog) twice, K9, rep from * to end, finishing last rep K5. 85 sts.
Row 12 K to end.
Cut off B and join on A.**
Inc 1 st at each end of first row, work in Staggered Eyelets patt as follows:
Row 1 (RS) K to end.
Row 2 P to end.
Row 3 K2tog, *yfd, K4, K2tog, rep from * to last st, yfd, K1.
Rows 4 to 8 Beg with a P row, work 5 rows st st.
Row 9 K3, *K2tog, yfd, K4, rep from * to end.
Rows 10 to 12 Beg with a P row, work 3 rows st st.
These 12 rows form the patt.
Cont in patt until work measures 25cm (10in) from beg, ending with a WS row.

Shape shoulders

Cast off 10 sts at beg of next 4 rows and 9 sts at beg of foll 2 rows. Cut off yarn and leave rem 29 sts on a holder.

LEFT FRONT

Using 3.25mm (size 3) needles and B, cast on 55 sts.
Work as given for back from ** to **. 43 sts.
Beg row 7, cont in Staggered Eyelets patt as given for back, work 8 rows inc 1 st at each end of first row. 45 sts.

Shape front edge

Keeping patt correct, dec 1 st at end of next and every foll 4th row until 29 sts rem. Cont without shaping until front measures same as back to shoulder, ending at side edge.

Shape shoulder

Cast off 10 sts at beg of next and foll alt row. Work 1 row.
Cast off.

RIGHT FRONT
Work as given for left front but dec 1 st at beg of row for front edge shaping.

SLEEVES
Using 2.75mm (size 2) needles and A, cast on 49 sts.
Rib row 1 (RS) K1, (P1, K1) to end.
Rib row 2 P1, (K1, P1) to end.
Rep these 2 rows once more, then work the first row again.
Change to 3.25mm (size 3) needles.
Next row K to end.
Inc row K3, inc in next st, (K5, inc in next st) to last 3 sts, K3. 57 sts.
Beg row 8, cont in Staggered Eyelets patt, but inc 1 st at each end of every 4th row until there are 69 sts.
Cont without shaping until work measures 10cm (4in) from beg, ending with a WS row.
Cast off.

BAND
Join shoulder seams. With right side of work facing, join A to first row of Staggered Eyelets patt on right front and, using 2.75mm (size 2) needles, K up 60 sts along front edge, K sts from holder, then K up 60 sts along left front edge to top of edging. 149 sts.
Next row K to end.
Rib row 1 (RS) K1, (P1, K1) to end.
Rib row 2 P1, (K1, P1) to end.
Buttonhole row 1 Rib 3, cast off 3, rib to end.
Buttonhole row 2 Rib to end, casting on 3 sts at buttonhole.
Next row K to end.
Cast off knitwise.

lesson 13 lace panels

The textural contrast of a lace panel set within a neutral knitted background is not only visually dramatic but makes a perfect starting point for a knitter new to lace for whom an all-over lace pattern might be a little daunting. Whether the design is large or small, simple or complex, a lace panel isolated in a stocking stitch or reverse stocking stitch background provides visual impact for home accessories and garments alike.

Lace panels can consist of a single large lace motif, or a block of repeated motifs worked together. They can be worked horizontally or vertically and are a great way to customise basic stocking stitch designs.

For a larger item such as a sweater, the panel can be repeated in a series with each repeat 'framed' in a border of neutral background knitting. You can create your own design easily by combining panels of different patterns, working them side-by-side to create an exquisite lace patchwork.

Lace panels worked on their own can be used in a number of eye-catching ways. A long, narrow panel makes a pretty trim for the leading edge of a curtain – match the yarn weight to the weight of the curtain fabric. A long wide panel creates an intriguing and unusual wrap for a fabric cushion cover.

Practice pattern
Use this pattern to work through the step-by-step exercise overleaf to make the sample as shown.

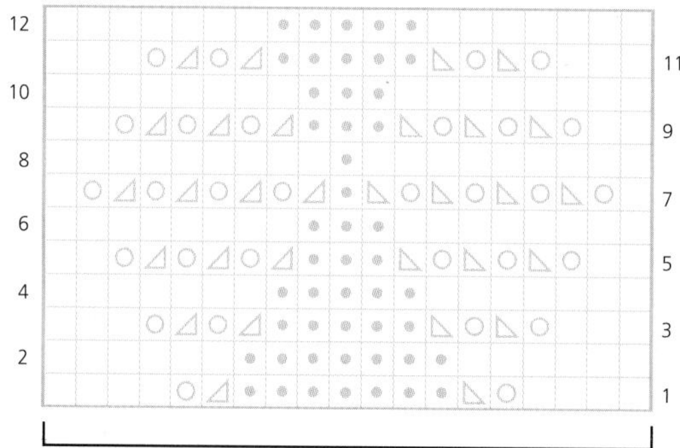

Panel of 19 stitches

Pattern

Row 1 (RS) K4, yfd, skpo, P7, K2tog, yfd, K4.
Row 2 P6, K7, P6.
Row 3 K3, (yfd, skpo) twice, P5, (K2tog, yfd) twice, K3.
Row 4 P7, K5, P7.
Row 5 K2, (yfd, skpo) 3 times, P3, (K2tog, yfd) 3 times, K2.
Row 6 P8, K3, P8.
Row 7 K1, (yfd, skpo) 4 times, P1, (K2tog, yfd) 4 times, K1.
Row 8 P9, K1, P9.
Row 9 As row 5.
Row 10 As row 6.
Row 11 As row 3.
Row 12 As row 4.
These 12 rows form the patt.

diamond mesh

Panel of 19 stitches. Worked on a background of reverse stocking stitch.

12
11
10
9
8
7
6
5
4
3
2
1

3.25mm
(size 3)

4-ply wool

eyelets in diagonal lines

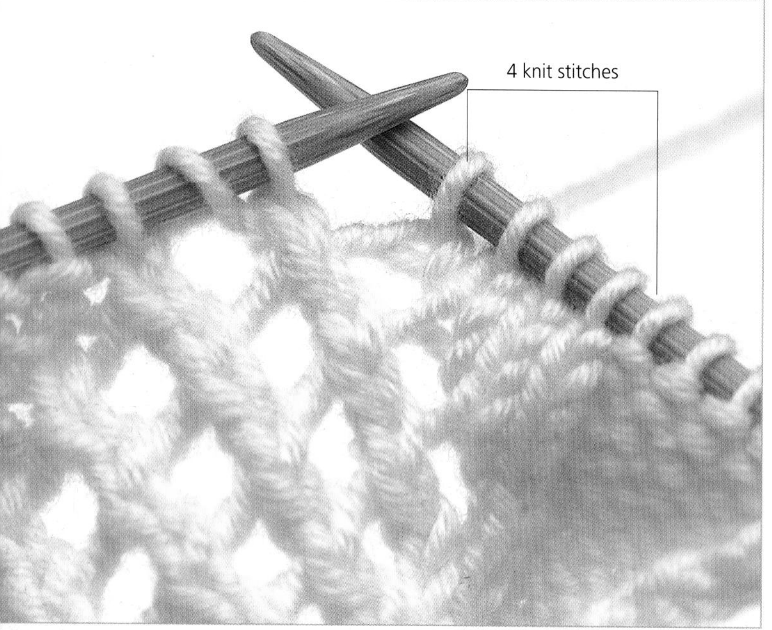

1 The eyelets in this pattern form diagonal lines – on the first side of the panel they slope from right to left and on the second side from left to right. The direction of the slope is determined by the type of decrease used. The eyelet at the beginning of the row is formed by working yarn forward (abbreviated as yfd) followed by a decrease. On row 1 the first four stitches of the panel are knitted.

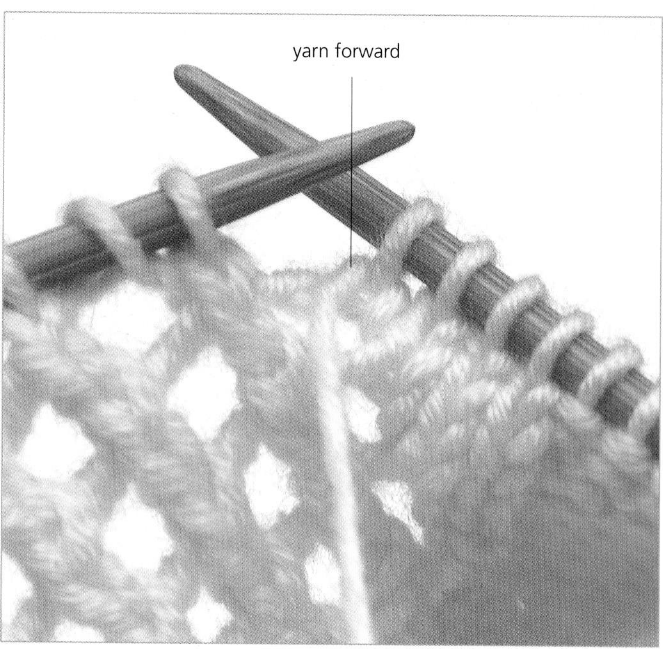

2 For the eyelet the yarn is taken to the front of the knitting (yfd) ready to work the next stitch. The eyelet is formed once the next row is worked.

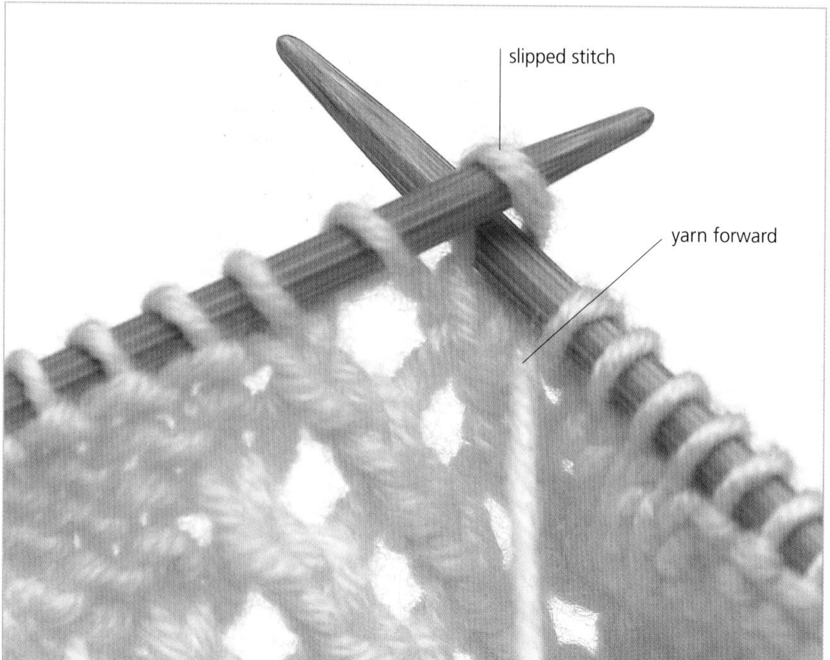

3 To form the diagonal slope from right to left, the decrease slip 1, knit 1, pass slipped stitch over is worked (abbreviated as skpo). Slip the next stitch knitwise from the left-hand needle to the right-hand needle.

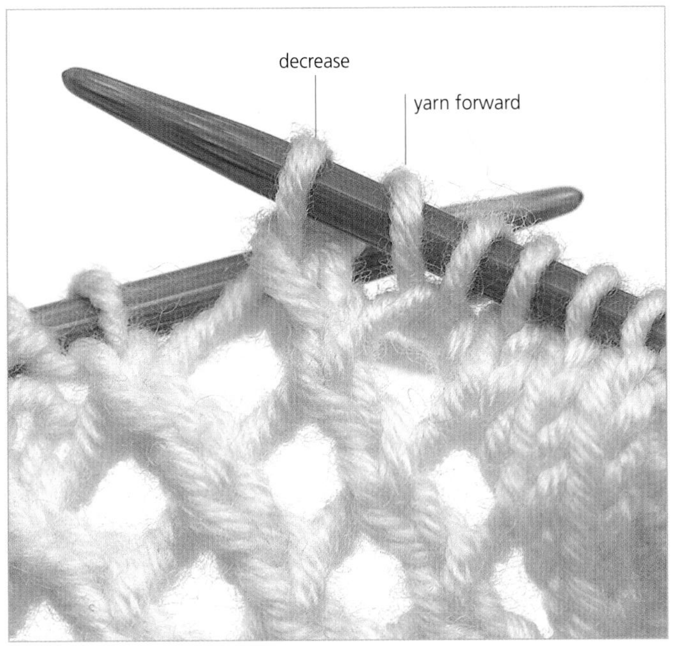

4 Knit the next stitch, then insert the left-hand needle, from left to right, into the slipped stitch on the right-hand needle and lift it over the stitch just knitted and off the needle – decrease formed. The decrease slopes from right to left. The yarn forward has made a stitch on the right-hand needle.

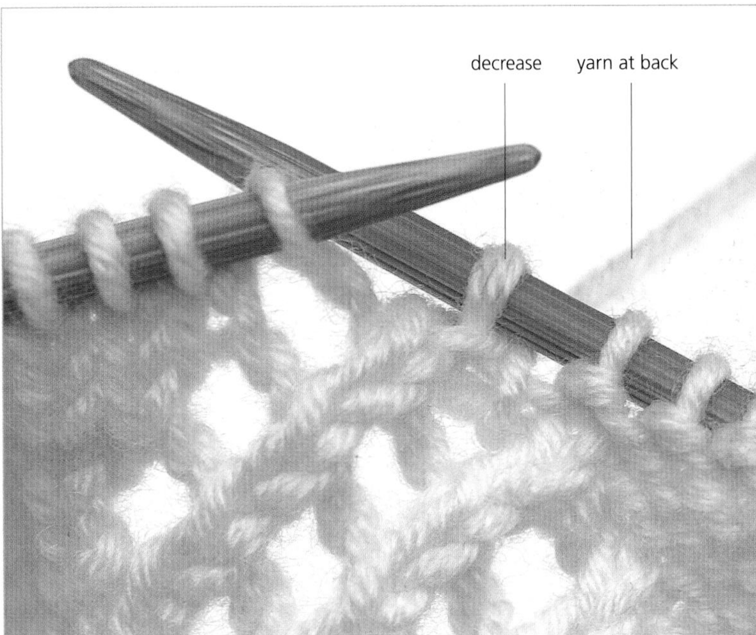

5 On the second side of the panel the eyelet is worked after the decrease. The decrease is worked by knitting two stitches together (abbreviated as K2tog). Purl the next seven stitches, then take the yarn to the back and knit the next two stitches together – decrease formed. The decrease slopes from left to right.

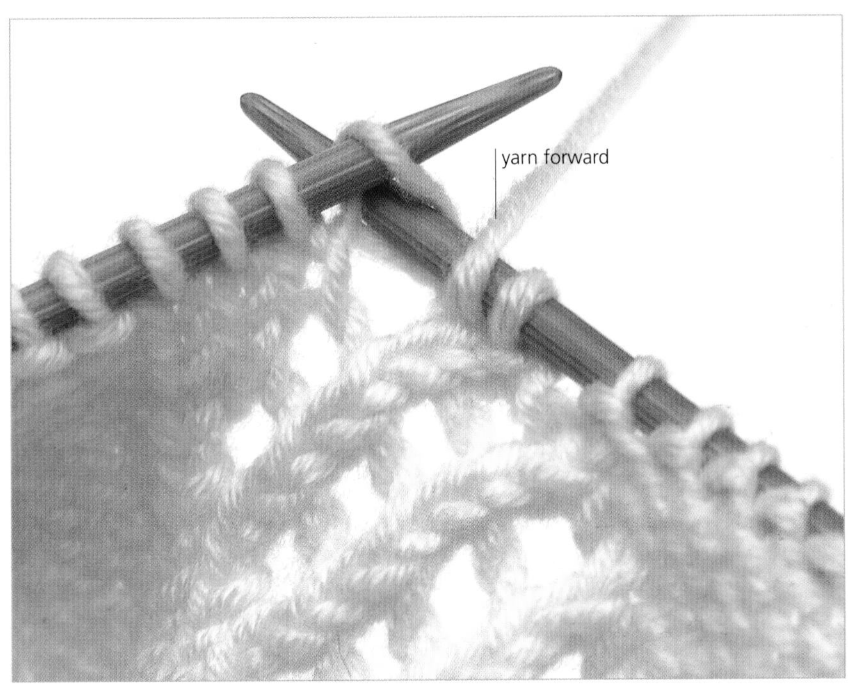

6 For the eyelet, bring the yarn to the front of the knitting and knit the next stitch – the yarn is automatically taken over the needle, so making a stitch. The eyelet is formed once the next row is worked.

single diamond

Panel of 9 stitches. Worked on a background of stocking stitch.

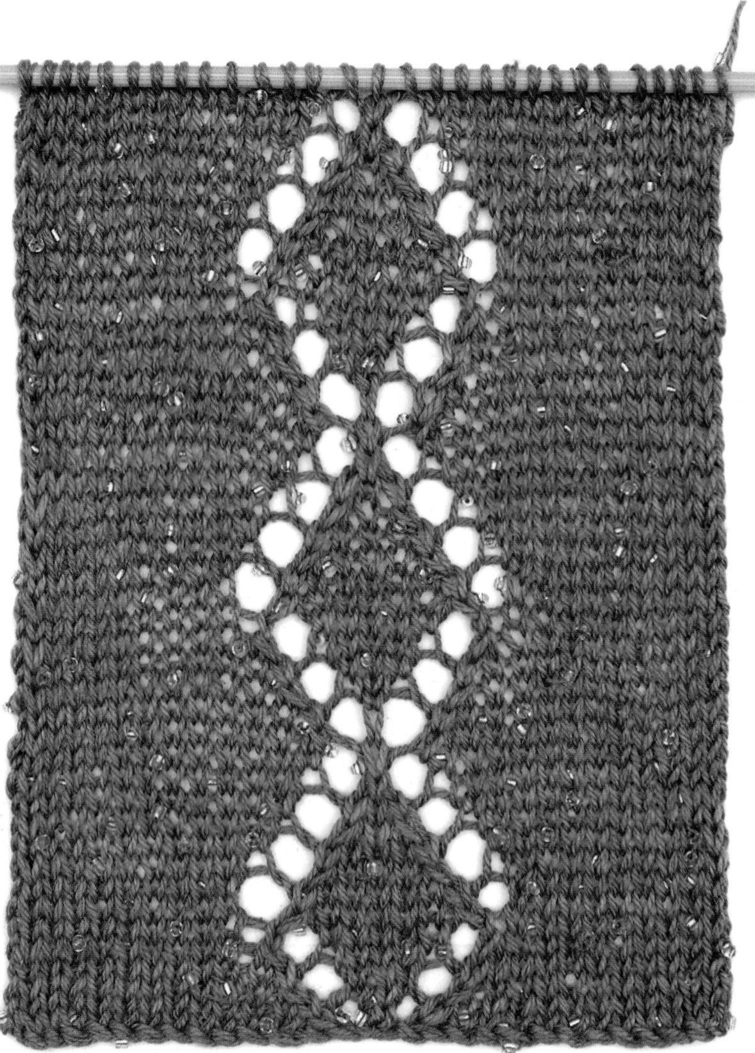

3.75mm (size 5)

Beaded 3-ply

Pattern

Row 1 (RS) K2, K2tog, yfd, K1, yfd, skpo, K2.
Row 2 and every alt row P to end.
Row 3 K1, K2tog, yfd, K3, yfd, skpo, K1.
Row 5 K2tog, yfd, K5, yfd, skpo.
Row 7 Yfd, skpo, K5, K2tog, yfd.
Row 9 K1, yfd, skpo, K3, K2tog, yfd, K1.
Row 11 K2, yfd, skpo, K1, K2tog, yfd, K2.
Row 13 K3, yfd, sl 2 as if to K2tog, K1, p2sso, yfd, K3.
Row 14 P to end.
These 14 rows form the patt.

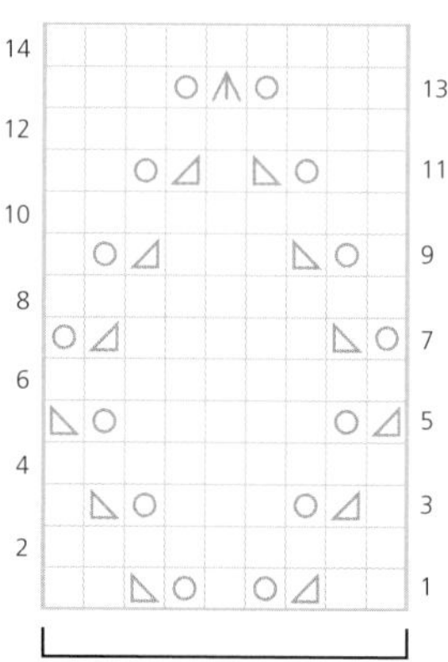

Panel of 9 stitches

variation

Panel of 23 stitches. Worked on a background of stocking stitch.

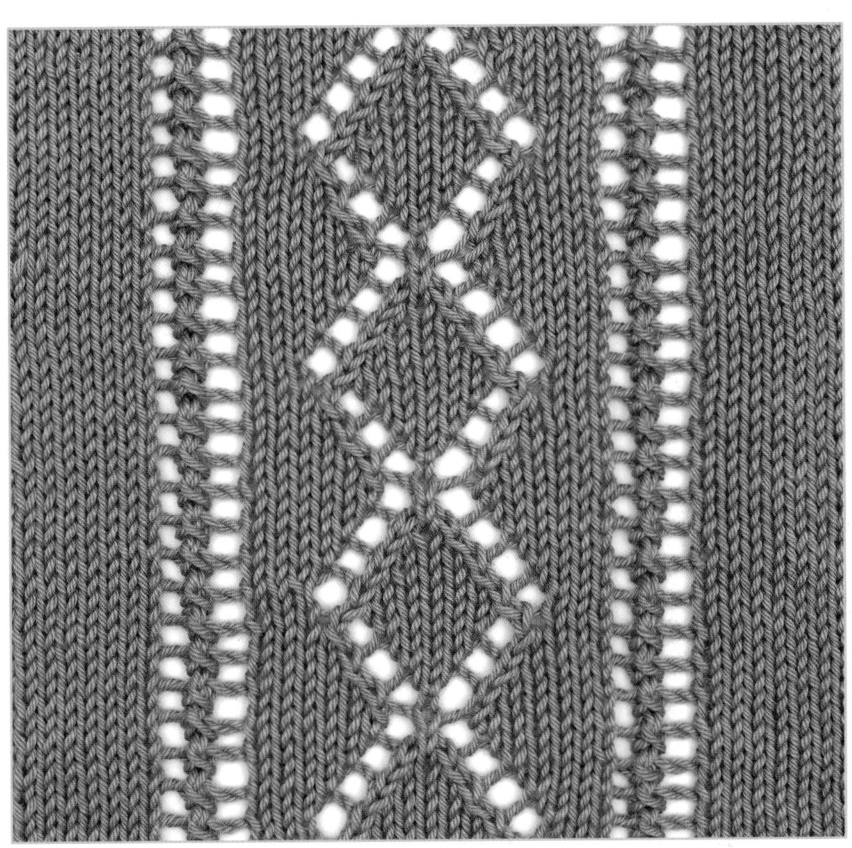

3.75mm (size 5)

DK cotton

Pattern

Row 1 (RS) K1, yfd, sl 1, K2tog, psso, yfd, K5, K2tog, yfd, K1, yfd, skpo, K5, yfd, sl 1, K2tog, psso, yfd, K1.
Row 2 and every alt row P to end.
Row 3 K1, yfd, sl 1, K2tog, psso, yfd, K4, K2tog, yfd, K3, yfd, skpo, K4, yfd, sl 1, K2tog, psso, yfd, K1.
Row 5 K1, yfd, sl 1, K2tog, psso, yfd, K3, K2tog, yfd, K5, yfd, skpo, K3, yfd, sl 1, K2tog, psso, yfd, K1.
Row 7 K1, yfd, sl 1, K2tog, psso, yfd, K3, yfd, skpo, K5, K2tog, yfd, K3, yfd, sl 1, K2tog, psso, yfd, K1.
Row 9 K1, yfd, sl 1, K2tog, psso, yfd, K4, yfd, skpo, K3, K2tog, yfd, K4, yfd, sl 1, K2tog, psso, yfd, K1.
Row 11 K1, yfd, sl 1, K2tog, psso, yfd, K5, yfd, skpo, K1, K2tog, yfd, K5, yfd, sl 1, K2tog, psso, yfd, K1.
Row 13 K1, yfd, sl 1, K2tog, psso, yfd, K6, yfd, sl 2 as if to K2tog, K1, p2sso, yfd, K6, yfd, sl 1, K2tog, psso, yfd, K1.
Row 14 P to end.
These 14 rows form the patt.

Panel of 23 stitches

double diamonds

Panel of 19 stitches. Worked on a background of reverse stocking stitch.

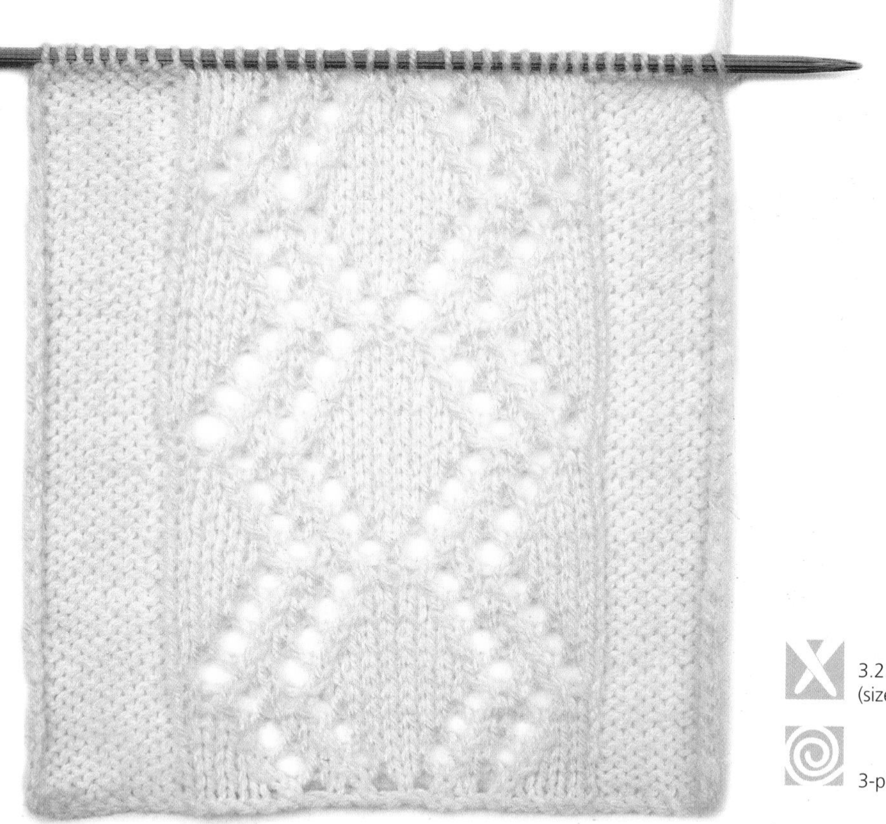

3.25mm (size 3)

3-ply wool

Pattern

Row 1 (RS) K4, (K2tog, yfd, K1) twice, (yfd, skpo, K1) twice, K3.
Row 2 and every alt row P to end.
Row 3 K3, K2tog, yfd, K1, K2tog, yfd, K3, (yfd, skpo, K1) twice, K2.
Row 5 K2, K2tog, yfd, K1, K2tog, yfd, K5, (yfd, skpo, K1) twice, K1.
Row 7 K1, K2tog, yfd, K1, K2tog, yfd, K7, (yfd, skpo, K1) twice.
Row 9 (K1, yfd, skpo) twice, K7, (K2tog, yfd, K1) twice.
Row 11 K2, yfd, skpo, K1, yfd, skpo, K5, (K2tog, yfd, K1) twice, K1.
Row 13 K3, yfd, skpo, K1, yfd, skpo, K3, (K2tog, yfd, K1) twice, K2.
Row 15 K4, (yfd, skpo, K1) twice, (K2tog, yfd, K1) twice, K3.
Row 16 P to end.
These 16 rows form the patt.

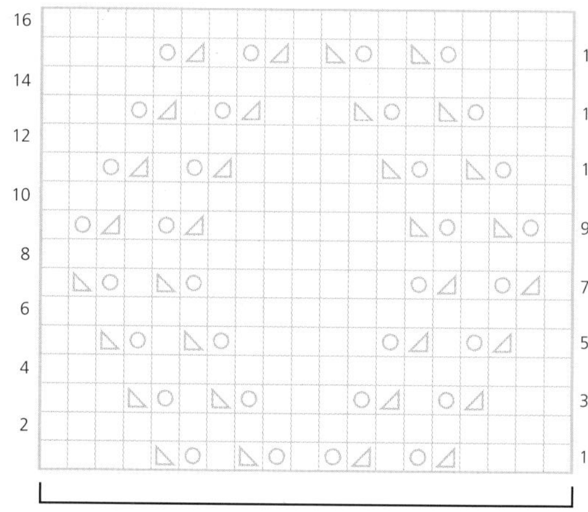

Panel of 19 stitches

variation

Panel of 23 stitches. Worked on a background of reverse stocking stitch.

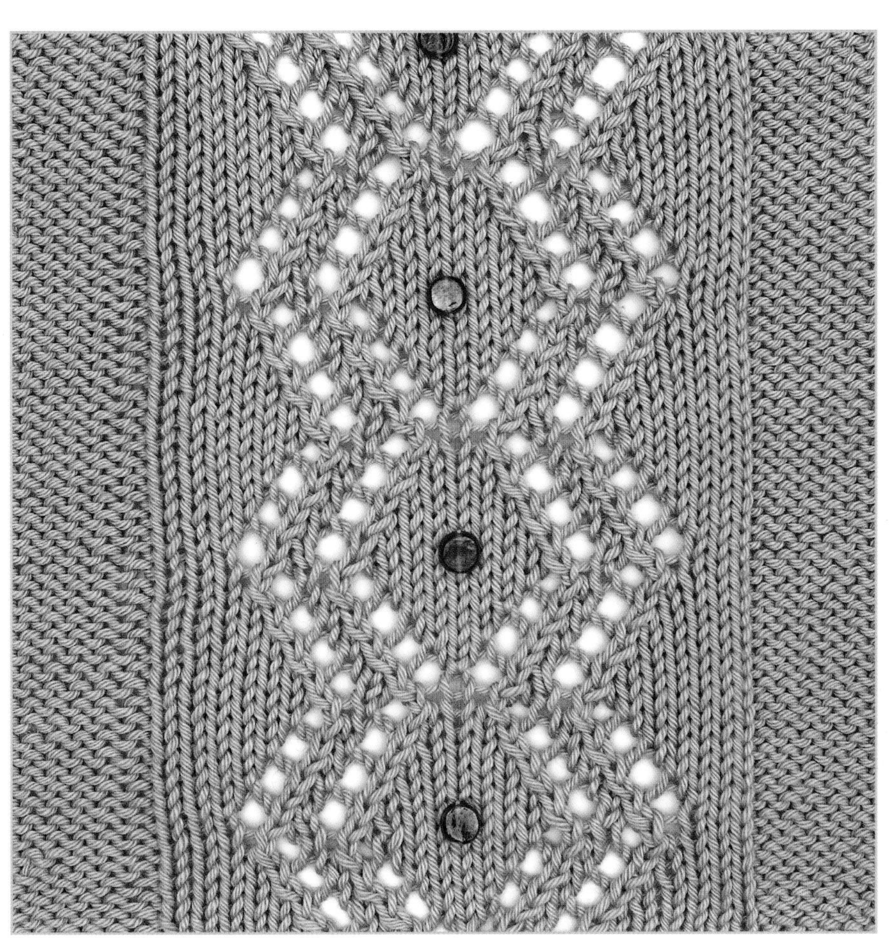

3.25mm (size 3)

4-ply perlé cotton

Crisp texture

Worked in 4-ply perlé cotton yarn, the pattern has a crisp texture. The panel has been widened by working two extra stitches at each side in stocking stitch and the diamonds have been embellished with beads at the centres.

diamond spiral

Panel of 15 stitches. Worked on a background of stocking stitch.

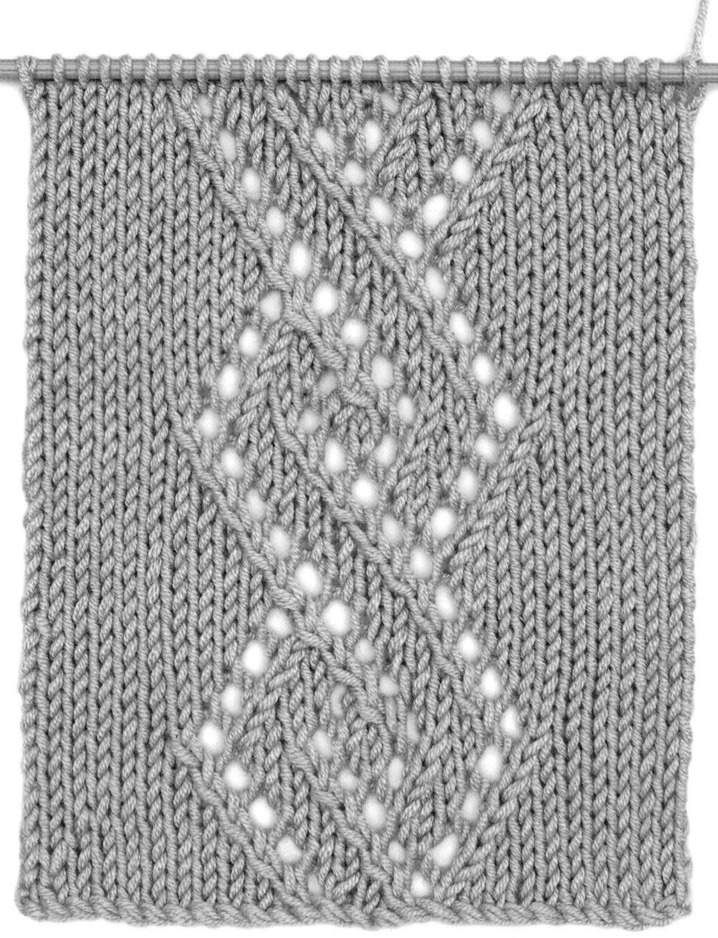

3.75mm (size 5)

DK cotton

Pattern

Row 1 (RS) K5, yfd, skpo, K2, yfd, skpo, K4.
Row 2 and every alt row P to end.
Row 3 K3, K2tog, yfd, K1, yfd, skpo, K2, yfd, skpo, K3.
Row 5 K2, K2tog, yfd, K3, yfd, skpo, K2, yfd, skpo, K2.
Row 7 K1, K2tog, yfd, K2, K2tog, yfd, K1, yfd, skpo, K2, yfd, skpo, K1.
Row 9 K2tog, yfd, K2, K2tog, yfd, K3, yfd, skpo, K2, yfd, skpo.
Row 11 K2, yfd, skpo, K2, yfd, sl 1, K2tog, psso, yfd, K2, K2tog, yfd, K2.
Row 13 K3, yfd, skpo, K2, yfd, skpo, K1, K2tog, yfd, K3.
Row 15 K4, yfd, skpo, K2, yfd, sl 1, K2tog, psso, yfd, K4.
Row 16 P to end.
These 16 rows form the patt.

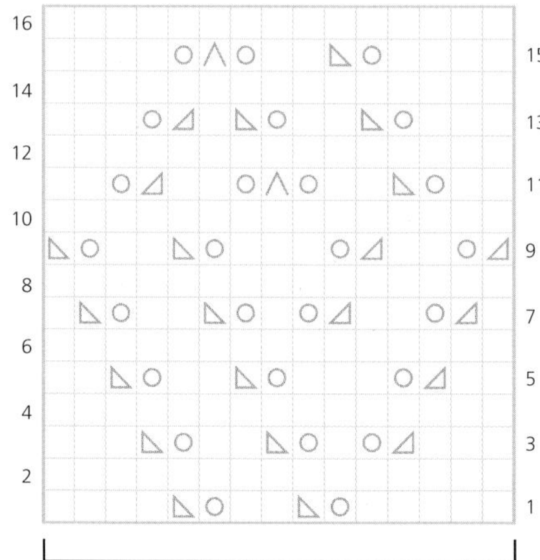

Panel of 15 stitches

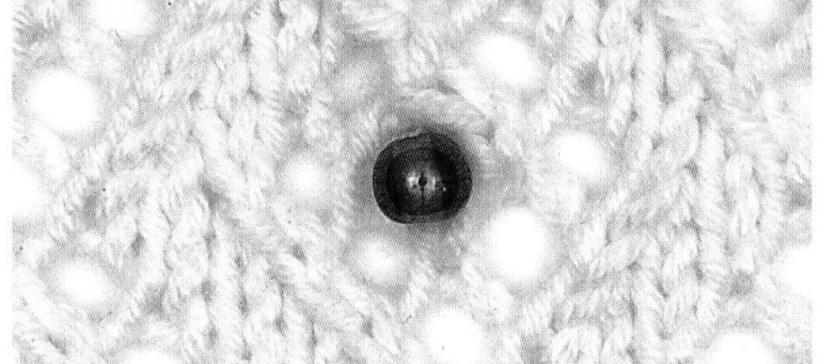

variation

Panel of 15 stitches. Worked on a background of reverse stocking stitch.

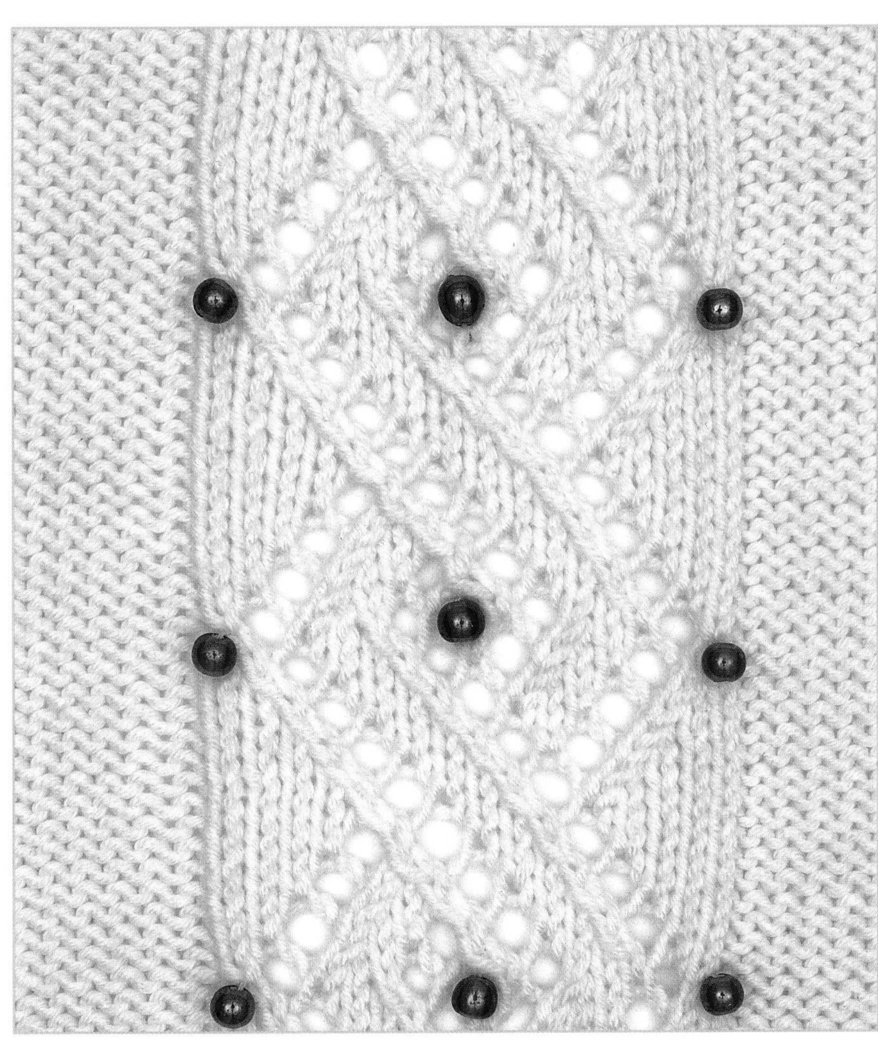

3.25mm (size 3)

4-ply wool

Embellishment

The outer edge and centre of each diamond has been trimmed with a bead.

arrowhead

Panel of 21 stitches. Worked on a background of stocking stitch.

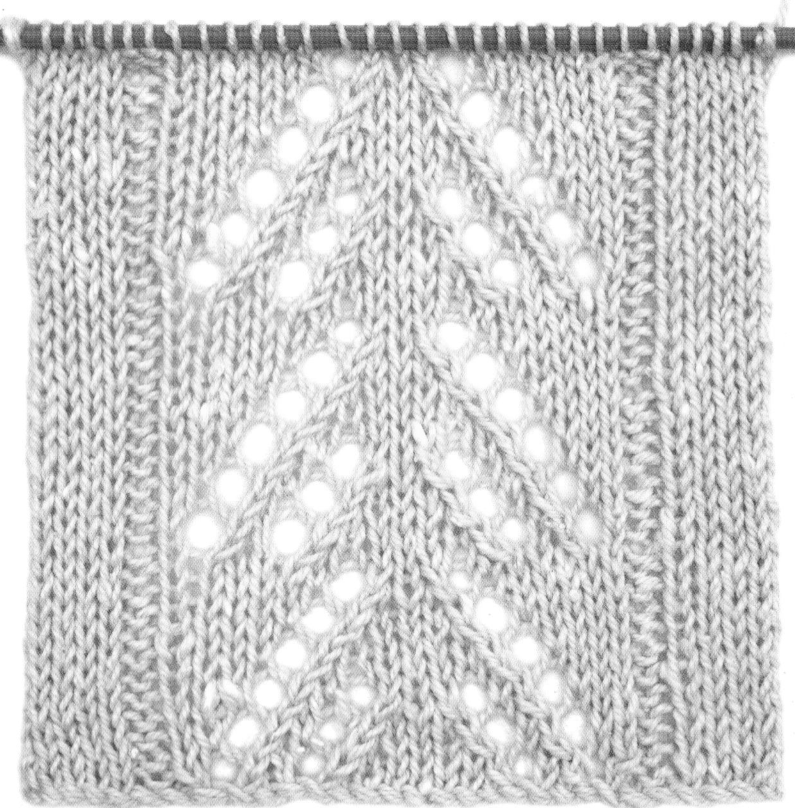

3.75mm (size 5)

DK slubbed cotton

Pattern

Row 1 (RS) P2, (K1, yfd, skpo) twice, K5, (K2tog, yfd, K1) twice, P2.
Row 2 and every alt row K2, P17, K2.
Row 3 P2, K2, yfd, skpo, K1, yfd, skpo, K3, K2tog, yfd, K1, K2tog, yfd, K2, P2.
Row 5 P2, K3, (yfd, skpo, K1) twice, K2tog, yfd, K1, K2tog, yfd, K3, P2.
Row 7 P2, K4, yfd, skpo, K5, K2tog, yfd, K4, P2.
Row 9 P2, K5, yfd, skpo, K3, K2tog, yfd, K5, P2.
Row 11 P2, K6, yfd, skpo, K1, K2tog, yfd, K6, P2.
Row 12 K2, P17, K2.
These 12 rows form the patt.

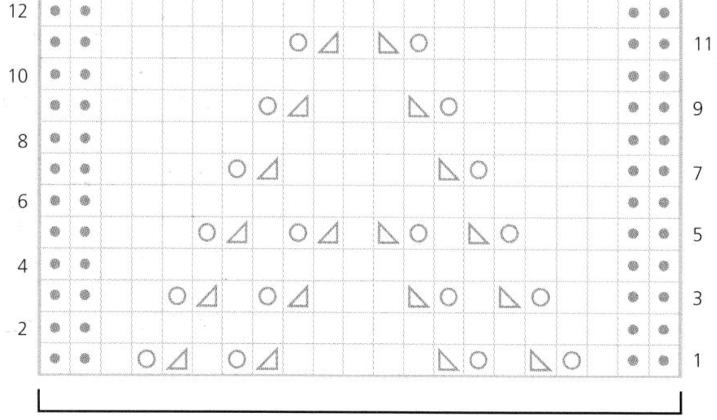

Panel of 21 stitches

variation

Panel of 25 stitches. Worked on a background of stocking stitch.

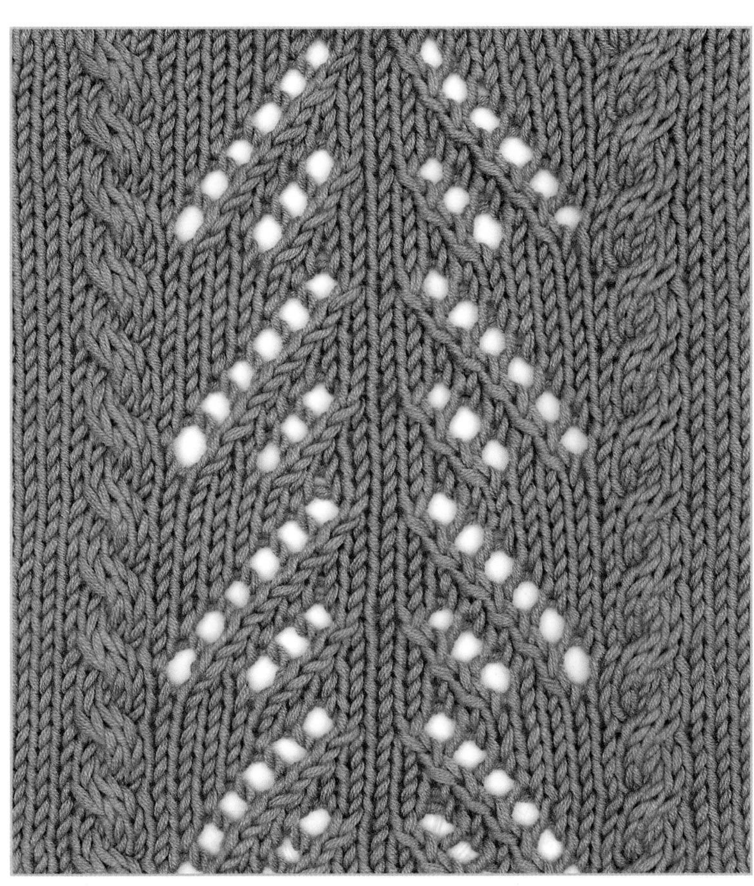

3.75mm (size 5)

DK cotton

Pattern

Row 1 (RS) K5, yfd, skpo, K1, yfd, skpo, K5, K2tog, yfd, K1, K2tog, yfd, K5.
Row 2 and every alt row P to end.
Row 3 C4B, K2, yfd, skpo, K1, yfd, skpo, K3, K2tog, yfd, K1, K2tog, yfd, K2, C4F.
Row 5 K7, (yfd, skpo, K1) twice, K2tog, yfd, K1, K2tog, yfd, K7.
Row 7 C4B, K4, yfd, skpo, K5, K2tog, yfd, K4, C4F.
Row 9 K9, yfd, skpo, K3, K2tog, yfd, K9.
Row 11 C4B, K6, yfd, skpo, K1, K2tog, yfd, K6, C4F.
Row 12 P to end.
These 12 rows form the patt.

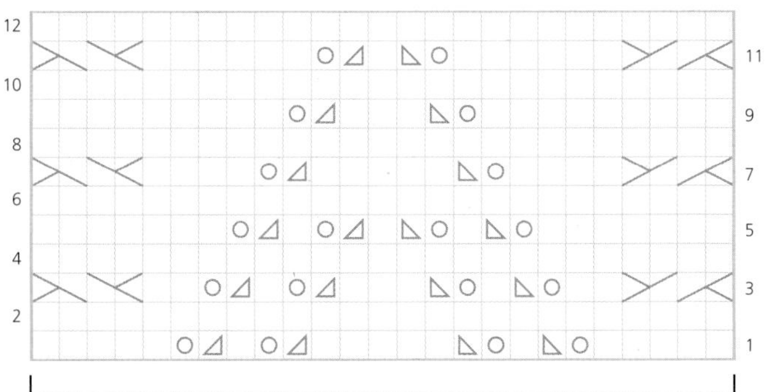

Panel of 25 stitches

small diamonds

Panel of 15 stitches. Worked on a background of reverse stocking stitch.

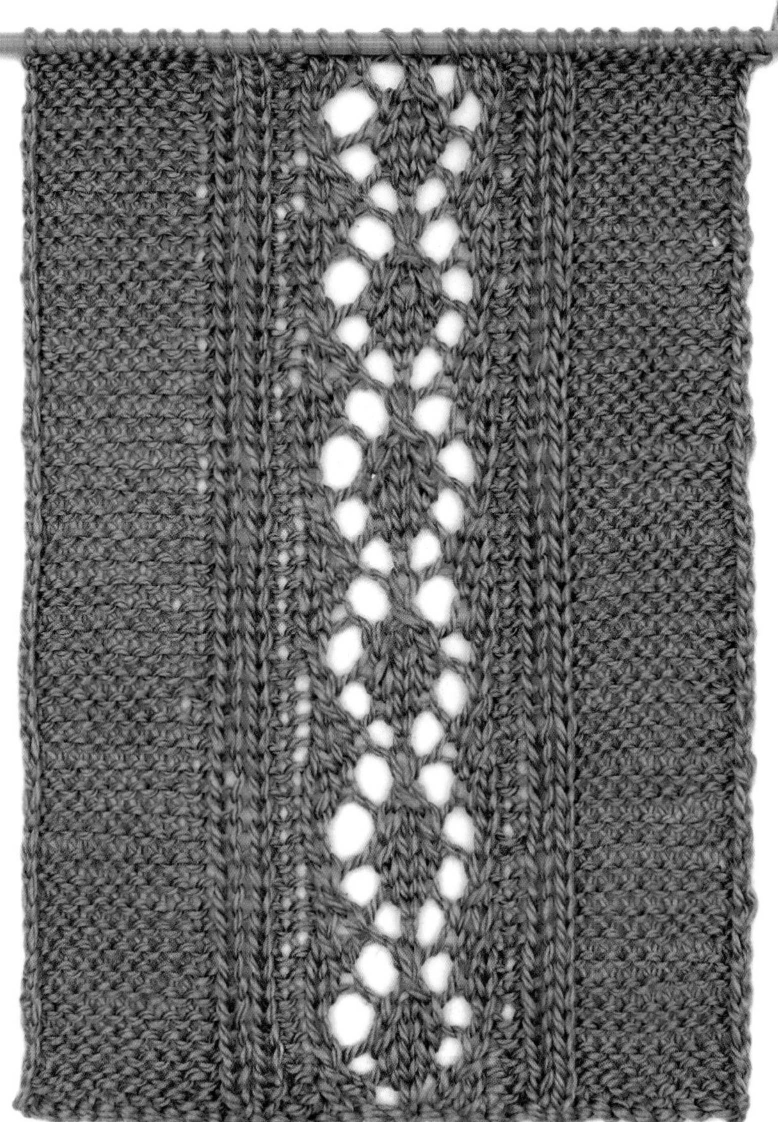

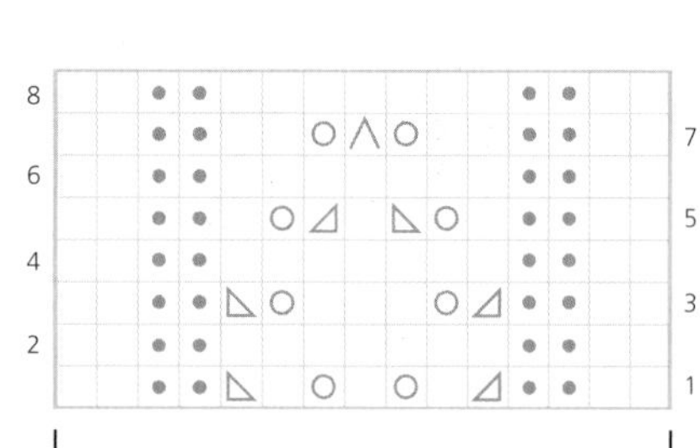

Panel of 15 stitches

Pattern

Row 1 (RS) K2, P2, K2tog, K1, (yfd, K1) twice, skpo, P2, K2.
Row 2 and every alt row P2, K2, P7, K2, P2.
Row 3 K2, P2, K2tog, yfd, K3, yfd, skpo, P2, K2.
Row 5 K2, P2, K1, yfd, skpo, K1, K2tog, yfd, K1, P2, K2.
Row 7 K2, P2, K2, yfd, sl 1, K2tog, psso, yfd, K2, P2, K2.
Row 8 P2, K2, P7, K2, P2.
These 8 rows form the patt.

2.75mm (size 2)

3-ply silk

variation

This sample shows two panels with 5 stitches worked in moss stitch between. Worked on a multiple of 20 stitches plus 5.

3.25mm (size 3)

4-ply cotton

Pattern

Row 1 (RS) P1, (K1, P1) twice, *K2, P2, K2tog, K1, (yfd, K1) twice, skpo, P2, K2, P1, (K1, P1) twice, rep from * to end.
Row 2 and every alt row P1, (K1, P1) twice, *P2, K2, P7, K2, P3, (K1, P1) twice, rep from * to end.
Row 3 P1, (K1, P1) twice, *K2, P2, K2tog, yfd, K3, yfd, skpo, P2, K2, P1, (K1, P1) twice, rep from * to end.
Row 5 P1, (K1, P1) twice, *K2, P2, K1, yfd, skpo, K1, K2tog, yfd, K1, P2, K2, P1, (K1, P1) twice, rep from * to end.
Row 7 P1, (K1, P1) twice, *K2, P2, K2, yfd, sl 1, K2tog, psso, yfd, K2, P2, K2, P1, (K1, P1) twice, rep from * to end.
Row 8 As row 2.
These 8 rows form the patt.

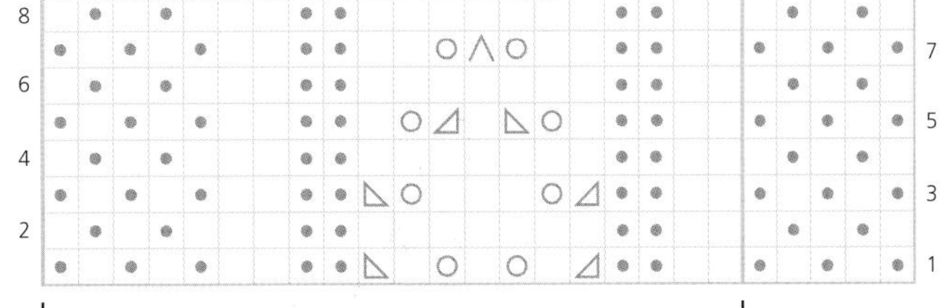

20-stitch repeat

horseshoe and bobbles

Panel of 15 stitches. Worked on a background of stocking stitch.

3.75mm (size 5)

DK alpaca

Pattern

Row 1 (WS) P to end.
Row 2 K2, MB-2, K2, K2tog, yfd, K1, yfd, skpo, K2, MB-2, K2.
Row 3 and every alt row P to end.
Row 4 K1, MB-2, K2, K2tog, yfd, K3, yfd, skpo, K2, MB-2, K1.
Row 6 MB-2, K2, K2tog, yfd, K5, yfd, skpo, K2, MB-2.
Row 8 MB-2, K2, skpo, yfd, K5, yfd, K2tog, K2, MB-2.
Row 10 K1, MB-2, K11, MB-2, K1.
Row 11 P to end.
Rows 2 to 11 form the patt.

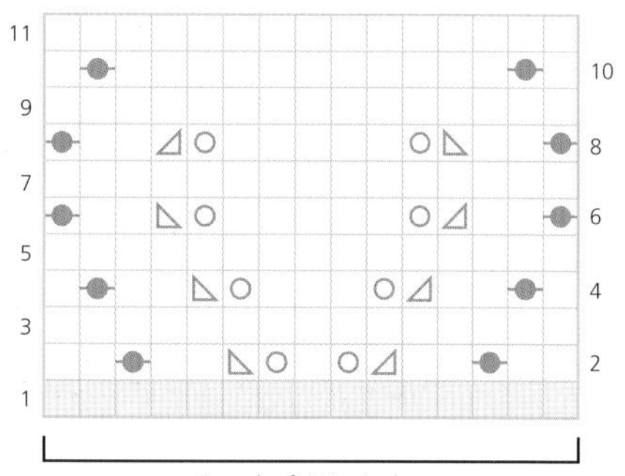

Panel of 15 stitches

variation

Panel of 15 stitches. Worked on a background of stocking stitch.

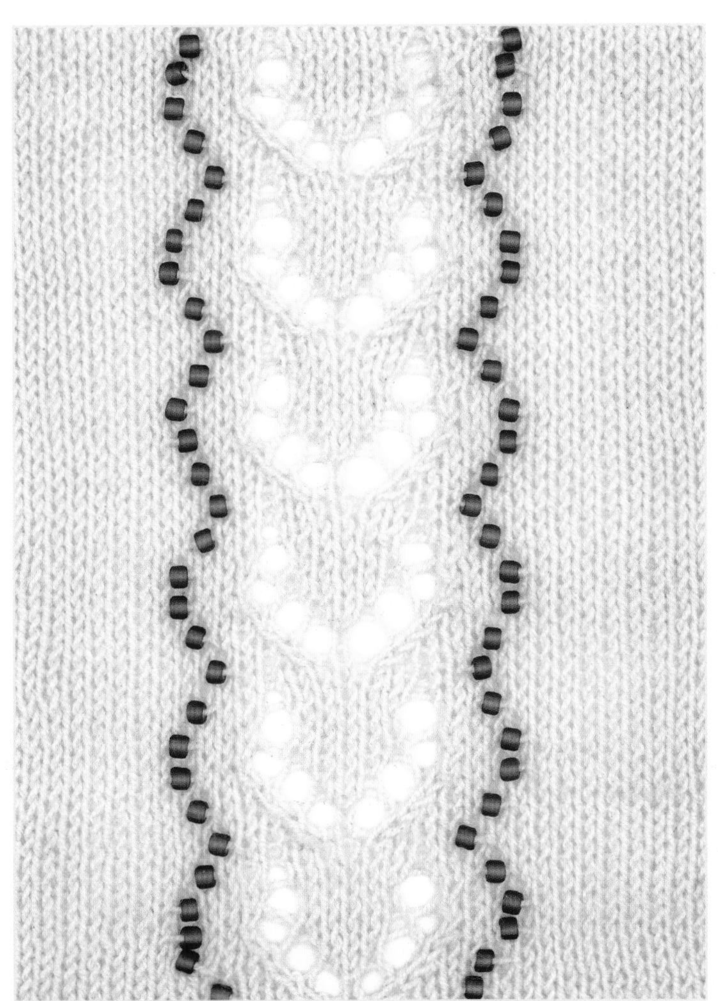

3.25mm (size 3)

3-ply wool

Beads instead of bobbles

Thread small beads onto a ball of yarn. Push the beads along the yarn until you are ready to work with them. Work the 10 rows of horseshoe and bobbles pattern, but knit a bead (B1) into the pattern on rows 2, 4, 6, 8 and 10 instead of working a bobble.

Special abbreviation

B1 (bead 1) = With yarn at front, slip the next stitch purlwise and push the bead against the right-hand needle ready to work the next stitch.

paired leaves

Panel of 29 stitches. Worked on a background of stocking stitch.

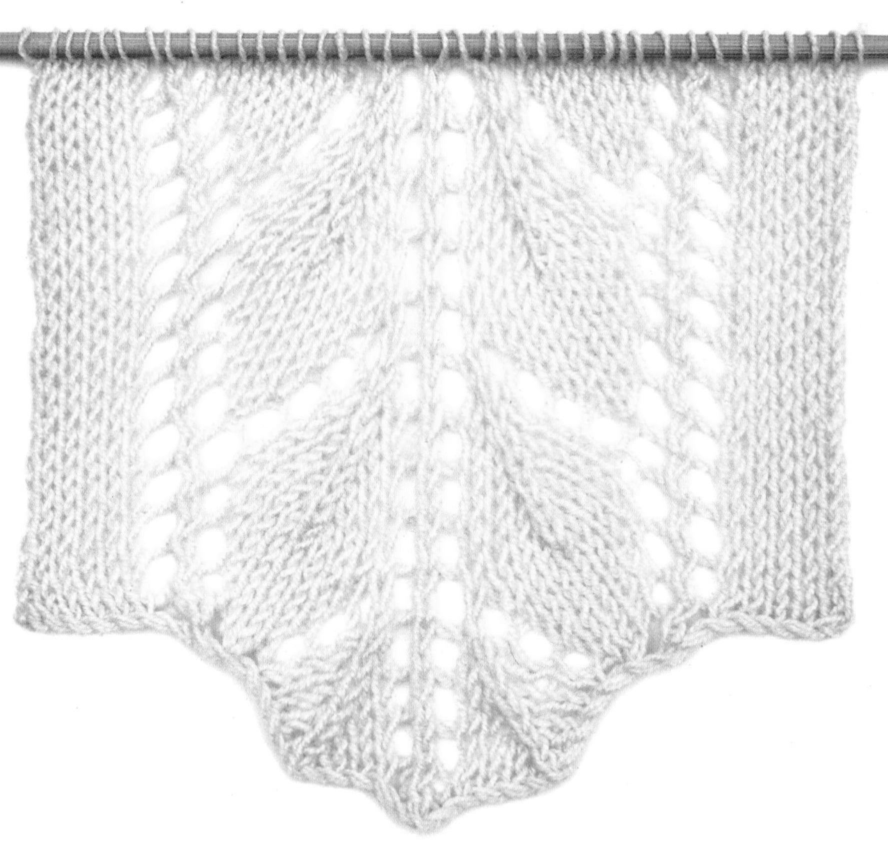

3.25mm (size 3)

3-ply wool

Pattern

Row 1 (RS) K1, yfd, K2tog, yfd, K1, yfd, K3, sl 2 as if to K2tog, K1, p2sso, K3, yfd, sl 2 as if to K2tog, K1, p2sso, yfd, K3, sl 2 as if to K2tog, K1, p2sso, K3, yfd, K1, yfd, skpo, yfd, K1.
Row 2 and every alt row P to end.
Row 3 K1, yfd, K2tog, yfd, K3, yfd, K2, sl 2 as if to K2tog, K1, p2sso, K2, yfd, sl 2 as if to K2tog, K1, p2sso, yfd, K2, sl 2 as if to K2tog, K1, p2sso, K2, yfd, K3, yfd, skpo, yfd, K1.
Row 5 K1, yfd, K2tog, yfd, K5, yfd, K1, sl 2 as if to K2tog, K1, p2sso, K1, yfd, sl 2 as if to K2tog, K1, p2sso, yfd, K1, sl 2 as if to K2tog, K1, p2sso, K1, yfd, K5, yfd, skpo, yfd, K1.
Row 7 K1, yfd, K2tog, yfd, K7, (yfd, sl 2 as if to K2tog, K1, p2sso) 3 times, yfd, K7, yfd, skpo, yfd, K1.
Row 9 K1, yfd, K2tog, yfd, K8, K2tog, yfd, sl 2 as if to K2tog, K1, p2sso, yfd, skpo, K8, yfd, skpo, yfd, K1.
Row 10 P to end.
These 10 rows form the patt.

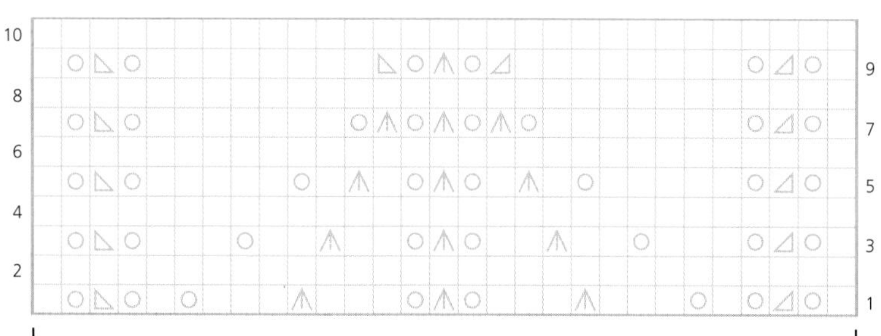

Panel of 29 stitches

variation

Panel of 29 stitches. Worked on a background of stocking stitch.

Ribbon trim
The eyelet borders that frame the leaves can be threaded with a narrow ribbon for added emphasis.

4mm
(size 6)

DK cotton

spirals and berries

Panel of 25 stitches. Worked on a background of stocking stitch.

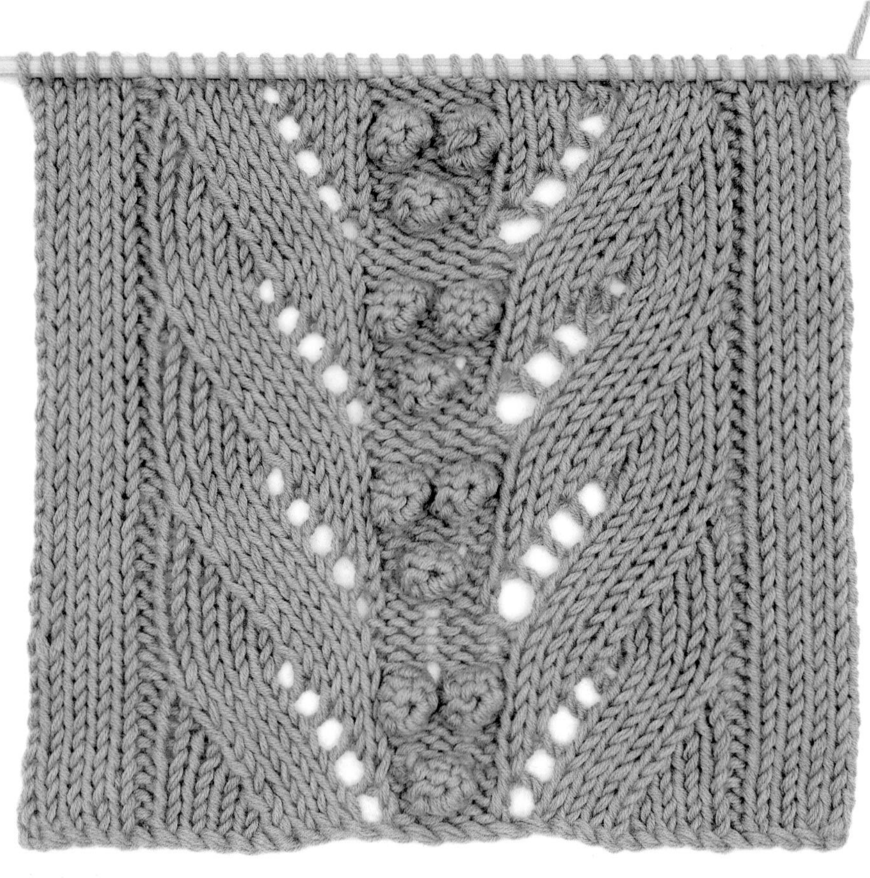

3.25mm (size 3)

4-ply cotton

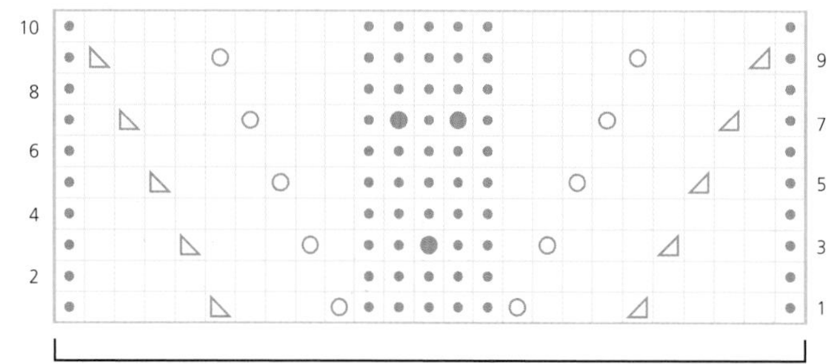

Panel of 25 stitches

Pattern

Row 1 (RS) P1, K4, K2tog, K3, yfrn, P5, yon, K3, skpo, K4, P1.
Row 2 and every alt row K1, P9, K5, P9, K1.
Row 3 P1, K3, K2tog, K3, yfd, K1, P2, MB-1, P2, K1, yfd, K3, skpo, K3, P1.
Row 5 P1, K2, K2tog, K3, yfd, K2, P5, K2, yfd, K3, skpo, K2, P1.
Row 7 P1, K1, K2tog, K3, yfd, K3, P1, (MB-1, P1) twice, K3, yfd, K3, skpo, K1, P1.
Row 9 P1, K2tog, K3, yfd, K4, P5, K4, yfd, K3, skpo, P1.
Row 10 K1, P9, K5, P9, K1.
These 10 rows form the patt.

variation

Panel of 14 stitches. Worked on a background of reverse stocking stitch.

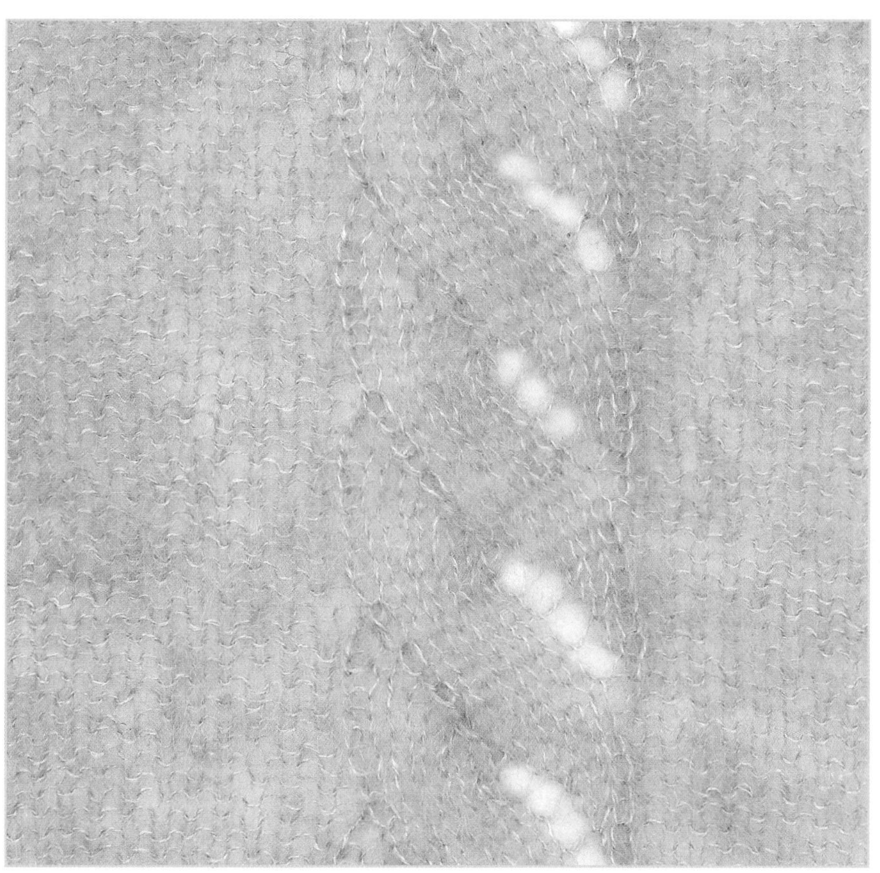

3.25mm (size 3)

Fine mohair

Pattern

Row 1 (RS) P2, yon, K4, skpo, K4, P2.
Row 2 and every alt row K2, P10, K2.
Row 3 P2, K1, yfd, K4, skpo, K3, P2.
Row 5 P2, K2, yfd, K4, skpo, K2, P2.
Row 7 P2, K3, yfd, K4, skpo, K1, P2.
Row 9 P2, K4, yfd, K4, skpo, P2.
Row 10 K2, P10, K2.
These 10 rows form the patt.

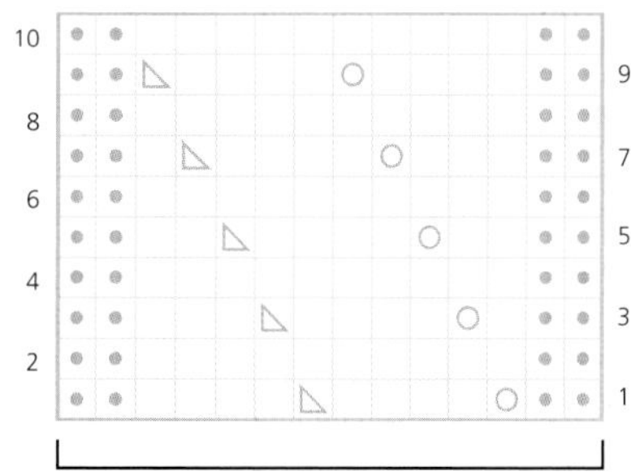

Panel of 14 stitches

project 4: cushion wraps

Dress up a plain cushion cover with an elegant knitted wrap. There are two designs to choose from – simple diamonds or a textured berry pattern.

YOU WILL NEED

- 100g (3½oz) 4-ply cotton in lilac
- 100g (3½oz) 4-ply cotton in lavender
- 3.25mm (size 3) knitting needles
- 4 buttons for each wrap
- Small buttons to trim lilac wrap
- Sequins and seed beads to trim lavender wrap
- Needle and matching sewing thread

SIZE

Lilac wrap: 13 x 84cm (5 x 33in)
Lavender wrap: 14.5 x 84cm (5¾ x 33in)
Adjust the length to fit your cushion

TENSION

26 sts and 34 rows to 10cm (4in) over st st
Single Diamond panel width: 8cm (3in)
Spirals and Berries panel width: 9cm (3½in)

Lilac wrap

TO MAKE

Using 3.25mm (size 3) needles, cast on 35 sts.
K 2 rows.
Next row K3, P to last 3 sts, K3.
Next row K to end.
Rep last 2 rows once more, then work the first of these 2 rows again.
Work in Single Diamond patt as follows:
Row 1 (RS) K7, yfd, sl 1, K2tog, psso, yfd, K5, K2tog, yfd, K1, yfd, skpo, K5, yfd, sl 1, K2tog, psso, yfd, K7.
Row 2 and every alt row K3, P to last 3 sts, K3.
Row 3 K7, yfd, sl 1, K2tog, psso, yfd, K4, K2tog, yfd, K3, yfd, skpo, K4, yfd, sl 1, K2tog, psso, yfd, K7.
Row 5 K7, yfd, sl 1, K2tog, psso, yfd, K3, K2tog, yfd, K5, yfd, skpo, K3, yfd, sl 1, K2tog, psso, yfd, K7.
Row 7 K7, yfd, sl 1, K2tog, psso, yfd, K3, yfd, skpo, K5, K2tog, yfd, K3, yfd, sl 1, K2tog, psso, yfd, K7.
Row 9 K7, yfd, sl 1, K2tog, psso, yfd, K4, yfd, skpo, K3, K2tog, yfd, K4, yfd, sl 1, K2tog, psso, yfd, K7.
Row 11 K7, yfd, sl 1, K2tog, psso, yfd, K5, yfd, skpo, K1, K2tog, yfd, K5, yfd, sl 1, K2tog, psso, yfd, K7.
Row 13 K7, yfd, sl 1, K2tog, psso, yfd, K6, yfd, sl 2 as if to K2tog, K1, p2sso, yfd, K6, yfd, sl 1, K2tog, psso, yfd, K7.
Row 14 K3, P to last 3 sts, K3.
These 14 rows form the patt.
Cont in patt until work measures 84cm (33in) from beg, ending row 14. Length can be adjusted here.
Next row K to end.
Next row K3, P to last 3 sts, K3.
Next row K to end.
Buttonhole row K3, P2, (yrn, P2tog, P6) 3 times, yrn, P2tog, P2, K3.
Next row K to end.
Next row K3, P to last 3 sts, K3.
Next row K to end.
Cast off knitwise.

TO FINISH

Block knitting to size. Sew in the ends. Sew on buttons to correspond with buttonholes. Sew a small button in the centre of each diamond on the lilac wrap. Sew a sequin and seed bead between each group of bobbles on the lavender wrap.

Lavender wrap

TO MAKE
Using 3.25mm (size 3) needles, cast on 41 sts.
K 2 rows.
Next row K3, P to last 3 sts, K3.
Next row K to end.
Rep last 2 rows once more, then work the first of these 2 rows again.
Work in Spirals and Berries patt as follows:
Row 1 (RS) K8, P1, K4, K2tog, K3, yfrn, P5, yon, K3, skpo, K4, P1, K8.
Row 2 and every alt row K3, P5, K1, P9, K5, P9, K1, P5, K3.
Row 3 K8, P1, K3, K2tog, K3, yfd, K1, P2, MB-1, P2, K1, yfd, K3, skpo, K3, P1, K8.
Row 5 K8, P1, K2, K2tog, K3, yfd, K2, P5, K2, yfd, K3, skpo, K2, P1, K8.
Row 7 K8, P1, K1, K2tog, K3, yfd, K3, P1, (MB-1, P1) twice, K3, yfd, K3, skpo, K1, P1, K8.
Row 9 K8, P1, K2tog, K3, yfd, K4, P5, K4, yfd, K3, skpo, P1, K8.
Row 10 K3, P5, K1, P9, K5, P9, K1, P5, K3.
These 10 rows form the patt.
Cont in patt until work measures 84cm (33in) from beg, ending row 10.
Length can be adjusted here.
Next row K to end.
Next row K3, P to last 3 sts, K3.
Next row K to end.
Buttonhole row K3, P3, (yrn, P2tog, P7) 3 times, yrn, P2tog, P3, K3.
Next row K to end.
Next row K3, P to last 3 sts, K3.
Next row K to end.
Cast off knitwise.

project 5: jewellery purse

Knit a chic purse to store your favourite pieces of jewellery. The lined purse is edged with satin ribbon and trimmed with a beautiful beaded tassel.

YOU WILL NEED

- 50g (1¾oz) 4-ply cotton in mauve
- 3.25mm (size 3) knitting needles
- 2m (2yd) narrow ribbon
- Ribbon and beads for tassel (see page 135)
- Fabric for lining
- Needle and matching sewing thread

SIZE

14 x 15.5cm (5½ x 6¼in)

TENSION

Small Diamonds panel (15 sts) to 5cm (2in) and 5 patt reps (40 rows) to 10cm (4in)

Pattern

TO MAKE (made in one piece)

Using 3.25mm (size 3) needles, cast on 45 sts. Work in Small Diamonds patt with moss st as follows:

Row 1 (RS) P1, (K1, P1) twice, *K2, P2, K2tog, K1, (yfd, K1) twice, skpo, P2, K2, P1, (K1, P1) twice, rep from * to end.

Row 2 and every alt row P1, (K1, P1) twice, *P2, K2, P7, K2, P3, (K1, P1) twice, rep from * to end.

Row 3 P1, (K1, P1) twice, *K2, P2, K2tog, yfd, K3, yfd, skpo, P2, K2, P1, (K1, P1) twice, rep from * to end.

Row 5 P1, (K1, P1) twice, *K2, P2, K1, yfd, skpo, K1, K2tog, yfd, K1, P2, K2, P1, (K1, P1) twice, rep from * to end.

Row 7 P1, (K1, P1) twice, *K2, P2, K2, yfd, sl 1, K2tog, psso, yfd, K2, P2, K2, P1, (K1, P1) twice, rep from * to end.

Row 8 As row 2.

These 8 rows form the patt.

Cont in patt until work measures 34cm (13½in) from beg, ending row 8.

Cast off knitwise.

designer's tip

The lining fabric should sit within two stitches of the edges of the knitting so that the ribbon edging doesn't pierce the lining. Lay the lining on the knitting before sewing in place and check that you have sufficient along all edges; adjust as necessary.

TO FINISH

Block knitting to size. Sew in the ends. Cut a piece of lining fabric 17.5 x 36cm (7 x 14in). Press 1.5cm (⅝in) to wrong side along each edge. With wrong sides together, pin lining to the knitting (see designer's tip). Using a needle and matching sewing thread, slip stitch the lining in place. Measure 28cm (11in) from the cast-off edge and place a pin at each side edge to mark top of purse. With the lining on the inside, fold the cast-off edge level with the pins to form the purse. Pin side edges together. Using a length of narrow ribbon and working one stitch from the edge, oversew along one side edge of the purse, working through the double thickness, then continue around the flap and down the other side of the purse. Turn down the flap. Make a beaded tassel (see page 135) and sew to the centre of the flap.

project 6: women's sweaters

Simple lace panels can be added to a basic sweater shape for added interest. For a touch of luxury, trim the wide neckline with a length of marabou feathers.

YOU WILL NEED

- 350[350:400:400]g (12½[12½:14:14]oz) 4-ply yarn in cream
- 3.25mm (size 3) and 4mm (size 6) knitting needles
- Marabou trim (optional)
- Pearl beads (optional)
- Needle and matching sewing thread

SIZE

To fit bust 81[86:91:97]cm (32[34:36:38]in)
Length 55[56:57:58]cm (21½[22:22½:23]in)
Sleeve seam 12.5cm (5in)

TENSION

22 sts and 30 rows to 10cm (4in) over st st
Arrowhead panel 10cm (4in) wide
Double Diamonds panel 8cm (3¼in) wide

TO FINISH

Block knitting to size. Join shoulder and neckband seam. Mark depth of armholes 19[20:21:22]cm (7½[8:8¼:9]in) from shoulder seams on back and front. Sew sleeves to armholes between markers, then join side and sleeve seams. Press seams. Sew marabou trim around neck and trim diamond design with pearl beads, if desired.

Brackets

Figures in square brackets [ ] refer to larger sizes; where there is only one set of figures, this applies to all sizes.

Pattern – arrowhead design

BACK AND FRONT (alike)

Using 3.25mm (size 3) needles, cast on 103[109:115:121] sts.
Rib row 1 (RS) K1, (P1, K1) to end.
Rib row 2 P1, (K1, P1) to end.
Rep these 2 rows until work measures 4cm (1½in), ending rib row 2.
Change to 4mm (size 6) needles.
Cont in st st with Arrowhead panel as follows:
Row 1 (RS) K41[44:47:50], P2, (K1, yfd, skpo) twice, K5, (K2tog, yfd, K1) twice, P2, K to end.
Row 2 and every alt row
P41[44:47:50], K2, P17, K2, P to end.
Row 3 K41[44:47:50], P2, K2, yfd, skpo, K1, yfd, skpo, K3, K2tog, yfd, K1, K2tog, yfd, K2, P2, K to end.
Row 5 K41[44:47:50], P2, K3, (yfd, skpo, K1) twice, K2tog, yfd, K1, K2tog, yfd, K3, P2, K to end.
Row 7 K41[44:47:50], P2, K4, yfd, skpo, K5, K2tog, yfd, K4, P2, K to end.
Row 9 K41[44:47:50], P2, K5, yfd, skpo, K3, K2tog, yfd, K5, P2, K to end.
Row 11 K41[44:47:50], P2, K6, yfd, skpo, K1, K2tog, yfd, K6, P2, K to end.
Row 12 P41[44:47:50], K2, P17, K2, P to end.
These 12 rows form the patt.
Cont in patt until work measures 50[51:52:53]cm (19½[20:20½:21]in) from beg, ending with a WS row.
Shape neck
Next row K37[39:41:43], turn and leave rem sts on a spare needle.
Work on first set of sts as follows:
Cast off 6[7:7:8] sts at beg of next row and 6 sts at beg of foll alt row. Dec 1 st at neck edge on next and every foll alt row until 20[21:23:24] sts rem.
Work 3 rows. Cast off.
With RS of work facing, place next 29[31:33:35] sts on a holder, join yarn to next st and K to end of row.
Work 1 row.
Cast off 6[7:7:8] sts at beg of next row and 6 sts at beg of foll alt row. Dec 1 st at neck edge on next and every foll alt row until 20[21:23:24] sts rem.
Work 2 rows. Cast off.

SLEEVES

Using 3.25mm (size 3) needles, cast on 65[69:73:77] sts.
Work the 2 rib rows of back and front for 1.5cm (½in), ending rib row 2.
Change to 4mm (size 6) needles.
Cont in st st but inc 1 st at each end of 3rd and every foll alt row until there are 77[81:85:89] sts, then on every foll 4th row until there are 85[89:93:97] sts.
Cont without shaping until work measures 12.5cm (5in) from beg, ending with a P row. Cast off.

NECKBAND

Join one shoulder seam. With RS of work facing, join on yarn and, using 3.25mm (size 3) needles, K up 26[26:27:27] sts along side of neck, K sts from holder, K up 26[26:27:27] sts along side of neck to shoulder, K up 26[26:27:27] sts along side of neck, K sts from holder, then K up 25[25:26:26] sts from side of neck to shoulder. 161[165:173:177] sts.
Beg rib row 2, work the 2 rib rows of back and front for 2.5cm (1in), ending rib row 2. Cast off in rib.

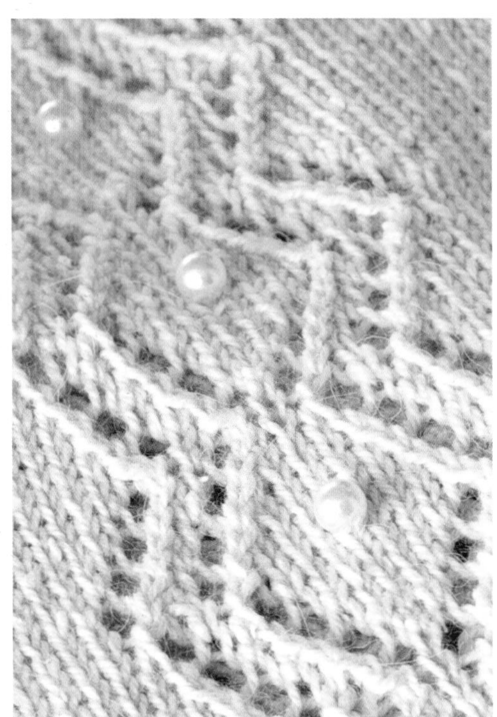

Pattern – double diamonds design

BACK AND FRONT (alike)
Using 3.25mm (size 3) needles, cast on 103[109:115:121] sts.
Rib row 1 (RS) K1, (P1, K1) to end.
Rib row 2 P1, (K1, P1) to end.
Rep these 2 rows until work measures 4cm (1½in), ending rib row 2.
Change to 4mm (size 6) needles.
Cont in st st with Double Diamonds panel as follows:
Row 1 (RS) K42[45:48:51], work panel K4, (K2tog, yfd, K1) twice, (yfd, skpo, K1) twice, K3, K to end.
Row 2 and every alt row P to end.
Row 3 K42[45:48:51], work panel K3, K2tog, yfd, K1, K2tog, yfd, K3, (yfd, skpo, K1) twice, K2, K to end.
Row 5 K42[45:48:51], work panel K2, K2tog, yfd, K1, K2tog, yfd, K5, (yfd, skpo, K1) twice, K1, K to end.
Row 7 K42[45:48:51], work panel K1, K2tog, yfd, K1, K2tog, yfd, K7, (yfd, skpo, K1) twice, K to end.
Row 9 K42[45:48:51], work panel (K1, yfd, skpo) twice, K7, (K2tog, yfd, K1) twice, K to end.
Row 11 K42[45:48:51], work panel K2, yfd, skpo, K1, yfd, skpo, K5, (K2tog, yfd, K1) twice, K1, K to end.
Row 13 K42[45:48:51], work panel K3, yfd, skpo, K1, yfd, skpo, K3, (K2tog, yfd, K1) twice, K2, K to end.
Row 15 K42[45:48:51], work panel K4, (yfd, skpo, K1) twice, (K2tog, yfd, K1) twice, K3, K to end.
Row 16 P to end.
These 16 rows form the patt.
Cont in patt until work measures 50[51:52:53]cm (19½[20:20½:21]in) from beg, ending with a WS row.
Shape neck
Next row K37[39:41:43], turn and leave rem sts on a spare needle.
Work on first set of sts as follows:
Cast off 6[7:7:8] sts at beg of next row and 6 sts at beg of foll alt row.
Dec 1 st at neck edge on next and every foll alt row until 20[21:23:24] sts rem.
Work 3 rows. Cast off.
With RS of work facing, place next 29[31:33:35] sts on a holder, join yarn to next st and K to end of row.
Work 1 row.
Cast off 6[7:7:8] sts at beg of next row and 6 sts at beg of foll alt row.
Dec 1 st at neck edge on next and every foll alt row until 20[21:23:24] sts rem.
Work 2 rows. Cast off.

SLEEVES
Work as given for sleeves of Arrowhead design.

NECKBAND
Work as given for neckband of Arrowhead design.

lesson 14 lace patterns

Traditionally, knitted lace focused on fine yarns and small needles. Today, however, the tempting array of modern yarns coupled with new and innovative approaches to lace knitting have broadened the horizons and taken the craft to new creative heights. There are no longer hard and fast rules – simply varying the yarn thickness and the needle size creates a breathtaking variety of effects that range from delicate and pretty to bold and contemporary, so that an array of different results can be achieved from the same lace pattern.

The combination of simple increasing and decreasing with basic knit and purl stitches creates an amazing variety of design possibilities. Making extra stitches (increasing) forms holes in the fabric and the size and placement of these holes creates the design. Corresponding decreases keep the number of stitches constant.

Most patterns can be equally successful in a variety of yarns and a little experimentation often brings intriguing results. Try fine yarn with different sized needles – the larger the needle, the more open and lacy the result. Investigate some of the more exotic yarns on offer – silk yarn creates soft and fluid lace fabrics, while heavier cottons give a firmer texture; delicate mohair creates a soft whisper of lace, and innovative chunky wools create thicker fabrics that alter the whole perception of lace and create show-stopping cushion covers and throws.

Adding embellishments such as beads, buttons and sequins gives yet another design dimension to knitted lace, providing extra visual focus and character that can be as bold or as subtle as you like.

Practice pattern

Use this pattern to work through the step-by-step exercise overleaf to make the sample as shown.

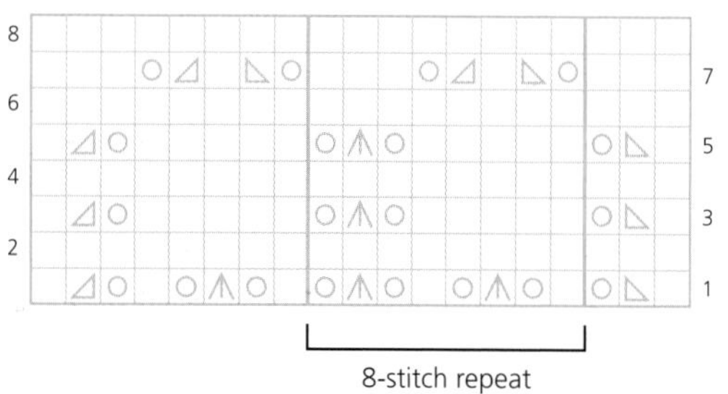

Pattern

Row 1 (RS) K1, skpo, yfd, *K1, yfd, sl 2 as if to K2tog, K1, p2sso, yfd, rep from * to last 4 sts, K1, yfd, K2tog, K1.
Row 2 and every alt row P to end.
Row 3 K1, skpo, yfd, *K5, yfd, sl 2 as if to K2tog, K1, p2sso, yfd, rep from * to last 8 sts, K5, yfd, K2tog, K1.
Row 5 As row 3.
Row 7 K3, *yfd, skpo, K1, K2tog, yfd, K3, rep from * to end.
Row 8 P to end.
These 8 rows form the patt.

harebell

This sample shows three pattern repeats.
Worked on a multiple of 8 stitches plus 11.

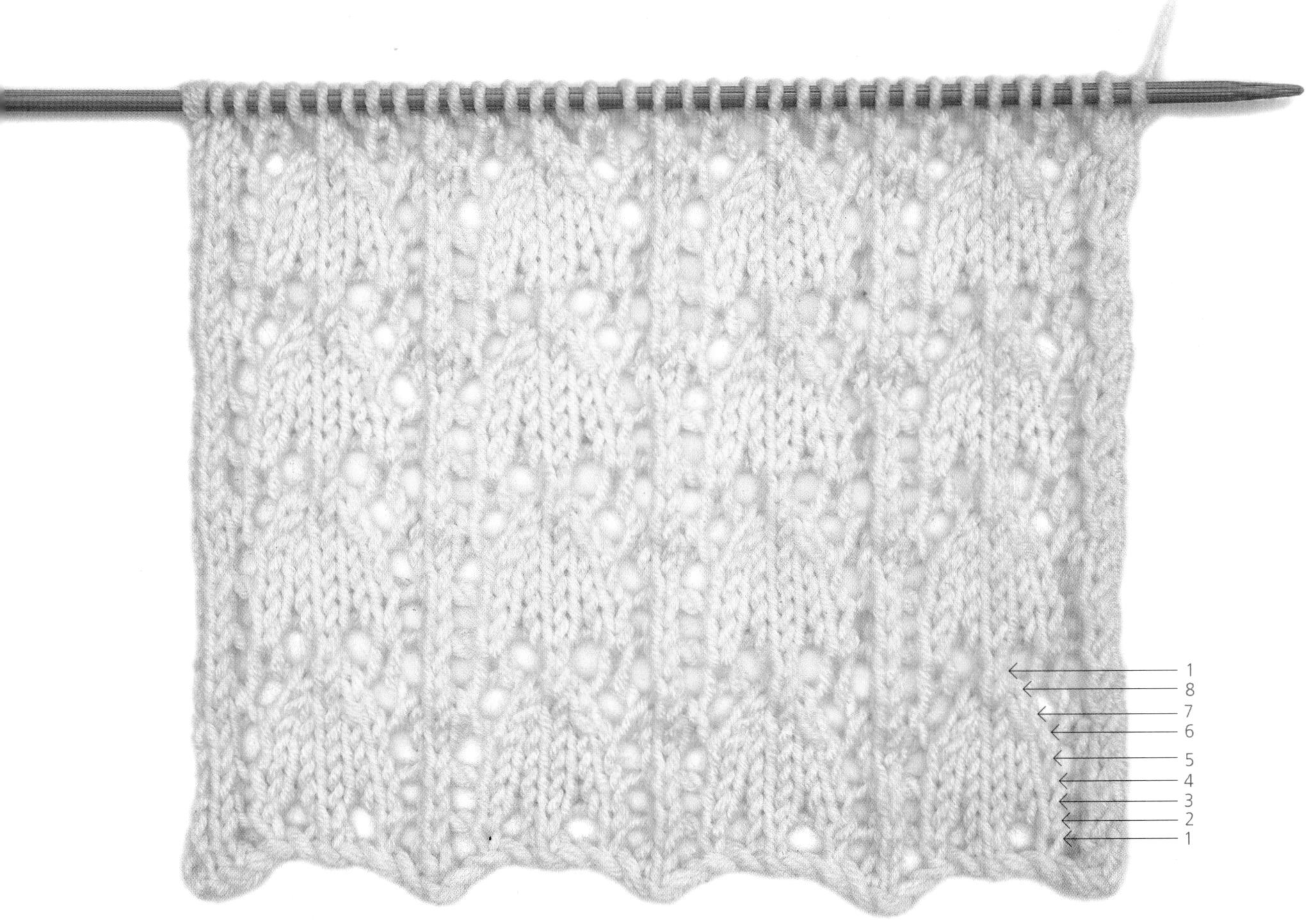

3.25mm
(size 3)

4-ply wool

double decrease

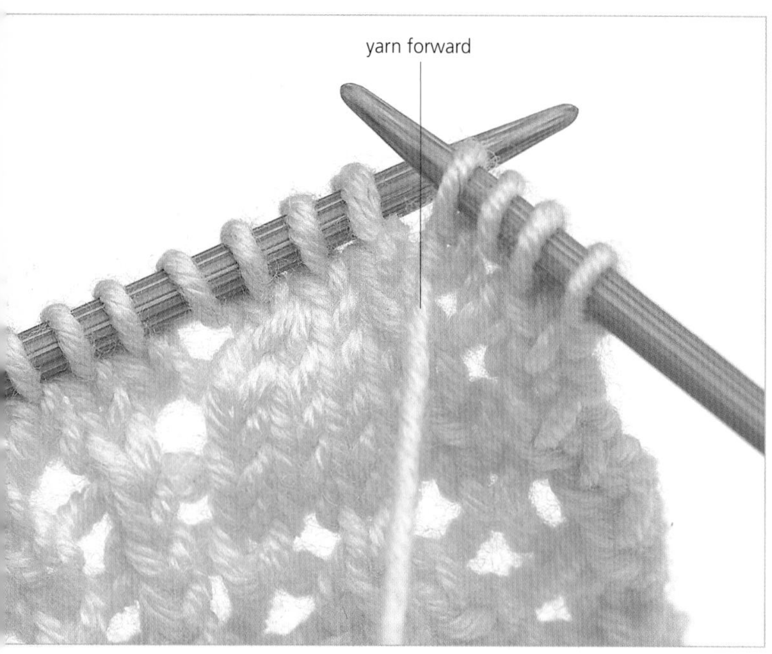

1 A double decrease is worked between each harebell and to curve the top of the harebells. It is important that the stitches are worked in the right order so that they lie on top of each other in the correct sequence. On row 1, pattern over the first four stitches (see page 78). Now work yarn forward (abbreviated as yfd) to form the eyelet.

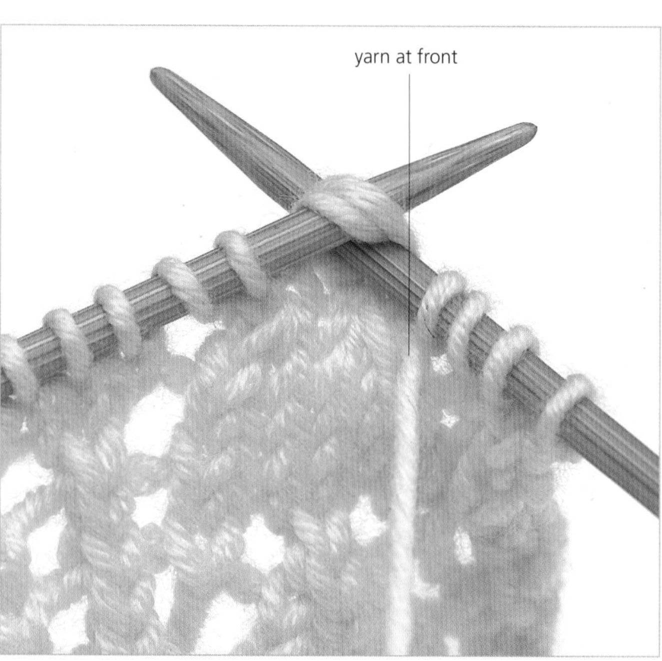

2 Keeping the yarn at the front of the knitting, insert the right-hand needle into the next two stitches knitwise as if knitting two together.

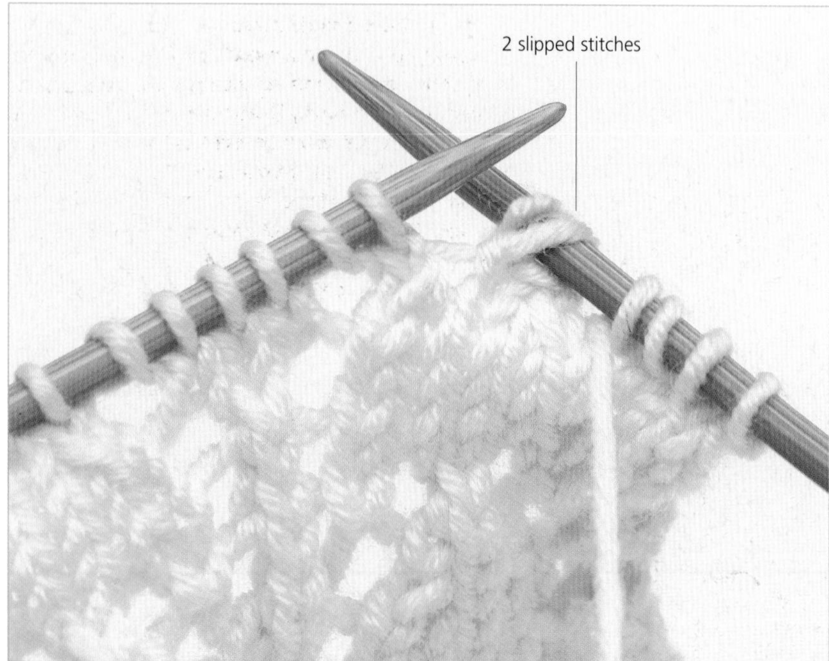

3 Do not knit the stitches but slip them onto the right-hand needle together – this forms the first part of the double decrease.

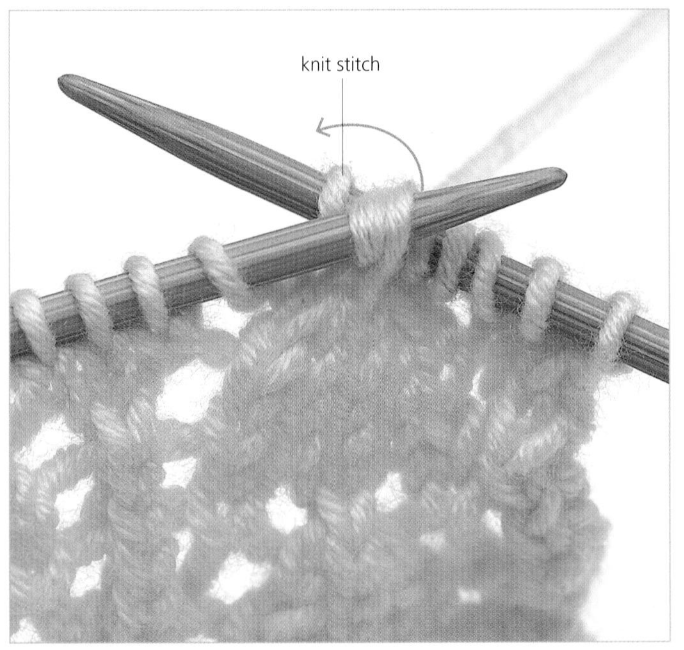

4 Knit the next stitch. The two slipped stitches are now passed over the knit stitch (abbreviated as p2sso); insert the left-hand needle, from left to right, into the two slipped stitches on the right-hand needle and carefully lift them over the knitted stitch and off the needle – double decrease worked.

5 The two slipped stitches sit on top of the knit stitch, so forming a neat double decrease. The number of stitches is kept consistent by making a stitch each side of the double decrease – the first stitch was made in steps 1 and 2.

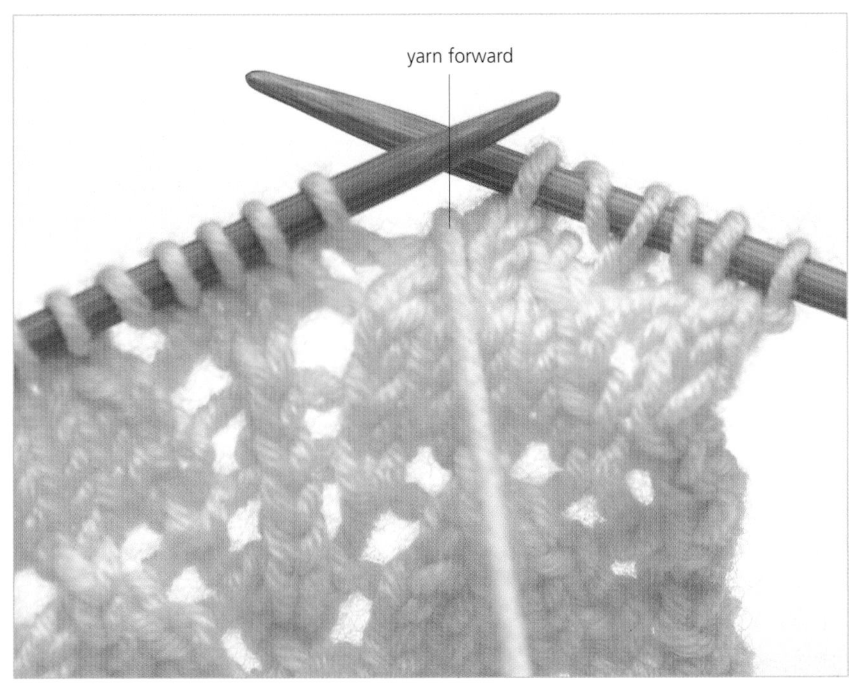

6 The second stitch is made by working yarn forward after the double decrease; the yarn will automatically lie across the needle when you work the next stitch. Bring the yarn to the front ready to work the next stitch. Each yarn forward will show as an eyelet once the next row has been worked.

staggered circles

This sample shows two pattern repeats. Worked on a multiple of 12 stitches plus 13.

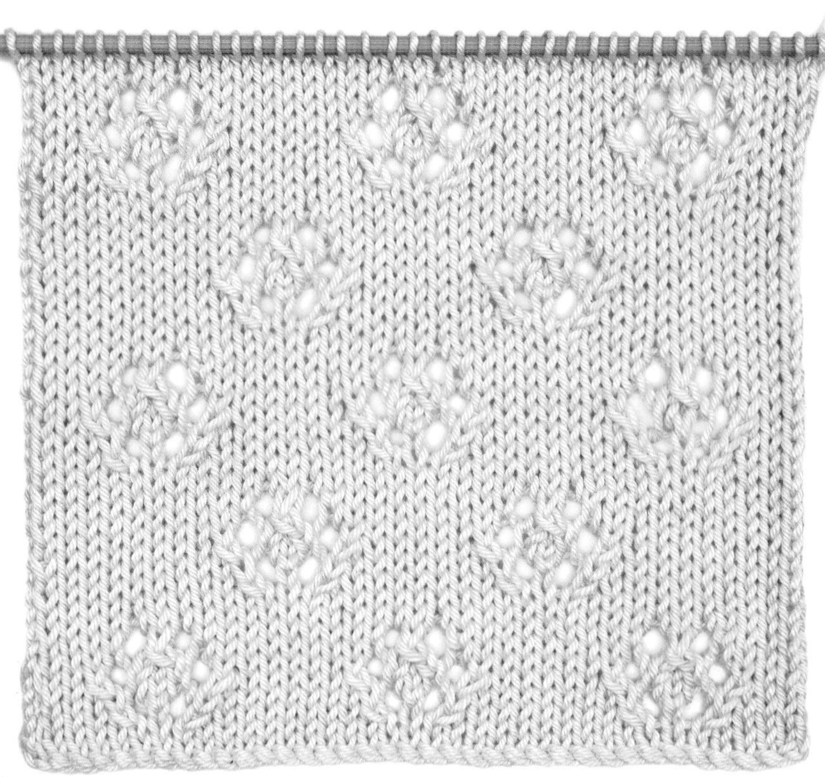

3.25mm (size 3)

4-ply cotton

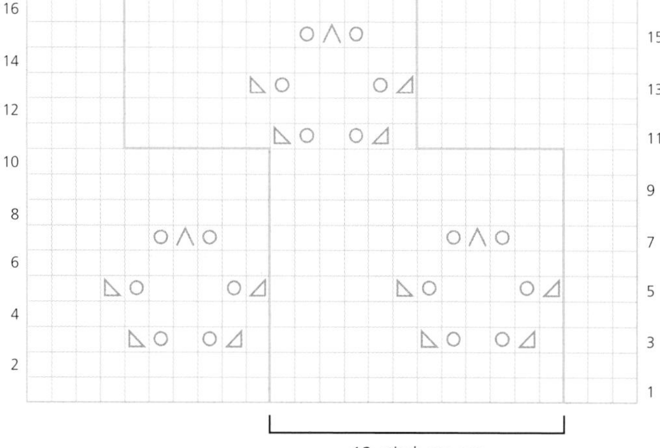

Pattern

Row 1 (RS) K to end.
Row 2 and every alt row P to end.
Row 3 K4, *K2tog, yfd, K1, yfd, skpo, K7, rep from * to end, finishing last rep K4.
Row 5 K3, *K2tog, yfd, K3, yfd, skpo, K5, rep from * to end, finishing last rep K3.
Row 7 K5, *yfd, sl 1, K2tog, psso, yfd, K9, rep from * to end, finishing last rep K5.
Row 9 K to end.
Row 11 K10, *K2tog, yfd, K1, yfd, skpo, K7, rep from * to last 3 sts, K3.
Row 13 K9, *K2tog, yfd, K3, yfd, skpo, K5, rep from * to last 4 sts, K4.
Row 15 K11, *yfd, sl 1, K2tog, psso, yfd, K9, rep from * to last 2 sts, K2.
Row 16 P to end.
These 16 rows form the patt.

variation

Worked on a multiple of 11 stitches plus 13.

3.25mm (size 3)

3-ply wool

Pattern

Row 1 (RS) K to end.
Row 2 and every alt row P to end.
Row 3 K to end.
Row 5 K4, *K2tog, yfd, K1, yfd, skpo, K6, rep from * to end, finishing last rep K4.
Row 7 K3, *K2tog, yfd, K3, yfd, skpo, K4, rep from * to end, finishing last rep K3.
Row 9 K5, *yfd, sl 1, K2tog, psso, yfd, K8, rep from * to end, finishing last rep K5.
Row 10 P to end.
These 10 rows form the patt.

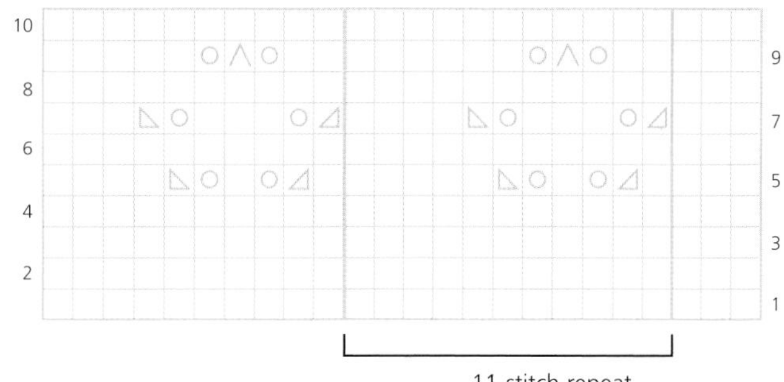

old shale

This sample shows two pattern repeats. Worked on a multiple of 18 stitches plus 1.

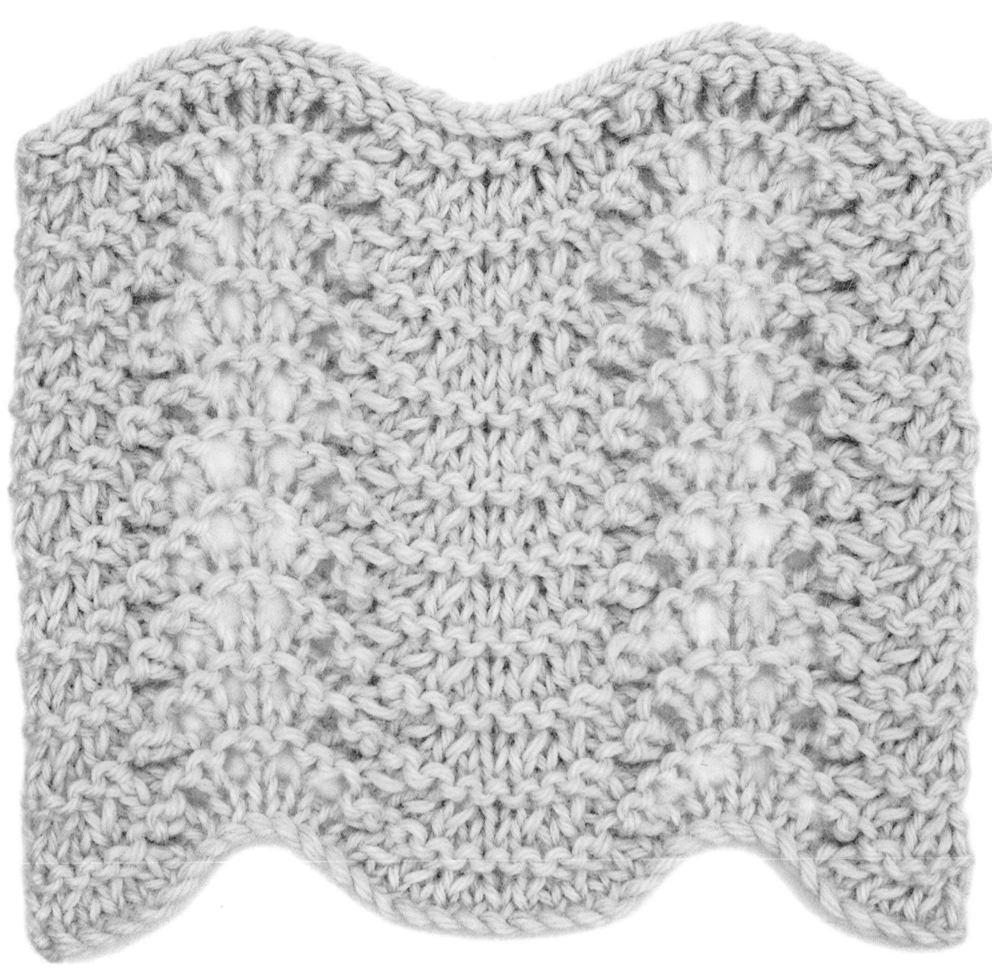

3.75mm (size 5)

DK alpaca

Pattern

Row 1 (RS) K to end.
Row 2 P to end.
Row 3 *K1, (K2tog) 3 times, (yfd, K1) 5 times, yfd, (K2tog) 3 times, rep from * to last st, K1.
Row 4 K to end.
These 4 rows form the patt.

Decorative edges

This pattern forms an interesting scallop at the cast-on and cast-off edges.

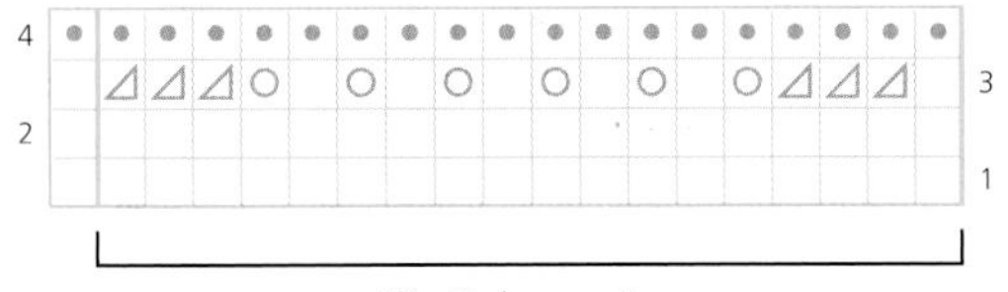

18-stitch repeat

variation

Worked on a multiple of 12 stitches plus 1.

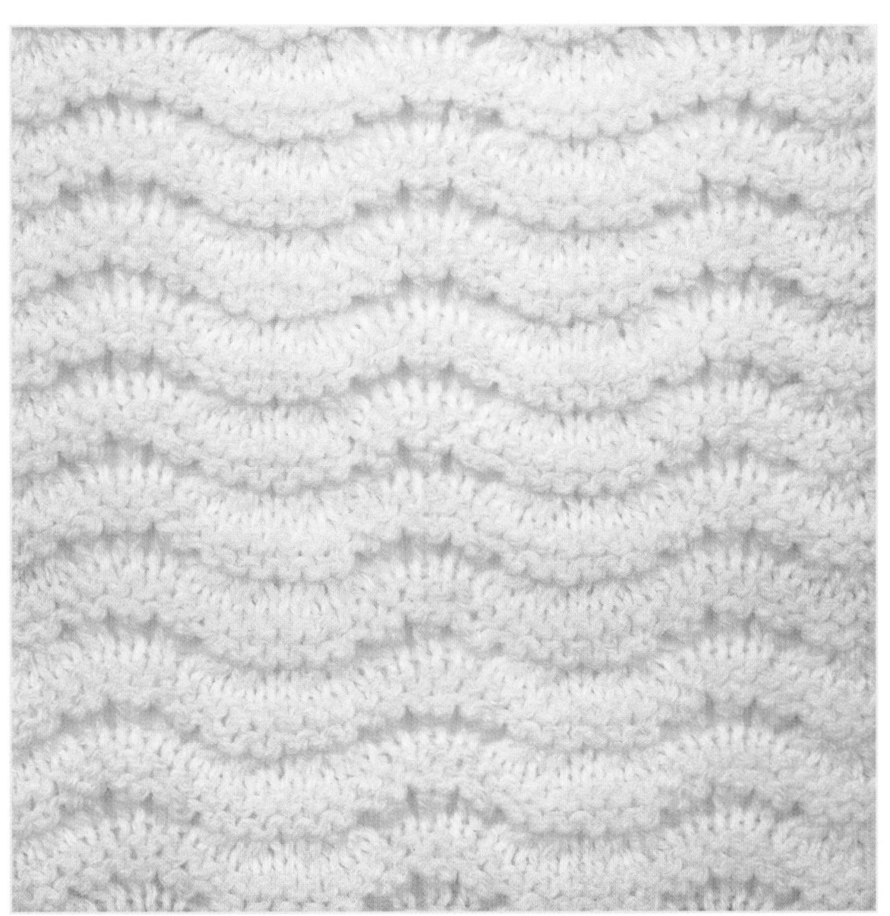

3.25mm (size 3)

3-ply wool

Pattern

Row 1 (RS) K to end.
Row 2 P to end.
Row 3 *K1, (K2tog) twice, (yfd, K1) 3 times, yfd, (K2tog) twice, rep from * to last st, K1.
Rows 4 to 6 K to end.
These 6 rows form the patt.

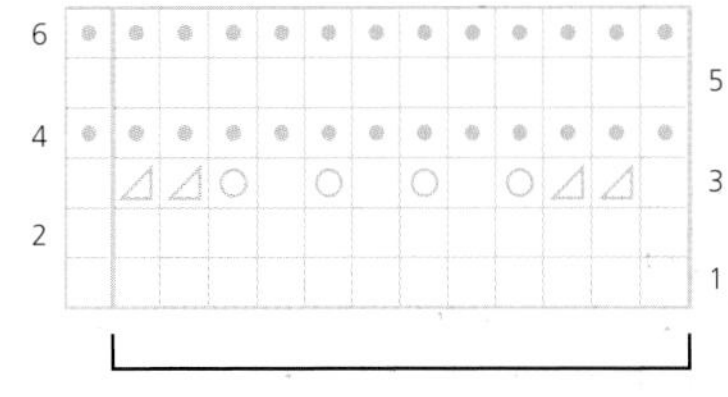

cockleshell lace

This sample shows three pattern repeats. Worked on a multiple of 14 stitches plus 1.

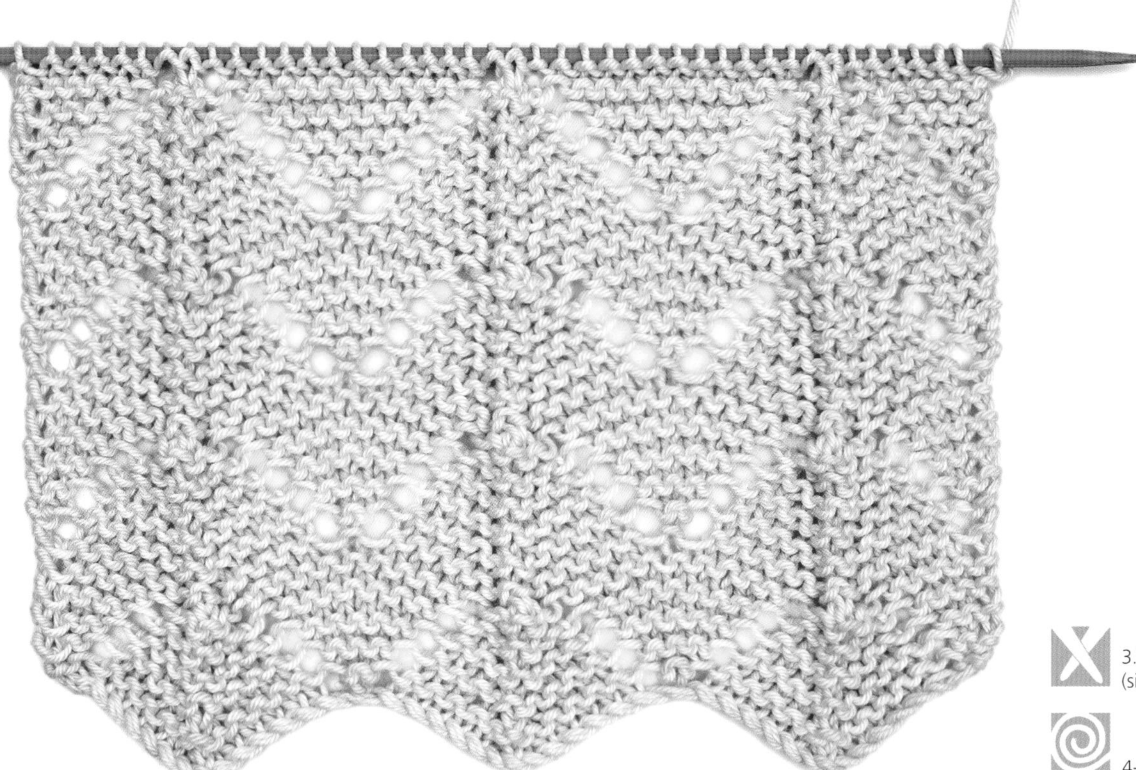

3.25mm (size 3)

4-ply cotton

Pattern

Row 1 (RS) *K1, yfd, K5, sl 2 as if to K2tog, K1, p2sso, K5, yfd, rep from * to last st, K1.
Row 2 and every alt row K to end.
Row 3 *K2, yfd, K4, sl 2 as if to K2tog, K1, p2sso, K4, yfd, K1, rep from * to last st, K1.
Row 5 *K3, yfd, K3, sl 2 as if to K2tog, K1, p2sso, K3, yfd, K2, rep from * to last st, K1.
Row 7 *K4, yfd, K2, sl 2 as if to K2tog, K1, p2sso, K2, yfd, K3, rep from * to last st, K1.
Row 9 *K5, yfd, K1, sl 2 as if to K2tog, K1, p2sso, K1, yfd, K4, rep from * to last st, K1.
Row 11 *K6, yfd, sl 2 as if to K2tog, K1, p2sso, yfd, K5, rep from * to last st, K1.
Row 12 K to end.
These 12 rows form the patt.

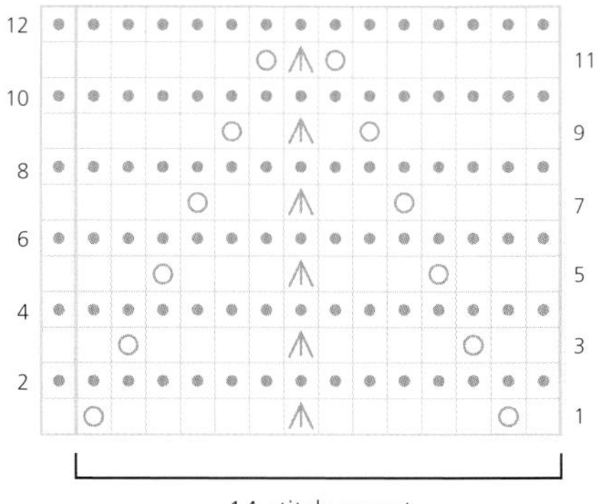

variation

Worked on a multiple of 14 stitches plus 1.

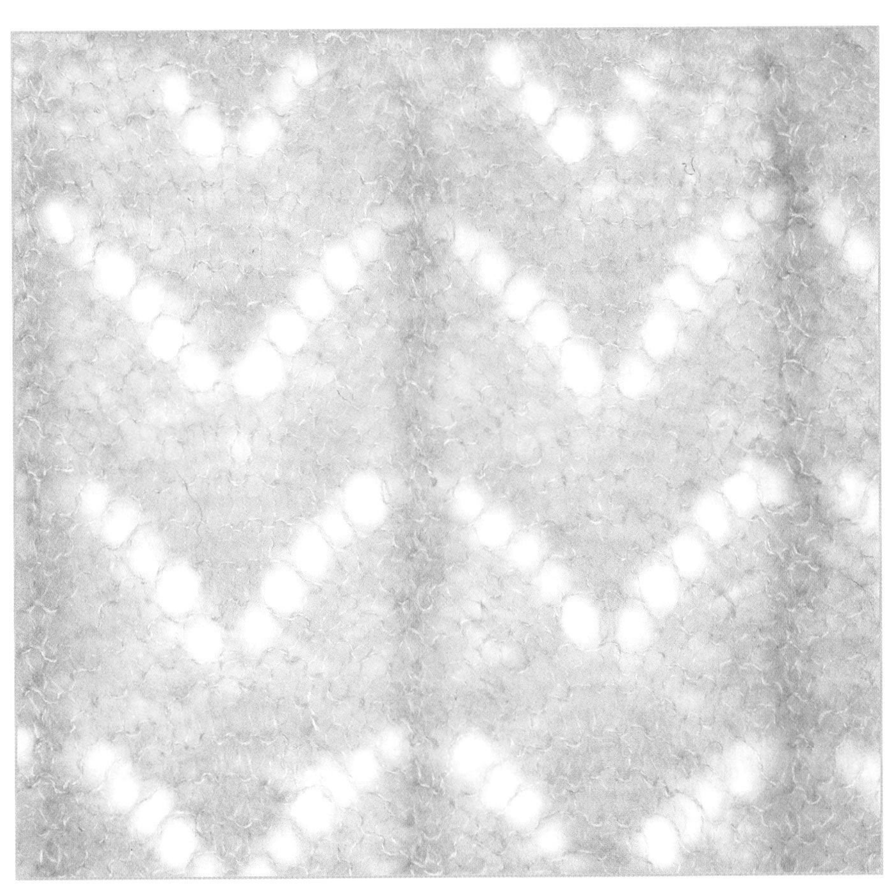

4mm (size 6)

Fine mohair

Gossamer
Worked in a fine mohair yarn on 4mm (size 6) knitting needles, the lacy pattern has a gossamer appearance.

fern leaf

This sample shows three pattern repeats. Worked on a multiple of 8 stitches plus 11.

3.25mm (size 3)

3-ply wool

Pattern

Row 1 (RS) K2, *yfd, K2, sl 1, K2tog, psso, K2, yfd, K1, rep from * to last st, K1.
Row 2 and every alt row P to end.
Row 3 K3, *yfd, K1, sl 1, K2tog, psso, K1, yfd, K3, rep from * to end.
Row 5 K4, *yfd, sl 1, K2tog, psso, yfd, K5, rep from * to end, finishing last rep K4.
Row 7 K1, K2tog, *K2, yfd, K1, yfd, K2, sl 1, K2tog, psso, rep from * to last 8 sts, K2, yfd, K1, yfd, K2, skpo, K1.
Row 9 K1, K2tog, *K1, yfd, K3, yfd, K1, sl 1, K2tog, psso, rep from * to last 8 sts, K1, yfd, K3, yfd, K1, skpo, K1.
Row 11 K1, K2tog, *yfd, K5, yfd, sl 1, K2tog, psso, rep from * to last 8 sts, yfd, K5, yfd, skpo, K1.
Row 12 P to end.
These 12 rows form the patt.

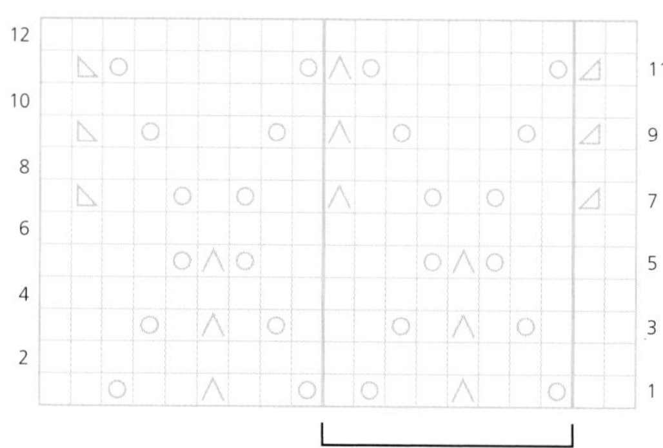

variation

Worked on a multiple of 10 stitches plus 13.

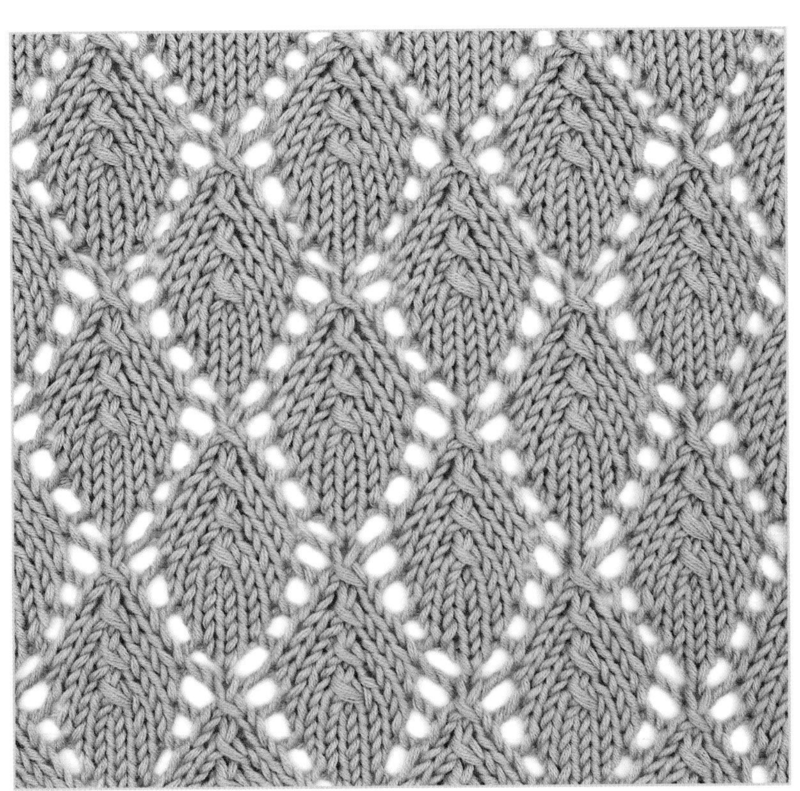

3.75mm (size 5)

DK cotton

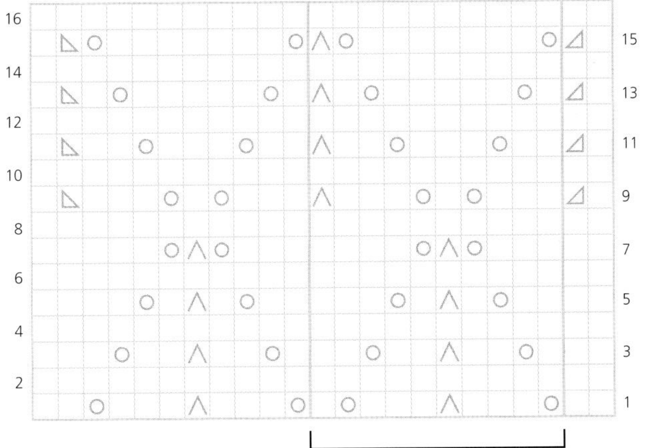

Pattern

Row 1 (RS) K2, *yfd, K3, sl 1, K2tog, psso, K3, yfd, K1, rep from * to last st, K1.
Row 2 and every alt row P to end.
Row 3 K3, *yfd, K2, sl 1, K2tog, psso, K2, yfd, K3, rep from * to end.
Row 5 K4, *yfd, K1, sl 1, K2tog, psso, K1, yfd, K5, rep from * to end, finishing last rep K4.
Row 7 K5, *yfd, sl 1, K2tog, psso, yfd, K7, rep from * to end, finishing last rep K5.
Row 9 K1, K2tog, K3, *yfd, K1, yfd, K3, sl 1, K2tog, psso, K3, rep from * to last 7 sts, yfd, K1, yfd, K3, skpo, K1.
Row 11 K1, K2tog, K2, *yfd, K3, yfd, K2, sl 1, K2tog, psso, K2, rep from * to last 8 sts, yfd, K3, yfd, K2, skpo, K1.
Row 13 K1, K2tog, K1, *yfd, K5, yfd, K1, sl 1, K2tog, psso, K1, rep from * to last 9 sts, yfd, K5, yfd, K1, skpo, K1.
Row 15 K1, K2tog, *yfd, K7, yfd, sl 1, K2tog, psso, rep from * to last 10 sts, yfd, K7, yfd, skpo, K1.
Row 16 P to end.
These 16 rows form the patt.

feather lace

This sample shows three pattern repeats. Worked on a multiple of 8 stitches plus 11.

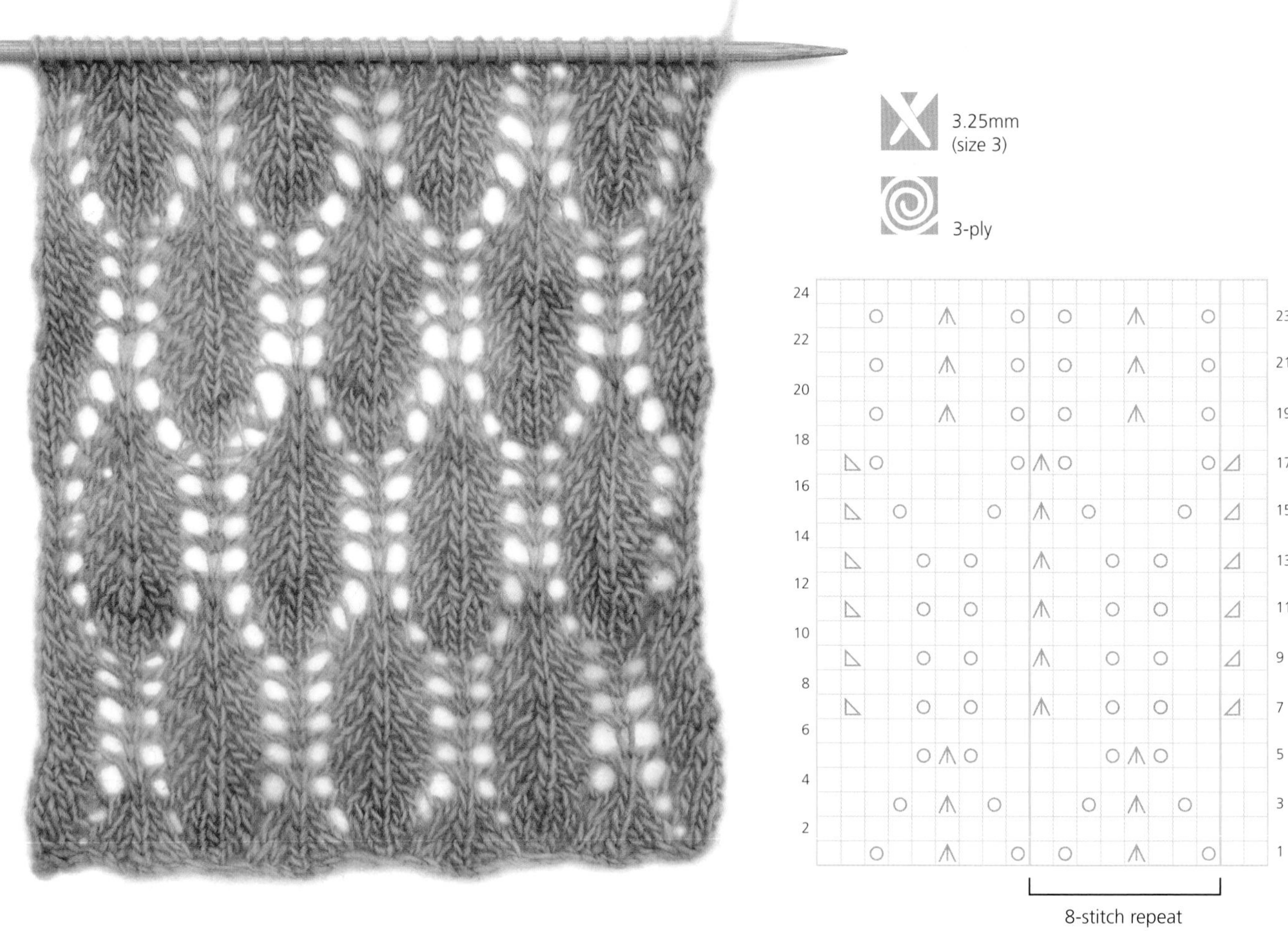

Pattern

Row 1 (RS) K2, *yfd, K2, sl 2 as if to K2tog, K1, p2sso, K2, yfd, K1, rep from * to last st, K1.
Row 2 and every alt row P to end.
Row 3 K3, *yfd, K1, sl 2 as if to K2tog, K1, p2sso, K1, yfd, K3, rep from * to end.
Row 5 K4, *yfd, sl 2 as if to K2tog, K1, p2sso, yfd, K5, rep from * to end, finishing last rep K4.
Rows 7, 9, 11 and 13 K1, K2tog, K2, yfd, K1, yfd, K2, *sl 2 as if to K2tog, K1, p2sso, K2, yfd, K1, yfd, K2, rep from * to last 3 sts, skpo, K1.
Row 15 K1, K2tog, K1, yfd, K3, *yfd, K1, sl 2 as if to K2tog, K1, p2sso, K1, yfd, K3, rep from * to last 4 sts, yfd, K1, skpo, K1.
Row 17 K1, K2tog, yfd, K5, *yfd, sl 2 as if to K2tog, K1, p2sso, yfd, K5, rep from * to last 3 sts, yfd, skpo, K1.
Rows 19, 21 and 23 K2, *yfd, K2, sl 2 as if to K2tog, K1, p2sso, K2, yfd, K1, rep from * to last st, K1.
Row 24 P to end.
These 24 rows form the patt.

variation

Worked on a multiple of 8 stitches plus 11.

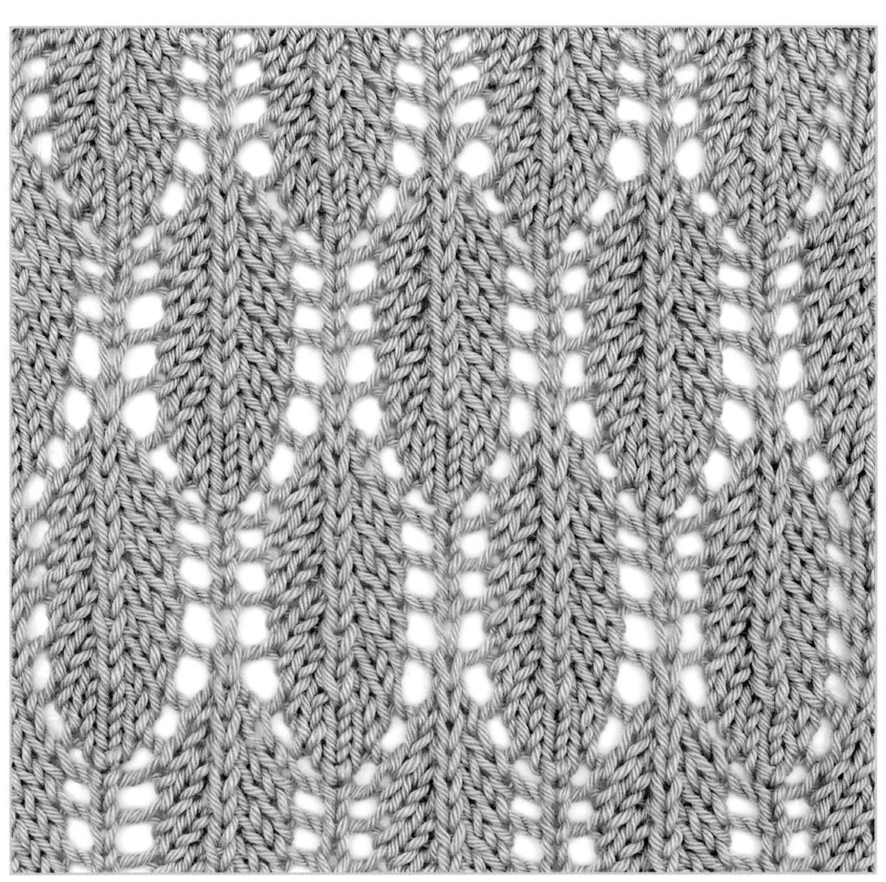

4mm (size 6)

DK cotton

Crisp outlines

A crisp cotton yarn gives clear definition to the feathers, particularly along the centre spine where the stitches are raised.

diamonds and eyelets

This sample shows two pattern repeats. Worked on a multiple of 10 stitches plus 11.

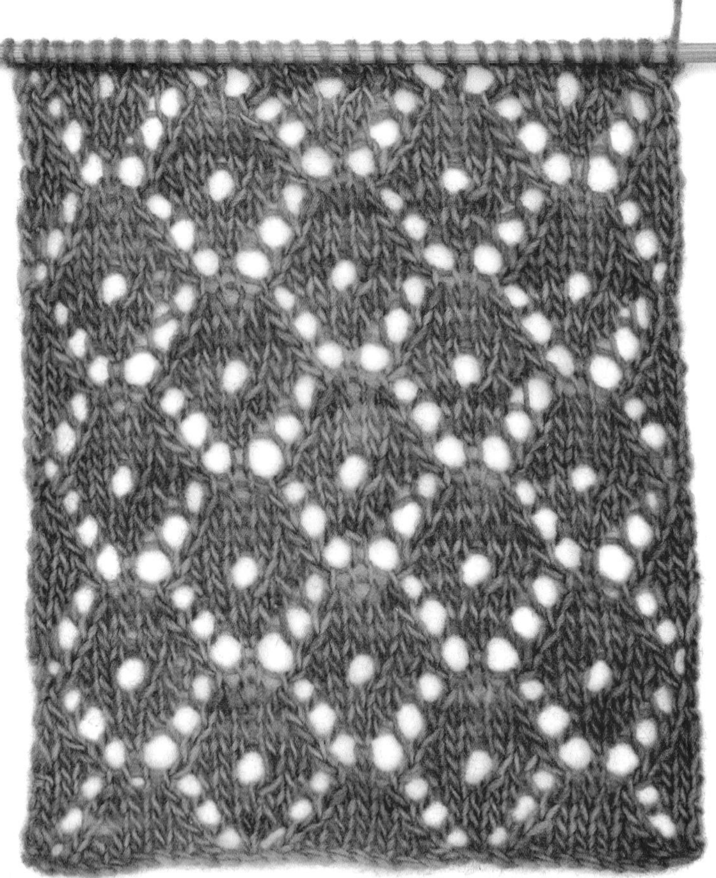

3.25mm
(size 3)

3-ply wool

Pattern

Row 1 (RS) K1, *yfd, skpo, K5, K2tog, yfd, K1, rep from * to end.
Row 2 P to end.
Row 3 K2, *yfd, skpo, K3, K2tog, yfd, K3, rep from * to end, finishing last rep K2.
Row 4 P to end.
Row 5 K3, *yfd, skpo, K1, K2tog, yfd, K5, rep from * to end, finishing last rep K3.
Row 6 P10, *yrn, P2tog, P8, rep from * to last st, P1.
Row 7 K3, *K2tog, yfd, K1, yfd, skpo, K5, rep from * to end, finishing last rep K3.
Row 8 P to end.
Row 9 K2, *K2tog, yfd, K3, yfd, skpo, K3, rep from * to end, finishing last rep K2.
Row 10 P to end.
Row 11 K1, *K2tog, yfd, K5, yfd, skpo, K1, rep from * to end.
Row 12 P5, *yrn, P2tog, P8, rep from * to end, finishing last rep P4.
These 12 rows form the patt.

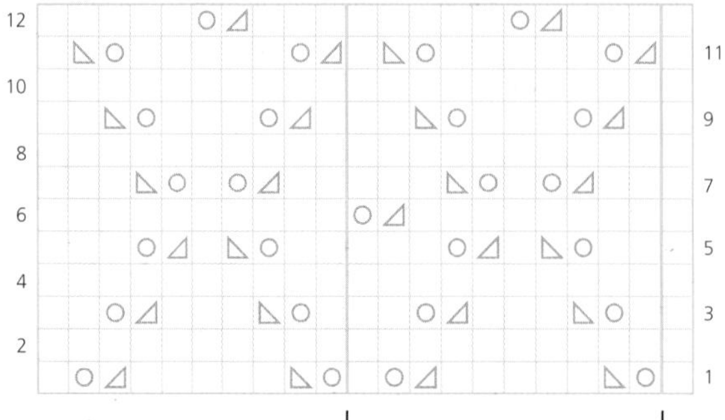

variation

Worked on a multiple of 10 stitches plus 1.

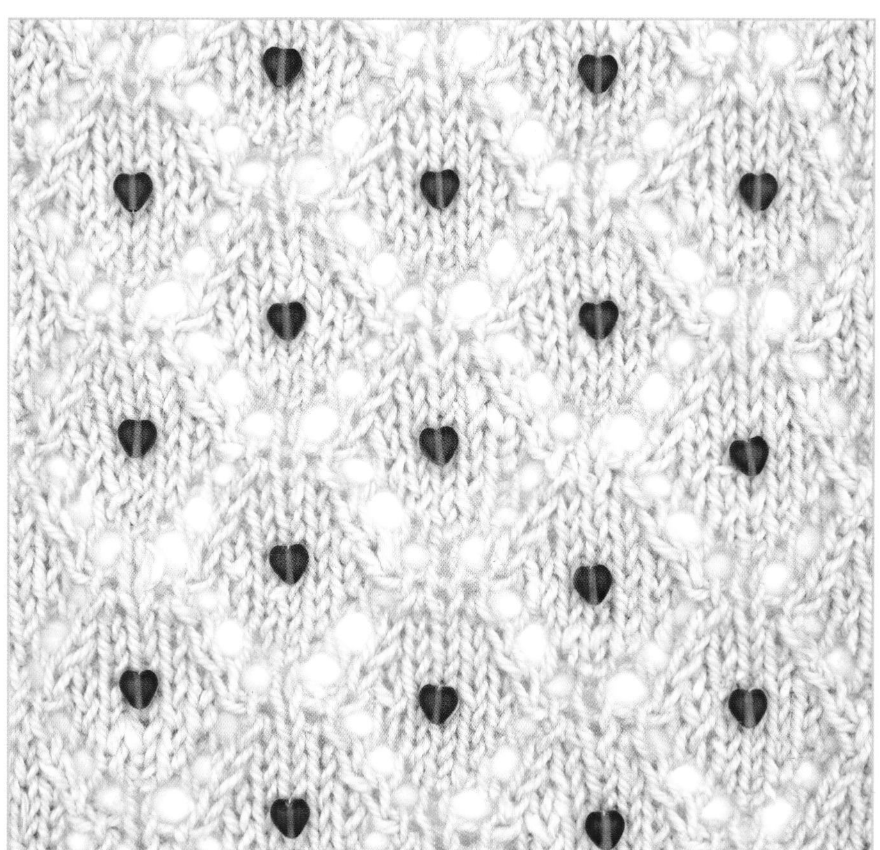

Embellishment
A small heart-shaped bead has been added to the centre of each diamond.

3.75mm (size 5)

DK slubbed yarn

Pattern

Row 1 (RS) K1, *yfd, skpo, K5, K2tog, yfd, K1, rep from * to end.
Row 2 and every alt row P to end.
Row 3 *K2, yfd, skpo, K3, K2tog, yfd, K1, rep from * to last st, K1.
Row 5 *K3, yfd, skpo, K1, K2tog, yfd, K2, rep from * to last st, K1.
Row 7 *K3, K2tog, yfd, K1, yfd, skpo, K2, rep from * to last st, K1.
Row 9 *K2, K2tog, yfd, K3, yfd, skpo, K1, rep from * to last st, K1.
Row 11 K1, *K2tog, yfd, K5, yfd, skpo, K1, rep from * to end.
Row 12 P to end.
These 12 rows form the patt.

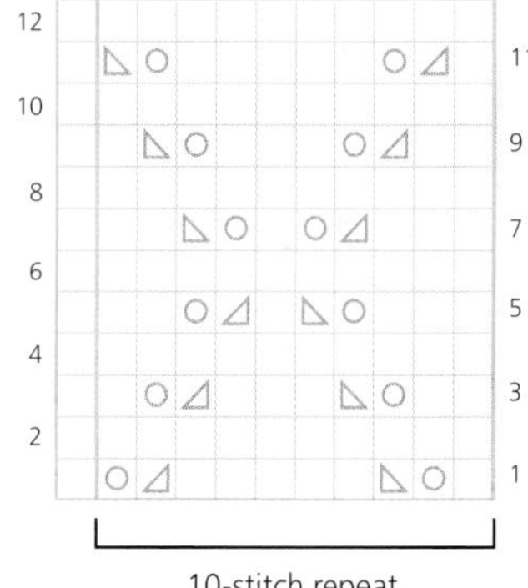

cable lace

This sample shows three pattern repeats. Worked on a multiple of 11 stitches plus 11.

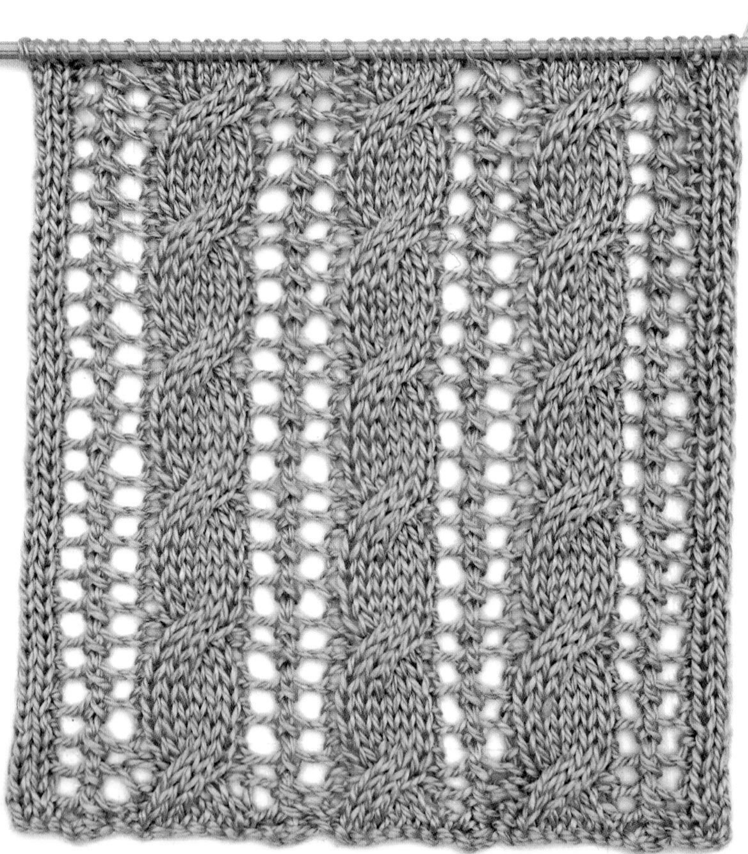

2.75mm
(size 2)

3-ply silk

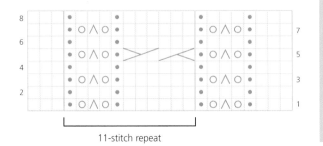

Pattern

Row 1 (RS) K3, P1, yon, sl 1, K2tog, psso, yfrn, P1, *K6, P1, yon, sl 1, K2tog, psso, yfrn, P1, rep from * to last 3 sts, K3.
Row 2 (P3, K1) twice, *P6, K1, P3, K1, rep from * to last 3 sts, P3.
Rows 3 and 4 As rows 1 and 2.
Row 5 K3, P1, yon, sl 1, K2tog, psso, yfrn, P1, *C6B, P1, yon, sl 1, K2tog, psso, yfrn, P1, rep from * to last 3 sts, K3.
Row 6 As row 2.
Rows 7 and 8 As rows 1 and 2.
These 8 rows form the patt.

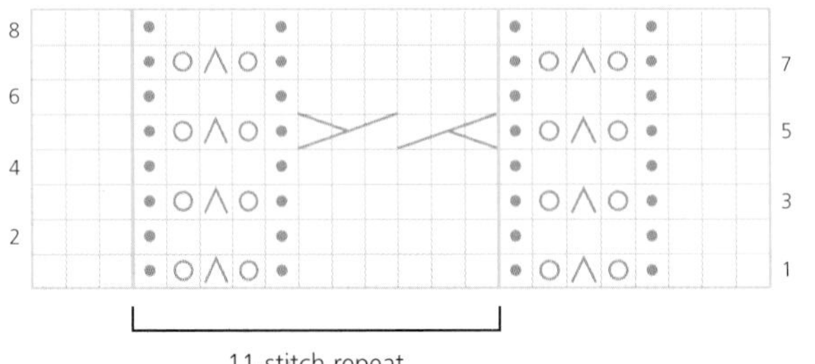

variation

Worked on a multiple of
9 stitches plus 9.

5mm
(size 8)

Chunky
cotton

Pattern

Row 1 (RS) K2, P1, yon, sl 1, K2tog, psso, yfrn, P1, *K4, P1, yon, sl 1, K2tog, psso, yfrn, P1, rep from * to last 2 sts, K2.
Row 2 P2, K1, P3, K1, *P4, K1, P3, K1, rep from * to last 2 sts, P2.
Rows 3 and 4 As rows 1 and 2.
Row 5 K2, P1, yon, sl 1, K2tog, psso, yfrn, P1, *C4F, P1, yon, sl 1, K2tog, psso, yfrn, P1, rep from * to last 2 sts, K2.
Row 6 As row 2.
These 6 rows form the patt.

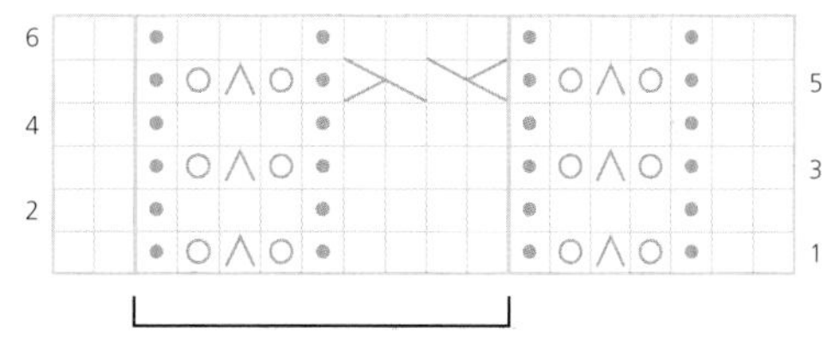

9-stitch repeat

horseshoe

This sample shows two pattern repeats. Worked on a multiple of 12 stitches plus 13.

3.25mm
(size 3)

3-ply wool

Pattern

Row 1 (RS) K2tog,*K4, yfd, K1, yfd, K4, sl 2 as if to K2tog, K1, p2sso, rep from * to end, finishing last rep skpo.
Row 2 and every alt row P to end.
Row 3 K2tog, *K3, (yfd, K3) twice, sl 2 as if to K2tog, K1, p2sso, rep from * to end, finishing last rep skpo.
Row 5 K2tog, *K2, yfd, K5, yfd, K2, sl 2 as if to K2tog, K1, p2sso, rep from * to end, finishing last rep skpo.
Row 7 K2tog, *(K1, yfd) twice, skpo, K1, K2tog, (yfd, K1) twice, sl 2 as if to K2tog, K1, p2sso, rep from * to end, finishing last rep skpo.
Row 9 K2tog, *yfd, K3, yfd, sl 2 as if to K2tog, K1, p2sso, rep from * to end, finishing last rep skpo.
Row 10 P to end.
These 10 rows form the patt.

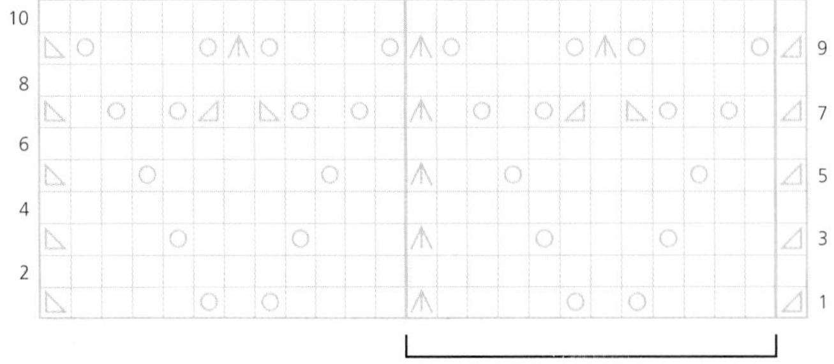

12-stitch repeat

variation

Worked on a multiple of 12 stitches plus 13.

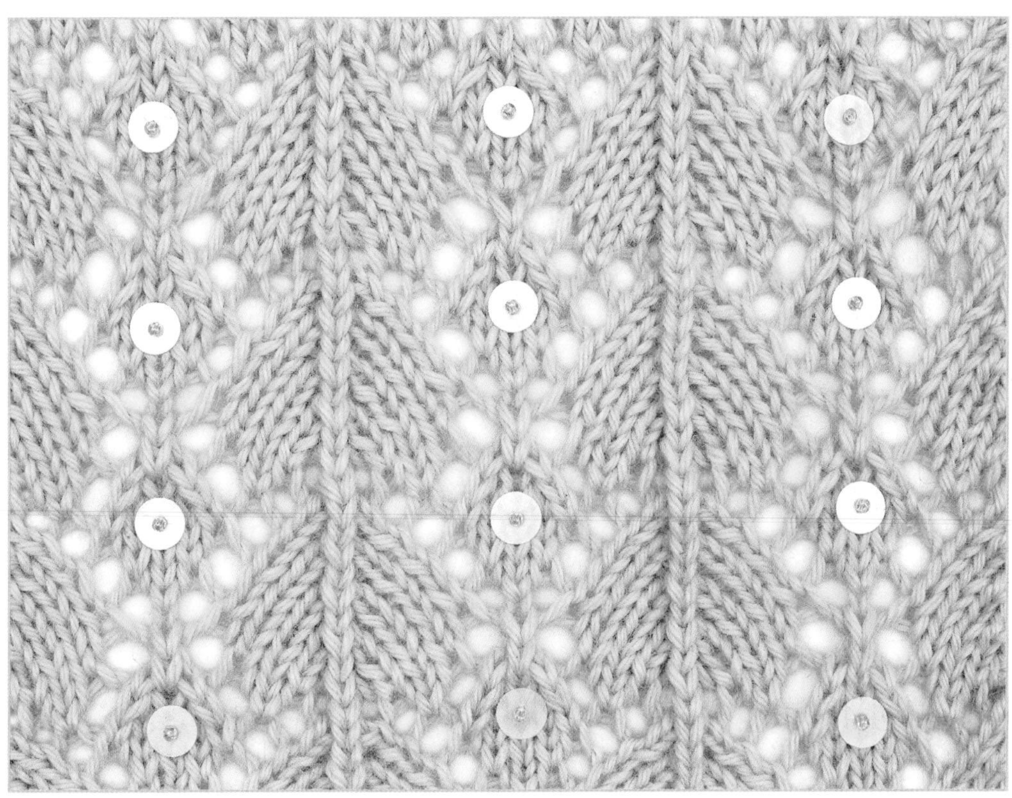

Embellishment

The small diamonds between the horseshoes lend themselves well to embellishment. Sequins and seed beads have been used on the sample shown.

3.75mm (size 5)

DK alpaca

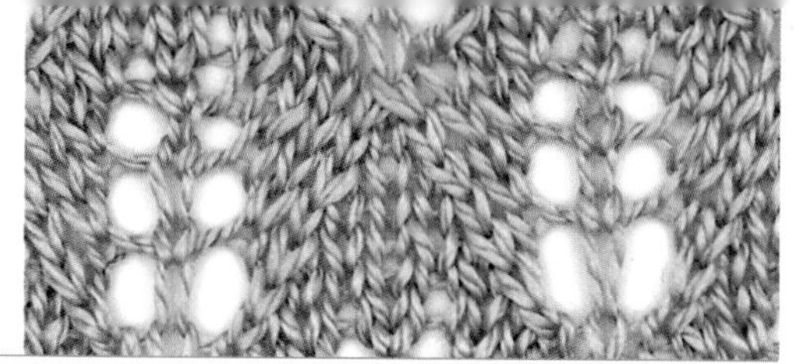

candlelight

This sample shows two pattern repeats. Worked on a multiple of 10 stitches plus 11.

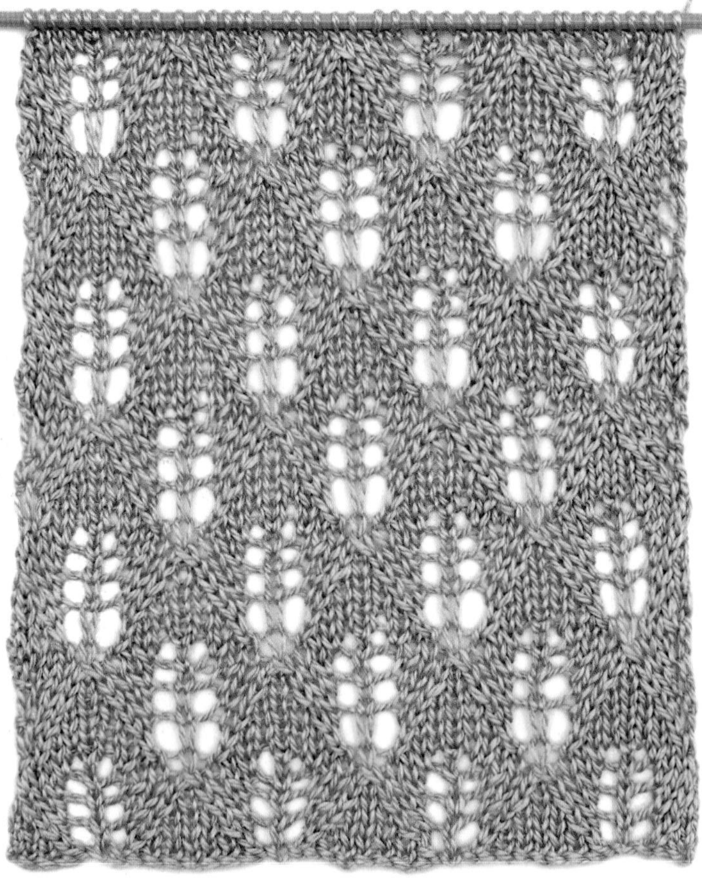

2.75mm (size 2)

3-ply silk

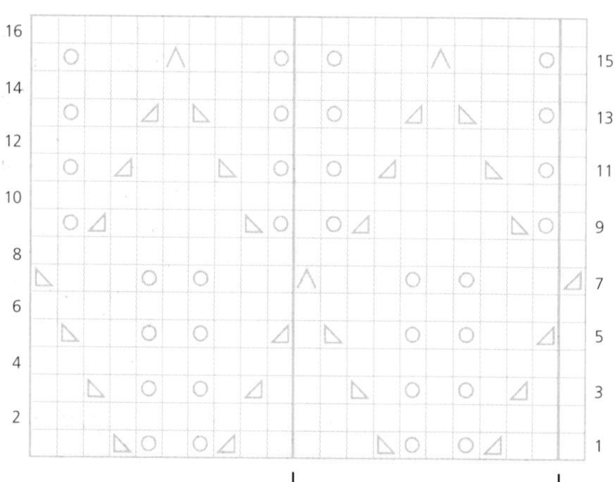

10-stitch repeat

Pattern

Row 1 (RS) K3, K2tog, yfd, K1, yfd, skpo, *K5, K2tog, yfd, K1, yfd, skpo, rep from * to last 3 sts, K3.
Row 2 and every alt row P to end.
Row 3 K2, K2tog, K1, (yfd, K1) twice, skpo, *K3, K2tog, K1, (yfd, K1) twice, skpo, rep from * to last 2 sts, K2.
Row 5 K1, *K2tog, K2, yfd, K1, yfd, K2, skpo, K1, rep from * to end.
Row 7 K2tog, K3, yfd, K1, yfd, K3, *sl 1, K2tog, psso, K3, yfd, K1, yfd, K3, rep from * to last 2 sts, skpo.
Row 9 K1, *yfd, skpo, K5, K2tog, yfd, K1, rep from * to end.
Row 11 K1, *yfd, K1, skpo, K3, K2tog, K1, yfd, K1, rep from to end.
Row 13 K1, *yfd, K2, skpo, K1, K2tog, K2, yfd, K1, rep from to end.
Row 15 K1, *yfd, K3, sl 1, K2tog, psso, K3, yfd, K1, rep from * to end.
Row 16 P to end.
These 16 rows form the patt.

variation

Worked on a multiple of 16 stitches plus 1.

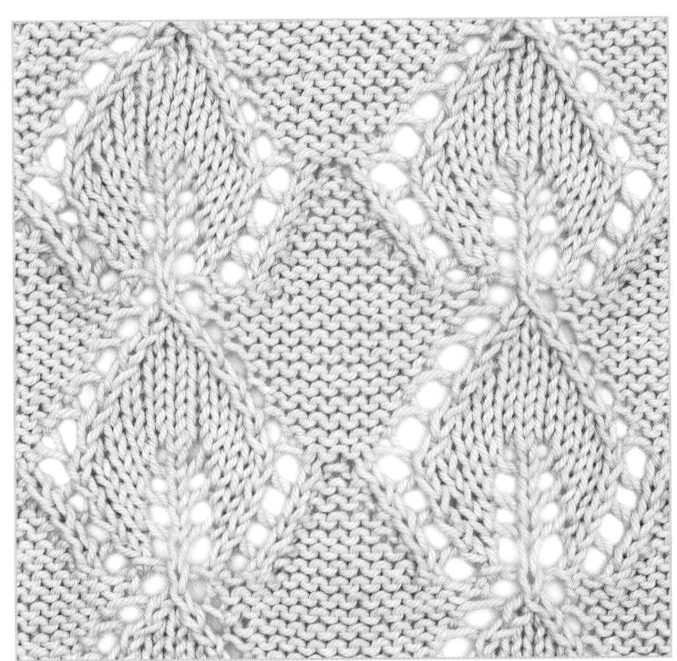

3.25mm (size 3)

4-ply cotton

Pattern

Row 1 (RS) *P4, (K2tog, yfd) twice, K1, (yfd, skpo) twice, P3, rep from * to last st, P1.
Row 2 *K4, P9, K3, rep from * to last st, K1.
Row 3 *P3, K2tog, yfd, K2tog, K1, (yfd, K1) twice, skpo, yfd, skpo, P2, rep from * to last st, P1.
Row 4 *K3, P11, K2, rep from * to last st, K1.
Row 5 *P2, K2tog, yfd, K2tog, K2, yfd, K1, yfd, K2, skpo, yfd, skpo, P1, rep from * to last st, P1.
Row 6 *K2, P13, K1, rep from * to last st, K1.
Row 7 *P1, K2tog, yfd, K2tog, K3, yfd, K1, yfd, K3, skpo, yfd, skpo, rep from * to last st, P1.
Row 8 As row 4.
Row 9 *P3, yon, skpo, K7, K2tog, yfrn, P2, rep from * to last st, P1.
Row 10 As row 2.
Row 11 *P4, yon, skpo, K5, K2tog, yfrn, P3, rep from * to last st, P1.
Row 12 *K5, P7, K4, rep from * to last st, K1.
Row 13 *P5, yon, skpo, K3, K2tog, yfrn, P4, rep from * to last st, P1.
Row 14 *K6, P5, K5, rep from * to last st, K1.
Row 15 *P6, yon, skpo, K1, K2tog, yfrn, P5, rep from * to last st, P1.
Row 16 *K7, P3, K6, rep from * to last st, K1.
Row 17 *P7, yon, sl 1, K2tog, psso, yfrn, P6, rep from * to last st, P1.
Row 18 *K8, P1, K7, rep from * to last st, K1.
These 18 rows form the patt.

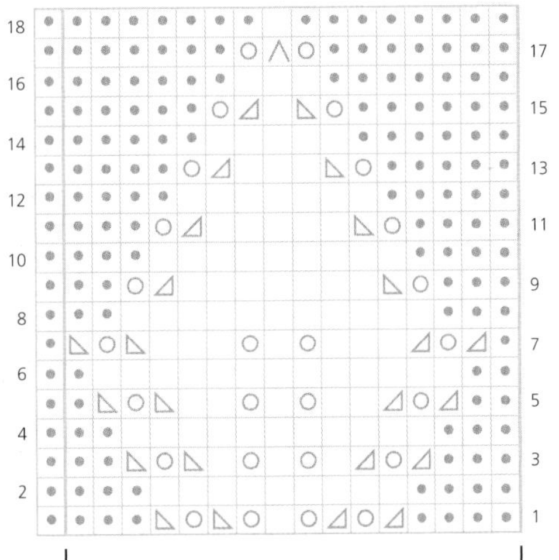

diamond trellis

This sample shows one pattern repeat. Worked on a multiple of 16 stitches plus 17.

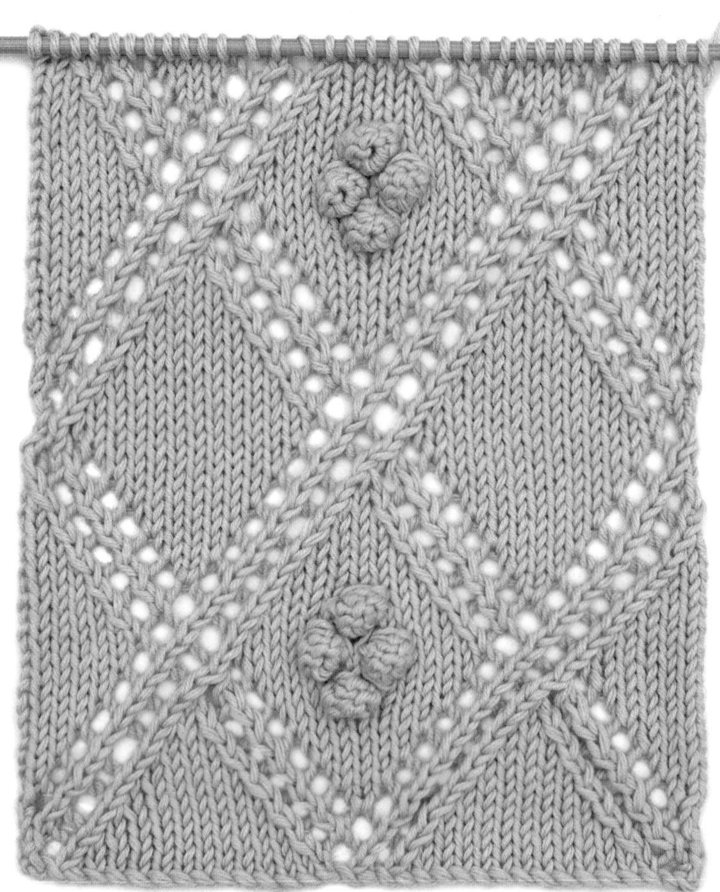

3.25mm (size 3)

4-ply cotton

Pattern

Row 1 (RS) K2tog, yfd, K12, *(K2tog, yfd) twice, K12, rep from * to last 3 sts, K2tog, yfd, K1.
Row 2 and every alt row P to end.
Row 3 K2, yfd, skpo, K9, *(K2tog, yfd) twice, K1, yfd, skpo, K9, rep from * to last 4 sts, K2tog, yfd, K2.
Row 5 K1, *(yfd, skpo) twice, K7, (K2tog, yfd) twice, K1, rep from * to end.
Row 7 K2, (yfd, skpo) twice, K5, (K2tog, yfd) twice, *K3, (yfd, skpo) twice, K5, (K2tog, yfd) twice, rep from * to last 2 sts, K2.
Row 9 K3, (yfd, skpo) twice, K3, (K2tog, yfd) twice, *K5, (yfd, skpo) twice, K3, (K2tog, yfd) twice, rep from * to last 3 sts, K3.
Row 11 K4, (yfd, skpo) twice, K1, (K2tog, yfd) twice, *K7, (yfd, skpo) twice, K1, (K2tog, yfd) twice, rep from * to last 4 sts, K4.
Row 13 K5, yfd, skpo, yfd, K3tog, yfd, K2tog, yfd, *K9, yfd, skpo, yfd, K3tog, yfd, K2tog, yfd, rep from * to last 5 sts, K5.

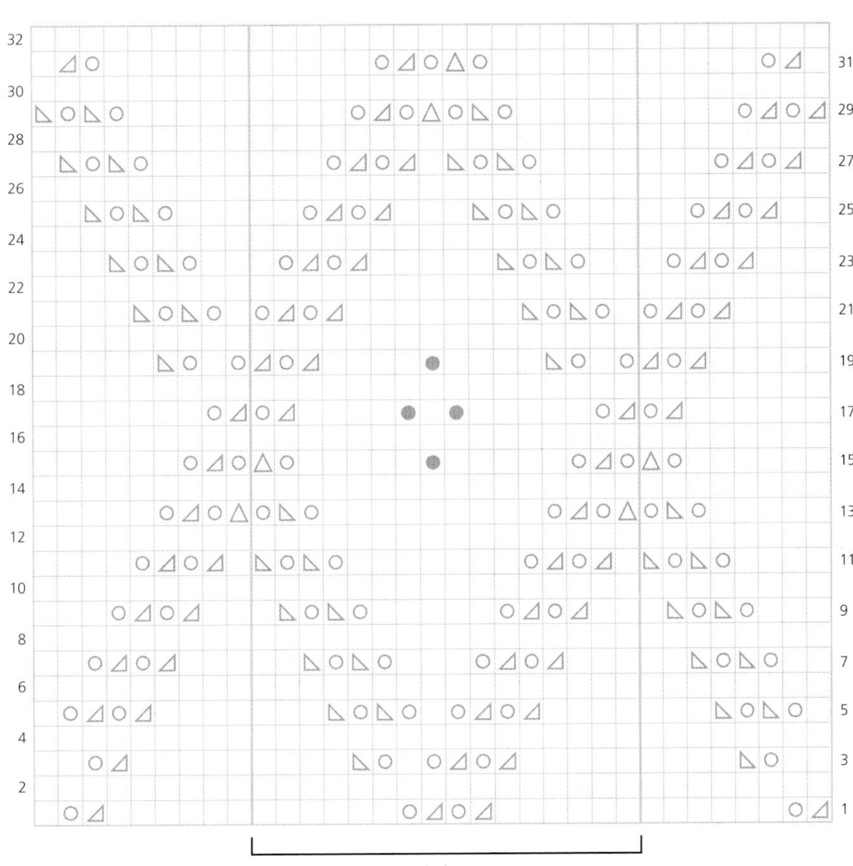

Row 15 K6, yfd, K3tog, yfd, K2tog, yfd, *K5, MB-1, K5, yfd, K3tog, yfd, K2tog, yfd, rep from * to last 6 sts, K6.
Row 17 K6, (K2tog, yfd) twice, *K5, MB-1, K1, MB-1, K4, (K2tog, yfd) twice, rep from * to last 7 sts, K7.
Row 19 K5, (K2tog, yfd) twice, K1, yfd, skpo, *K4, MB-1, K4, (K2tog, yfd) twice, K1, yfd, skpo, rep from * to last 5 sts, K5.
Row 21 K4, (K2tog, yfd) twice, K1, (yfd, skpo) twice, *K7, (K2tog, yfd) twice, K1, (yfd, skpo) twice, rep from * to last 4 sts, K4.
Row 23 K3, (K2tog, yfd) twice, K3, (yfd, skpo) twice, *K5, (K2tog, yfd) twice, K3, (yfd, skpo) twice, rep from * to last 3 sts, K3.
Row 25 K2, (K2tog, yfd) twice, K5, (yfd, skpo) twice, *K3, (K2tog, yfd) twice, K5, (yfd, skpo) twice, rep from * to last 2 sts, K2.
Row 27 *K1, (K2tog, yfd) twice, K7, (yfd, skpo) twice, rep from * to last st, K1.
Row 29 (K2tog, yfd) twice, K9, *yfd, skpo, yfd, K3tog, yfd, K2tog, yfd, K9, rep from * to last 4 sts, (yfd, skpo) twice.
Row 31 K1, K2tog, yfd, K11, *yfd, K3tog, yfd, K2tog, yfd, K11, rep from * to last 3 sts, yfd, K2tog, K1.
Row 32 P to end.
These 32 rows form the patt.

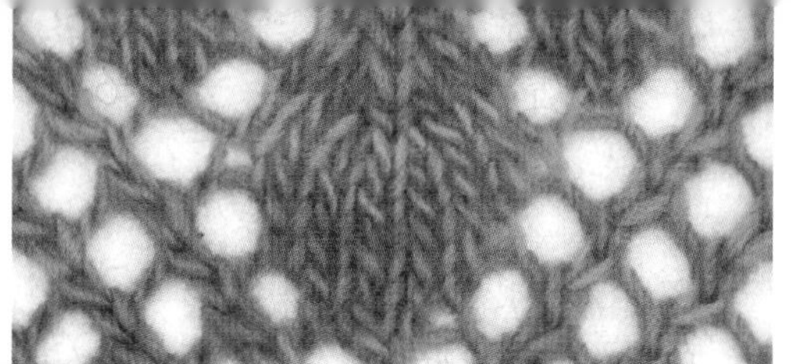

leaf cascade

This sample shows one repeat. Worked on a multiple of 16 stitches plus 17.

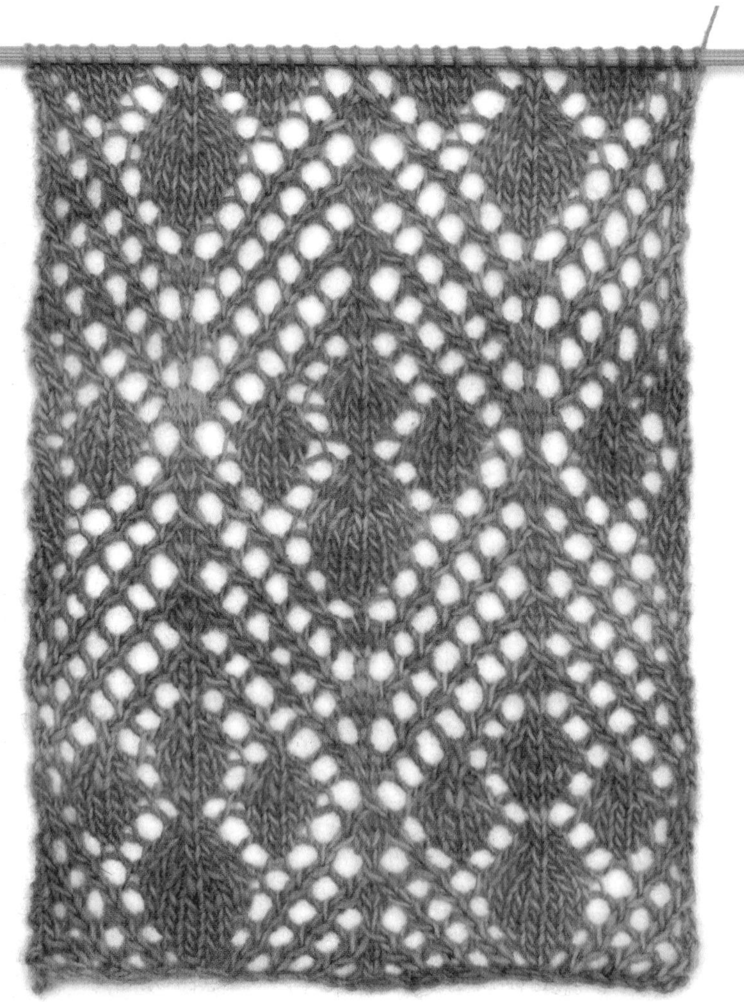

3.25mm (size 3)

3-ply wool

Pattern

Row 1 (RS) K2tog, *(yfd, K2tog) 3 times, yfd, K1, (yfd, skpo) 3 times, yfd, sl 1, K2tog, psso, rep from * to end, finishing last rep skpo.

Row 2 and every alt row P to end.

Row 3 K1, *(K2tog, yfd) 3 times, K3, (yfd, skpo) 3 times, K1, rep from * to end.

Row 5 K2tog, *(yfd, K2tog) twice, yfd, K5, (yfd, skpo) twice, yfd, sl 1, K2tog, psso, rep from * to end, finishing last rep skpo.

Row 7 K1, *(K2tog, yfd) twice, K7, (yfd, skpo) twice, K1, rep from * to end.

Row 9 K2tog, *yfd, K2tog, yfd, K1, yfd, K2, sl 2 as if to K2tog, K1, p2sso, K2, yfd, K1, yfd, skpo, yfd, sl 1, K2tog, psso, rep from * to end, finishing last rep skpo.

Row 11 K1, *K2tog, yfd, K3, yfd, K1, sl 2 as if to K2tog, K1, p2sso, K1, yfd, K3, yfd, skpo, K1, rep from * to end.

Row 13 K2tog, *yfd, K5, yfd, sl 2 as if to K2tog, K1, p2sso, yfd, K5, yfd, sl 1, K2tog, psso, rep from * to end, finishing last rep skpo.

Row 15 K2, *yfd, K1, sl 2 as if to K2tog, K1, p2sso, K1, yfd, K3, rep from * to end, finishing last rep K2.

Row 17 K1, *yfd, skpo, yfd, sl 2 as if to K2tog, K1, p2sso, yfd, K5, yfd, sl 2 as if to K2tog, K1, p2sso, yfd, K2tog, yfd, K1, rep from * to end.

Row 19 K2, *(yfd, skpo) twice, yfd, K1, sl 2 as if to K2tog, K1, p2sso, K1, (yfd, K2tog) twice, yfd, K3, rep from * to end, finishing last rep K2.

Row 21 K1, *(yfd, skpo) 3 times, yfd, sl 2 as if to K2tog, K1, p2sso, (yfd, K2tog) 3 times, yfd, K1, rep from * to end.

Row 23 K2, *(yfd, skpo) 3 times, K1, (K2tog, yfd) 3 times, K3, rep from * to end, finishing last rep K2.

Row 25 K1, *(yfd, skpo) 3 times, yfd, sl 1, K2tog, psso, (yfd, K2tog) 3 times, yfd, K1, rep from * to end.

Row 27 K2, *(yfd, skpo) 3 times, K1, (K2tog, yfd) 3 times, K3, rep from * to end, finishing last rep K2.
Row 29 K3, *(yfd, skpo) twice, yfd, sl 1, K2tog, psso, (yfd, K2tog) twice, yfd, K5, rep from * to end, finishing last rep K3.
Row 31 K4, *(yfd, skpo) twice, K1, (K2tog, yfd) twice, K7, rep from * to end, finishing last rep K4.
Row 33 K2tog, *K2, yfd, K1, yfd, skpo, yfd, sl 1, K2tog, psso, yfd, K2tog, yfd, K1, yfd, K2, sl 2 as if to K2tog, K1, p2sso, rep from * to end, finishing last rep skpo.
Row 35 K2tog, *K1, yfd, K3, yfd, skpo, K1, K2tog, yfd, K3, yfd, K1, sl 2 as if to K2tog, K1, p2sso, rep from * to end, finishing last rep skpo.
Row 37 K2tog, *yfd, K5, yfd, sl 1, K2tog, psso, yfd, K5, yfd, sl 2 as if to K2tog, K1, p2sso, rep from * to end, finishing last rep skpo.
Row 39 As row 15.
Row 41 K3, *yfd, sl 2 as if to K2tog, K1, p2sso, yfd, K2tog, yfd, K1, yfd, skpo, yfd, sl 2 as if to K2tog, K1, p2sso, yfd, K5, rep from * to end, finishing last rep K3.
Row 43 K2tog, *K1, (yfd, K2tog) twice, yfd, K3, (yfd, skpo) twice, yfd, K1, sl 2 as if to K2tog, K1, p2sso, rep from * to end, finishing last rep skpo.
Row 45 K2tog, *(yfd, K2tog) 3 times, yfd, K1, (yfd, skpo) 3 times, yfd, sl 2 as if to K2tog, K1, p2sso, rep from * to end, finishing last rep skpo.
Row 47 K1, *(K2tog, yfd) 3 times, K3, (yfd, skpo) 3 times, K1, rep from * to end.
Row 48 P to end.
These 48 rows form the patt.

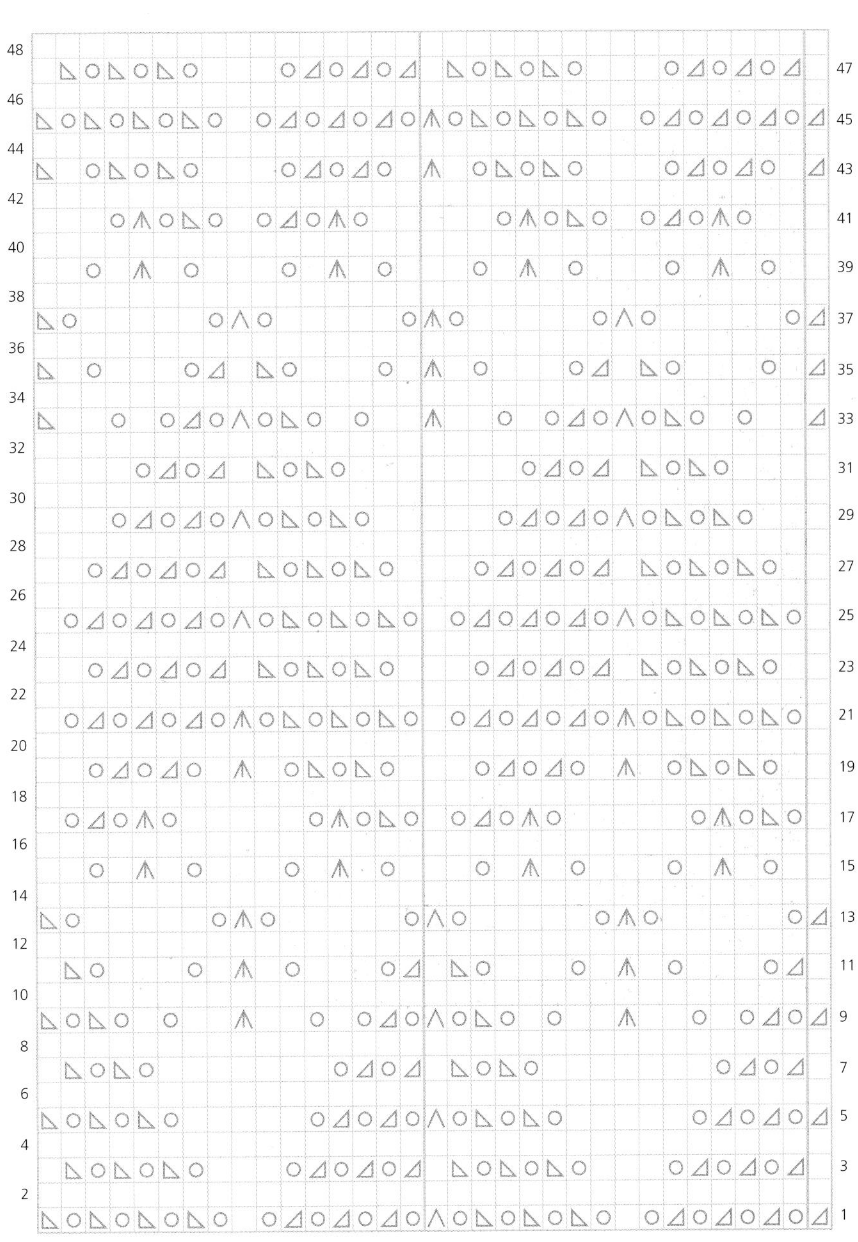

project 7: scarf

This delicate lightweight scarf can be worn to keep out the chill or as a fashion accessory to a favourite outfit. Knitted in a baby alpaca yarn it is both soft and warm.

YOU WILL NEED

- 50g (1¾oz) 3-ply alpaca yarn in cream
- 3.25mm (size 3) knitting needles
- Blocking wires

SIZE

17.5 x 80cm (6¾ x 31½in) excluding frills

TENSION

4 patt reps (32 sts) to 11cm (4½in)
2 patt reps (48 rows) to 15cm (6in)

Pattern

TO MAKE

Using 3.25mm (size 3) needles, cast on 51 sts.
Work in Feather Lace patt as follows:
Row 1 (RS) K2, *yfd, K2, sl 2 as if to K2tog, K1, p2sso, K2, yfd, K1, rep from * to last st, K1.
Row 2 and every alt row P to end.
Row 3 K3, *yfd, K1, sl 2 as if to K2tog, K1, p2sso, K1, yfd, K3, rep from * to end.
Row 5 K4, *yfd, sl 2 as if to K2tog, K1, p2sso, yfd, K5, rep from * to end, finishing last rep K4.
Rows 7, 9, 11 and 13 K1, K2tog, K2, yfd, K1, yfd, K2, *sl 2 as if to K2tog, K1, p2sso, K2, yfd, K1, yfd, K2, rep from * to last 3 sts, skpo, K1.
Row 15 K1, K2tog, K1, yfd, K3, *yfd, K1, sl 2 as if to K2tog, K1, p2sso, K1, yfd, K3, rep from * to last 4 sts, yfd, K1, skpo, K1.
Row 17 K1, K2tog, yfd, K5, *yfd, sl 2 as if to K2tog, K1, p2sso, yfd, K5, rep from * to last 3 sts, yfd, skpo, K1.
Rows 19, 21 and 23 K2, yfd, K2, sl 2 as if to K2tog, K1, p2sso, K2, *yfd, K1, yfd, K2, sl 2 as if to K2tog, K1, p2sso, K2, rep from * to last 2 sts, yfd, K2.
Row 24 P to end.
These 24 rows form the patt.
Rep them 9 times more, then work rows 1 to 18 again. Cast off loosely.

FRILLS (alike)

With RS facing, join on yarn and K up 50 sts along one end.
P 1 row.
Inc row K1, (puk, K1) to end. 99 sts.
Beg with a P row, work 3 rows st st.
Rep last 4 rows once more. 197 sts.
K 1 row. Cast off knitwise.

TO FINISH

Block knitting to size (see designer's tip), omitting the frills. Sew in the ends.

designer's tip

This lace pattern has a tendency to ruche and requires wet blocking. To ensure a straight, neat edge it is recommended that you use blocking wires to block your knitting (see page 129). Let the scarf dry completely before removing the pins and wires.

project 8: wrap

A sumptuous wrap knitted in the softest of yarns. A pretty harebell stitch has been used for the main piece and simple coiled flowers have been added along each end to create a dramatic border.

Pattern

MAIN PIECE

Using 6.5mm (size 10½) needles, cast on 75 sts.
K 1 row.
Work in Harebell patt as follows:
Row 1 (RS) K1, skpo, yfd, *K1, yfd, sl 2 as if to K2tog, K1, p2sso, yfd, rep from * to last 4 sts, K1, yfd, K2tog, K1.
Row 2 and every alt row P to end.
Row 3 K1, skpo, yfd, *K5, yfd, sl 2 as if to K2tog, K1, p2sso, yfd, rep from * to last 8 sts, K5, yfd, K2tog, K1.
Row 5 As row 3.
Row 7 K3, *yfd, skpo, K1, K2tog, yfd, K3, rep from * to end.
Row 8 P to end.
These 8 rows form the patt.
Rep them 32 times more, then work row 1 again.
Cast off loosely knitwise.

FLOWERS (make 18)

Using 4.5mm (size 7) needles, cast on 51 sts.
K 1 row.
Beg with a K row, work 4 rows st st.
Dec row (K1, K2tog) to end.
P 1 row.
Cast off, working K2tog across the row.

YOU WILL NEED

- 175g (6¼oz) mohair yarn in oyster for wrap
- 50g (1¾oz) mohair yarn in oyster for flowers
- 6.5mm (size 10½) knitting needles for wrap
- 4.5mm (size 7) knitting needles for flowers
- Blocking wires

SIZE

56 x 150cm (22 x 59in)

TENSION

2 patt reps (16 sts) to 12.5cm (5in)
2 patt reps (16 rows) to 9cm (3½in)

TO FINISH

Block wrap to size using blocking wires (see page 129). Sew in the ends. Let flowers coil, then sew nine flowers to each end of the wrap.

project 9: evening bag

A luxurious evening bag made from silk fabric and covered with a delicate mohair lace design. Beaded handles and ribbon flowers add that extra touch of elegance.

designer's tip

To make a ribbon flower cut an 11cm (4½in) length of 22mm- (¾in-) wide wired ribbon and tie a knot at one end. At the other end, pull out the wire along one edge, easing the ribbon along towards the knot so that the ribbon forms ruffles. Continue until the length of ribbon is completely gathered. Wind the wire around the knot to secure, then trim the end. Fold back the flat end and gently open out the flower.

YOU WILL NEED

- 25g (1oz) fine mohair in pale pink
- 4mm (size 6) knitting needles
- Silk dupion fabric for inner bag
- Needle and matching sewing thread
- Pair of metal bag handles for beading 11cm (4½in) wide x 9cm (3½in) high
- 40 x 12mm (½in) diameter beads with a large hole
- 12 ribbon flowers (see designer's tip)

SIZE

15 x 18cm (6 x 7in) excluding handles

TENSION

1 patt rep (14 sts) to 6cm (2½in)
2 patt reps (24 rows) to 7.5cm (3in)

Pattern

BACK AND FRONT (alike)

Using 4mm (size 6) needles, cast on 43 sts loosely.

Work in Cockleshell Lace patt as follows:

Row 1 (RS) *K1, yfd, K5, sl 2 as if to K2tog, K1, p2sso, K5, yfd, rep from * to last st, K1.

Row 2 and every alt row K to end.

Row 3 *K2, yfd, K4, sl 2 as if to K2tog, K1, p2sso, K4, yfd, K1, rep from * to last st, K1.

Row 5 *K3, yfd, K3, sl 2 as if to K2tog, K1, p2sso, K3, yfd, K2, rep from * to last st, K1.

Row 7 *K4, yfd, K2, sl 2 as if to K2tog, K1, p2sso, K2, yfd, K3, rep from * to last st, K1.

Row 9 *K5, yfd, K1, sl 2 as if to K2tog, K1, p2sso, K1, yfd, K4, rep from * to last st, K1.

Row 11 *K6, yfd, sl 2 as if to K2tog, K1, p2sso, yfd, K5, rep from * to last st, K1.

Row 12 K to end.

These 12 rows form the patt.

Rep them twice more, then work rows 1 to 11 again.

Cast off loosely knitwise.

TO FINISH

Block knitting to size. Join side seams.

INNER BAG

From silk fabric cut:
Outer piece (cut 1) 20 x 30cm (8 x 12in)
Lining (cut 1) 20 x 30cm (8 x 12in)
Handle strips (cut 4) 4 x 5cm (1½ x 2in)

Fold each handle strip in half lengthways with right sides together; stitch the long edge 1cm (⅜in) from the raw edges. Trim seam and turn to right side. Press with seam in centre. Trim off 2mm (1⁄16in) all around the lining piece. Fold outer piece in half widthways, right sides together, and pin. Sew side seams 1.5cm (⅝in) from raw edges. Trim corners. Press seams open, then turn to right side. Press 1.5cm (⅝in) to wrong side along top edge.

Fold lining piece in half widthways, right sides together, and pin. Join side seams 1.5cm (⅝in) from raw edges. Trim corners and press seams open. Press 1.5cm (⅝in) to wrong side along top edge. Thread 20 beads onto each handle. Fold handle strips around bars of handles, with seam on inside, and pin the ends together. Position handle strips centrally on each short edge of outer piece, with the raw edges level.

Insert lining inside bag, with wrong sides together and seams matching. Pin along top edge, enclosing the handle strips. Sew along top edge, stitching through all layers of fabric to secure handles. Pin top edge of knitted pieces around top of bag, then slip stitch in place. Sew ribbon flowers evenly around top edge.

project 10: pillow cover

This pretty pillow is made by slipping a knitted lacy cover over a silk pillow. A luxurious feather trim finishes the open edge to add a touch of frivolity!

Pattern

TO MAKE (made in one piece)
Using 3.25mm (size 3) needles, cast on 181 sts.
Work in Horseshoe patt as follows:
Row 1 (RS) K2tog,*K4, yfd, K1, yfd, K4, sl 2 as if to K2tog, K1, p2sso, rep from * to end, finishing last rep skpo.
Row 2 and every alt row P to end.
Row 3 K2tog, *K3, (yfd, K3) twice, sl 2 as if to K2tog, K1, p2sso, rep from * to end, finishing last rep skpo.
Row 5 K2tog, *K2, yfd, K5, yfd, K2, sl 2 as if to K2tog, K1, p2sso, rep from * to end, finishing last rep skpo.
Row 7 K2tog, *(K1, yfd) twice, skpo, K1, K2tog, (yfd, K1) twice, sl 2 as if to K2tog, K1, p2sso, rep from * to end, finishing last rep skpo.
Row 9 K2tog, *yfd, K3, yfd, sl 2 as if to K2tog, K1, p2sso, rep from * to end, finishing last rep skpo.
Row 10 P to end.
These 10 rows form the patt.
Rep them 9 times more.
K 2 rows. Cast off loosely.

YOU WILL NEED

- 50g (1¾oz) 3-ply yarn in pink
- 3.25mm (size 3) long knitting needles or circular needle
- 70cm (27½in) feather trim
- Needle and matching sewing thread
- 30 x 40cm (12 x 16in) silk pillow
- Blocking wires

SIZE
25 x 30cm (10 x 12in)

TENSION
1 patt rep (12 sts) to 4cm (1½in)
2 patt reps (20 rows) to 5cm (2in)

TO FINISH

Block knitting to size using blocking wires (see page 129). Sew in the ends. Join centre back seam, then with seam at centre back, join lower edge seam. Press seams, then turn cover to right side. Sew feather trim around top edge. Slip cover over silk pillow.

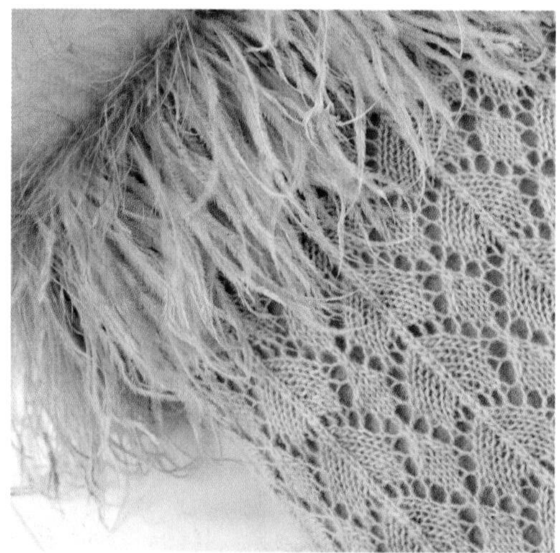

lesson 15 lace edgings

Lace edgings can be worked vertically or horizontally and in many different patterns, both flat and fluted. They can be worked on stitches picked up from the edge of a knitted piece, or knitted separately and slip stitched in place. Outer edges can be curved or pointed, and corners turned with a seamless mitred effect.

Worked in crisp cotton, they make perfect trimmings for bed linens. Bolder yarns are better for trimming soft furnishings – a cushion cover, for example. Vertical borders can be sewn to finished edges – try more than one border for added decorative impact.

A wide, whisper-soft lace edging perfectly frames a baby's blanket or shawl, while narrower edgings add finishing touches to welts, collars, bands or cuffs on knitted garments.

Lace edges can be taken a creative step further. Beads add extra decorative detailing, either threaded onto the yarn and knitted in or sewn on to embellish the finished piece. A row of eyelets along the inner side of a lace edging can be threaded with narrow ribbon. The decorative options are endless – a narrow edging can even be coiled and stitched to make a unique decorative corsage, colour-coordinated and decorated to complement a special outfit.

Edging patterns

Points and scallops on edgings are worked by increasing stitches followed by a group decrease – usually worked by binding the stitches. This detailed shaping doesn't always read clearly on a charted pattern; therefore, the edgings in this chapter have written pattern instructions along with two samples of the edging, one showing the knitting on the needle, the other a close-up of how the edging will look when it is hanging (with the exception of the ribbed flounce, which is knitted horizontally).

Practice pattern

Use this pattern to work through the step-by-step exercise overleaf to make the sample shown.

Pattern

Row 1 (RS) Sl 1, K2, (ytrn, K2tog) twice, K1.
Row 2 K2, (work K1 and P1 into double loop, K1) twice, K2. 10 sts.
Row 3 Sl 1, K to end.
Row 4 K to end.
Row 5 Sl 1, K2, (ytrn, K2tog) 3 times, K1. 13 sts.
Row 6 K2, (work K1 and P1 into double loop, K1) 3 times, K2.
Rows 7 and 8 As rows 3 and 4.
Row 9 As row 3.
Row 10 Cast off 5, K7. 8 sts.
These 10 rows form the patt.

pointed lace

This sample shows four pattern repeats.
Worked vertically on 8 stitches.

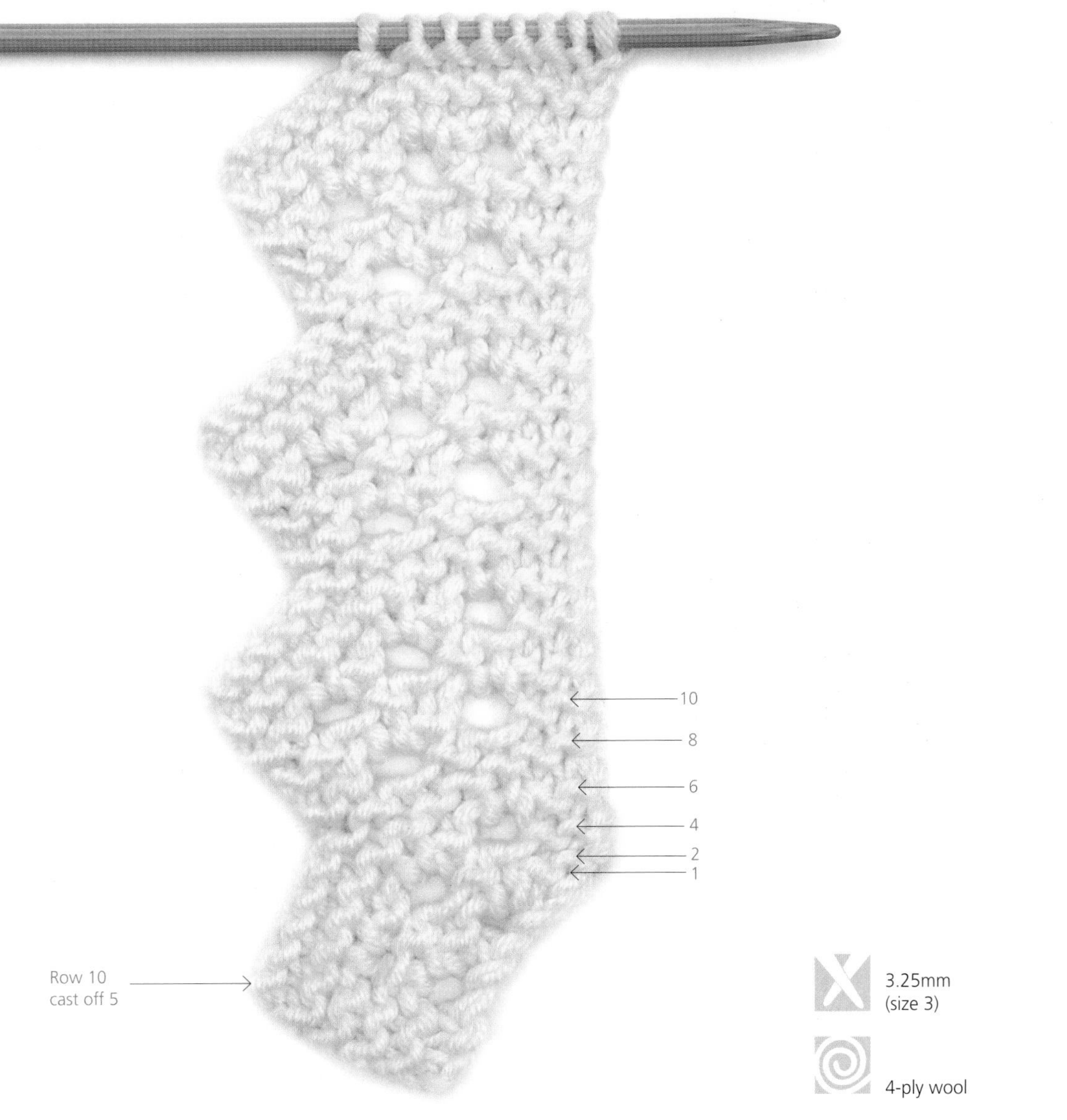

3.25mm
(size 3)

4-ply wool

double increase

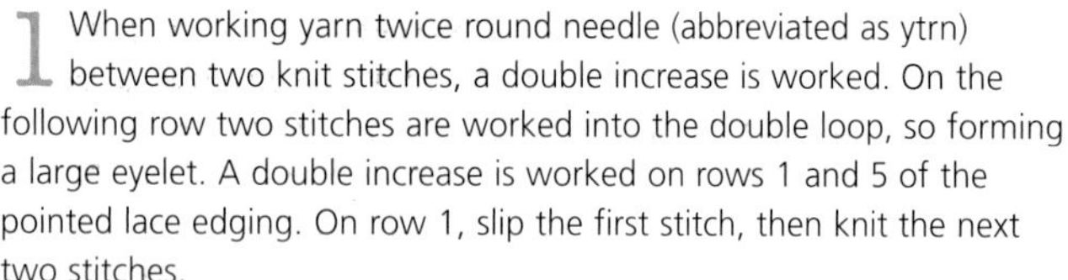

1 When working yarn twice round needle (abbreviated as ytrn) between two knit stitches, a double increase is worked. On the following row two stitches are worked into the double loop, so forming a large eyelet. A double increase is worked on rows 1 and 5 of the pointed lace edging. On row 1, slip the first stitch, then knit the next two stitches.

2 The yarn will be at the back of the knitting. Bring the yarn to the front then around the needle to the front again, so forming the first part of the double loop.

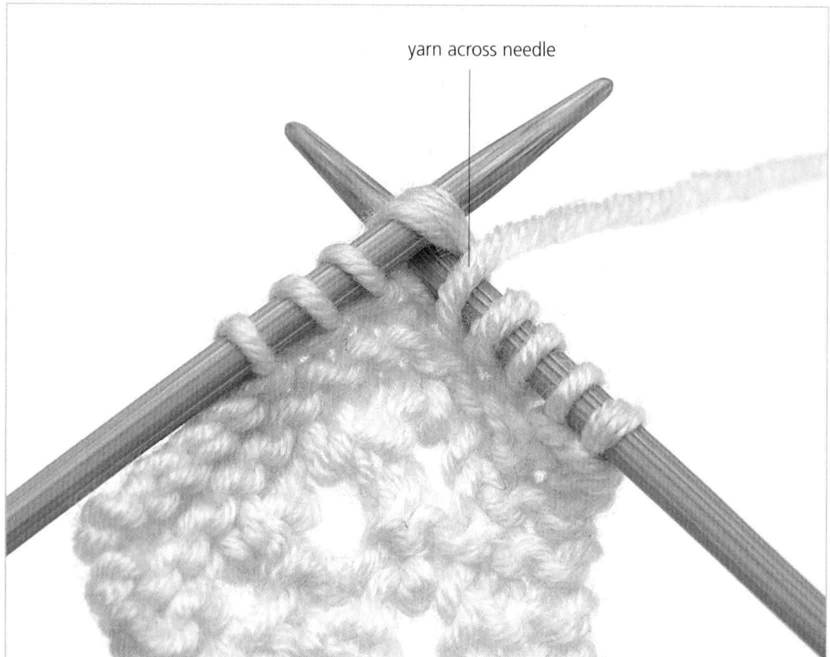

3 Knit the next two stitches together (abbreviated as K2tog). The yarn will lie across the right-hand needle from front to back, so forming the second part of the double loop.

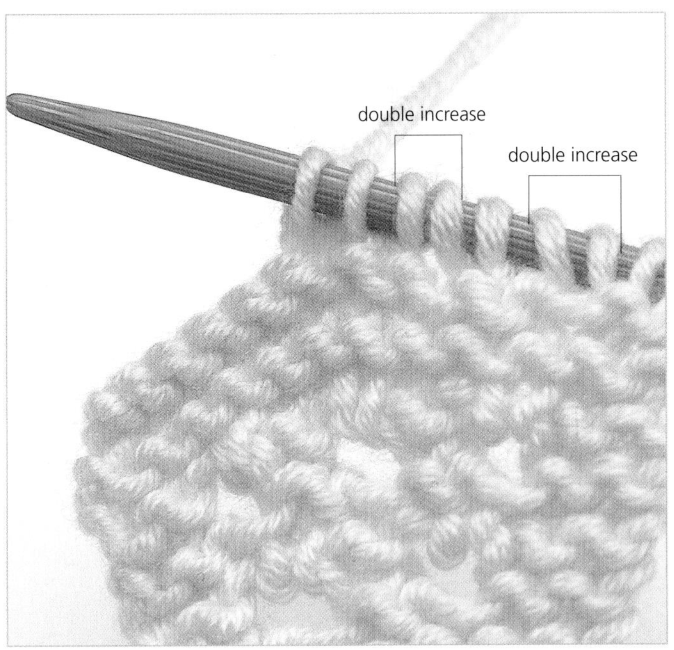

4 Repeat steps 2 and 3 again to form the second double increase – the second large eyelet – then knit the last stitch.

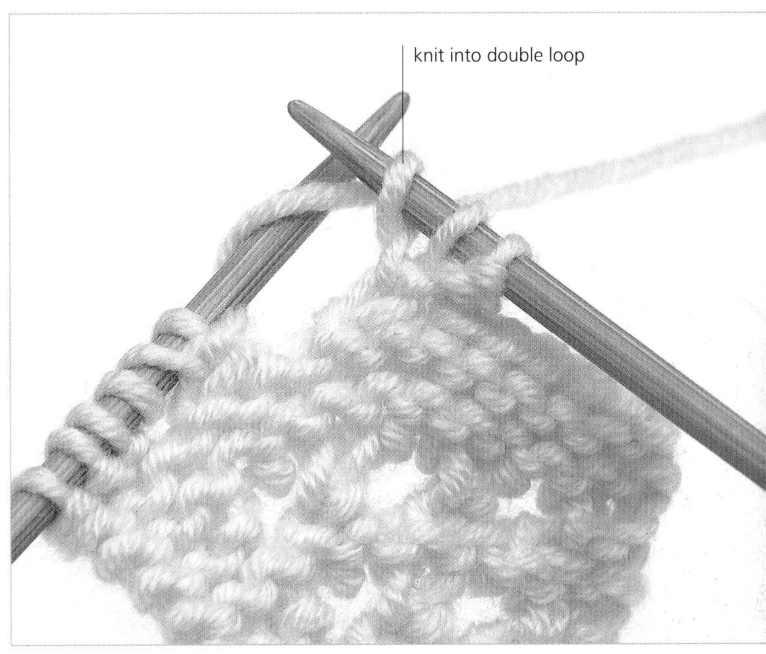

5 On the next row, row 2, two stitches are worked into the double loop. Knit the first two stitches, then knit the double loop but do not slip the loop off the left-hand needle – first stitch worked.

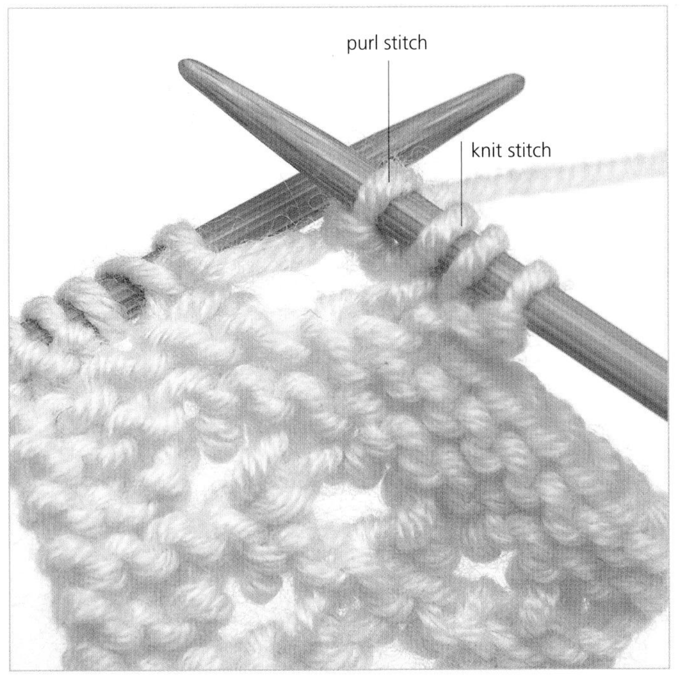

6 Now purl into the double loop and slip the double loop from the left-hand needle – second stitch worked and double loop completed. Pattern to the end of the row. Each double increase is followed by a single decrease – knit two together. Therefore, one stitch is made on each repeat, on row 1 there are two double loops, on row 2 there will be two extra stitches.

scallops

This sample shows four pattern repeats. Worked vertically on 8 stitches.

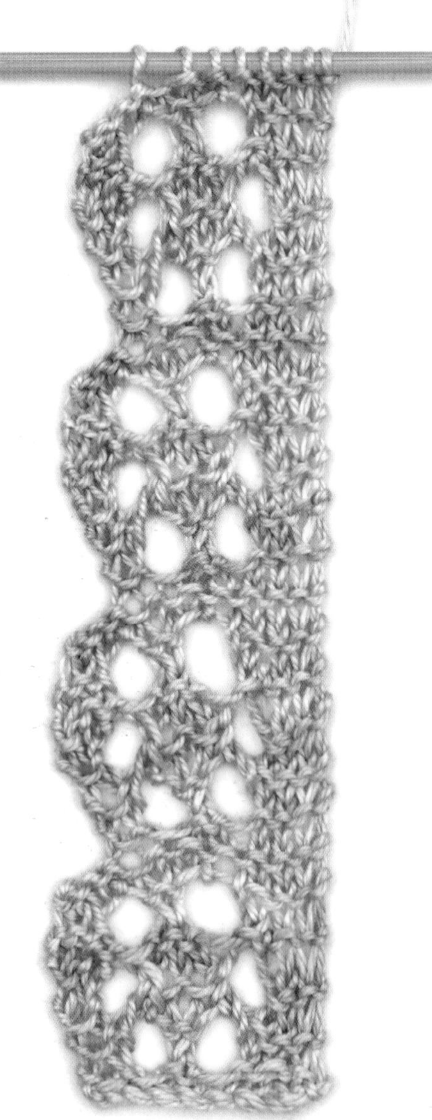

3.25mm (size 3)

4-ply cotton

Pattern

Row 1 (RS) Sl 1, K to end.
Row 2 K to end.
Row 3 Sl 1, K3, ytrn, K2tog, ytrn, K2. 11 sts.
Row 4 K2, work P1 and K1 into double loop, K1, work K1 and P1 into double loop, K4.
Row 5 Sl 1, K to end.
Row 6 K2, ytrn, skpo, K1, K2tog, ytrn, skpo, K2. 12 sts.
Row 7 Sl 1, K2, work P1 and K1 into double loop, K3, work K1 and P1 into double loop, K2.
Row 8 K to end.
Row 9 Sl 1, K2, K2tog, ytrn, sl 2 as if to K2tog, K1, p2sso, ytrn, (K2tog) twice. 11 sts.
Row 10 K2, work P1 and K1 into double loop, K1, work K1 and P1 into double loop, K4.
Row 11 Sl 1, K to end.
Row 12 Slipping first st, cast off 3, K to end. 8 sts.
These 12 rows form the patt.

bobbles and lace

This sample shows five pattern repeats. Worked vertically on 10 stitches.

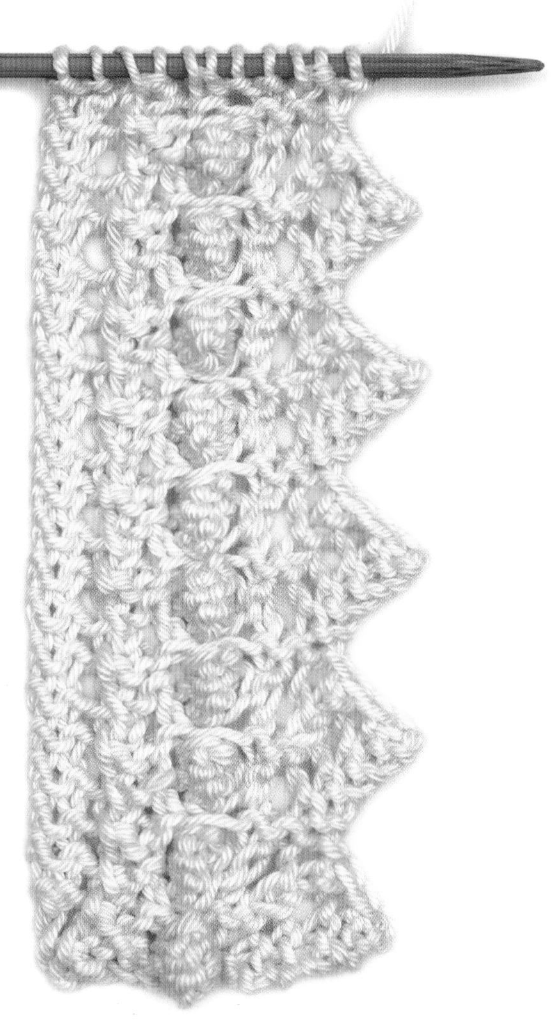

3.25mm (size 3)

4-ply cotton

Pattern

Row 1 (WS) K2, yfd, sl 1, K2tog, psso, yfd, K3, yfd, K2. 11 sts.
Row 2 K4, MB-3, P2, K4.
Row 3 K2, yfd, skpo, K2tog, K3, yfd, K2.
Row 4 K5, yfd, K1, P1, K4. 12 sts.
Row 5 K2, yfd, sl 1, K2tog, psso, yfd, K3, yfd, K2tog, yfd, K2. 13 sts.
Row 6 K6, MB-3, P2, K4.
Row 7 K2, yfd, skpo, K2tog, K3, yfd, K2tog, yfd, K2.
Row 8 Cast off 4, K2, yfd, K1, P1, K4. 10 sts.
These 8 rows form the patt.

ribbed flounce

This sample shows two pattern repeats. Worked horizontally on a multiple of 18 stitches plus 1, reducing to a multiple of 14 stitches plus 1.

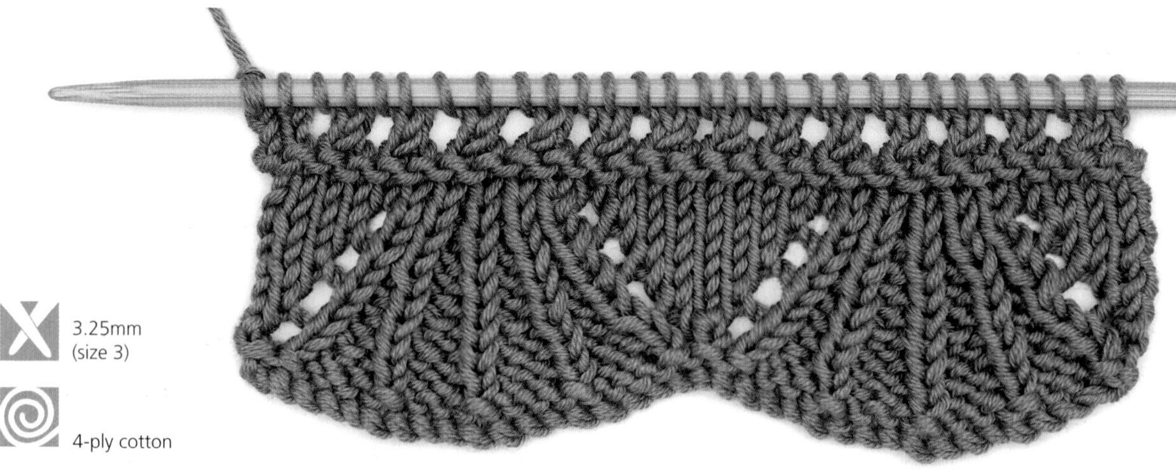

3.25mm (size 3)

4-ply cotton

Ribbon trim
Thread a length of narrow satin ribbon through the row of eyelets for added interest.

Pattern

Row 1 (RS) P to end.
Row 2 P2, *K3, (P1, K3) 3 times, P3, rep from * to end, finishing last rep P2.
Row 3 K1, *yfd, K1, P2tog, P1, (K1, P3) twice, K1, P1, P2tog, K1, yfd, K1, rep from * to end.
Row 4 P3, *K2, P1, (K3, P1) twice, K2, P5, rep from * to end, finishing last rep P3.
Row 5 K2, *yfd, K1, P2, (K1, P1, P2tog) twice, K1, P2, K1, yfd, K3, rep from * to end, finishing last rep K2.
Row 6 P4, *K2, (P1, K2) 3 times, P7, rep from * to end, finishing last rep P4.
Row 7 K3, *yfd, K1, P2tog, (K1, P2) twice, K1, P2tog, K1, yfd, K5, rep from * to end, finishing last rep K3.
Row 8 P5, *K1, (P1, K2) twice, P1, K1, P9, rep from * to end, finishing last rep P5.
Row 9 K4, *yfd, K1, P1, (K1, P2tog) twice, K1, P1, K1, yfd, K7, rep from * to end, finishing last rep K4.
Row 10 P6, *K1, (P1, K1) 3 times, P11, rep from * to end, finishing last rep P6.
Row 11 K5, *(skpo) twice, K1, (K2tog) twice, K9, rep from * to end, finishing last rep K5.
4 sts have been decreased on each repeat.
Rows 12 and 13 K to end.
Row 14 P2, *yrn, P2tog, rep from * to last st, P1.
Row 15 K to end.
Cast off knitwise.

wave edging

This sample shows three pattern repeats.
Worked vertically on 16 stitches.

Pattern

Row 1 (RS) Sl 1, (K5, yfd) twice, K2tog, yfd, K3. 18 sts.
Row 2 and every alt row K3, P to last 3 sts, K3.
Row 3 Sl 1, K6, ssk2po, K2, (yfd, K2tog) twice, K2. 16 sts.
Row 5 Sl 1, K5, K2tog, K2, (yfd, K2tog) twice, K2. 15 sts.
Row 7 Sl 1, K4, K2tog, K2, (yfd, K2tog) twice, K2. 14 sts.
Row 9 Sl 1, K3, K2tog, K2, (yfd, K2tog) twice, K2. 13 sts.
Row 11 Sl 1, K2, K2tog, K2, yfd, K1, yfd, K2tog, yfd, K3. 14 sts.
Row 13 Sl 1, K5, yfd, K3, yfd, K2tog, yfd, K3. 16 sts.
Row 14 K3, P to last 3 sts, K3.
These 14 rows form the patt.

3.25mm (size 3)

4-ply cotton

Special abbreviation

ssk2po = Slip 2 sts one at a time knitwise, insert left-hand needle in the front of these sts, K2tog, slip resulting st onto left-hand needle, slip next st over it, then slip it back onto right-hand needle.

project 11: shrug

An exquisite shrug knitted in a fine mohair yarn and trimmed with a beaded flounce edging – the perfect evening cover-up.

YOU WILL NEED

- 125g (4½oz) fine mohair in mink
- 5mm (size 8) and 5.5mm (size 9) knitting needles
- 3.25mm (size 3) long knitting needles or a circular needle for edging
- 29[31] x 6mm (¼in) round brown beads

SIZE

To suit bust 81–87[91–97]cm (32–34[36–38]in)
Length 37[40]cm (14½[16]in)

TENSION

18 sts and 22 rows to 10cm (4in) over g st

TO FINISH

Join side and underarm seams. Starting and finishing three pattern repeats from each end, sew cast-off edge of edging to fronts and back neck edges. Tie ends to fasten.

Pattern

BACK

Using 5mm (size 8) needles, cast on 91[109] sts.
**K 1 row.
Work in Old Shale patt as follows:
Row 1 (RS) K to end.
Row 2 P to end.
Row 3 *K1, (K2tog) 3 times, (yfd, K1) 5 times, yfd, (K2tog) 3 times, rep from * to last st, K1.
Row 4 K to end.
These 4 rows form the patt.
Rep them twice more.
Change to 5.5mm (size 9) needles and work in g st, as follows:
Work 2 rows.**

Shape for sleeves

Inc 1 st at each end of next and foll 7 alt rows. 107[125] sts.
Work 1 row.
Now cast on 6[8] sts at beg of next 4 rows and 11[13] sts at beg of foll 2 rows. 153[183] sts.
Cont without shaping until work measures 37[40]cm (14½[16]in), ending with WS facing. Cast off loosely.

LEFT FRONT

Using 5mm (size 8) needles, cast on 37 sts.
Work as given for back from ** to **.

Shape for sleeve and front edge

Inc 1 st at beg of next and foll 7 alt rows *at the same time* dec 1 st at end of next and every foll 6th row. 42 sts.
Work 1 row.
Cont to dec 1 st at end of every 6th row, cast on 6[8] sts at beg of next and foll alt row and 11[13] sts at beg of foll alt row. 64[70] sts.
Keeping sleeve edge straight, cont to dec at front edge on every 6th row until 57[62] sts rem. Cont without shaping until work measures 37[40]cm (14½[16]in), ending at sleeve edge.
Cast off loosely.

RIGHT FRONT

Using 5mm (size 8) needles, cast on 37 sts.
Work as given for back from ** to **.

Shape for sleeve and front edge

Inc 1 st at end of next and foll 7 alt rows *at the same time* dec 1 st at beg of next and every foll 6th row. 42 sts.
Work 2 rows.
Cont to dec 1 st at beg of every 6th row, cast on 6[8] sts at beg of next and foll alt row and 11[13] sts at beg of foll alt row. 64[70] sts.
Keeping sleeve edge straight, cont to dec at front edge on every 6th row until 57[62] sts rem. Cont without shaping until work measures 37[40]cm (14½[16]in), ending at front edge.
Cast off loosely.

SLEEVE EDGINGS (alike)

Join upper sleeve and shoulder seams. With RS facing, using 3.25mm (size 3) needles, join on yarn and K up 54[62] sts evenly along sleeve edge, K 5 rows. Cast off.

Brackets
Figures in square brackets [ ] refer to larger sizes; where there is only one set of figures, this applies to all sizes.

EDGING
Thread 29[31] beads onto a ball of yarn (see page 133).
Using 3.25mm (size 3) needles, cast on 541[577] sts.
Work in Ribbed Flounce patt as follows:
Row 1 (RS) P to end.
Row 2 P2, *K3, (P1, K3) 3 times, P3, rep from * to end, finishing last rep P2.
Row 3 K1, *yfd, K1, P2tog, P1, (K1, P3) twice, K1, P1, P2tog, K1, yfd, K1, rep from * to end.
Row 4 P3, *K2, P1, (K3, P1) twice, K2, P5, rep from * to end, finishing last rep P3.
Row 5 K2, *yfd, K1, P2, (K1, P1, P2tog) twice, K1, P2, K1, yfd, K3, rep from * to end, finishing last rep K2.
Row 6 P4, *K2, (P1, K2) 3 times, P7, rep from * to end, finishing last rep P4.
Row 7 K3, *yfd, K1, P2tog, (K1, P2) twice, K1, P2tog, K1, yfd, K2, B1, K2, rep from * to end, finishing last rep K3.
Row 8 P5, *K1, (P1, K2) twice, P1, K1, P9, rep from * to end, finishing last rep P5.
Row 9 K4, *yfd, K1, P1, (K1, P2tog) twice, K1, P1, K1, yfd, K7, rep from * to end, finishing last rep K4.
Row 10 P6, *K1, (P1, K1) 3 times, P11, rep from * to end, finishing last rep P6.
Row 11 K5, *(skpo) twice, K1, (K2tog) twice, K9, rep from * to end, finishing last rep K5.
4 sts have been decreased on each repeat.
Rows 12 and 13 K to end.
Row 14 P2, *yrn, P2tog, rep from * to last st, P1.
Row 15 K to end.
Cast off.

project 12: baby's shawl

A fine lace shawl is the perfect gift to welcome a new baby. The inner edge is trimmed with luxurious velvet ribbon and tiny seed beads.

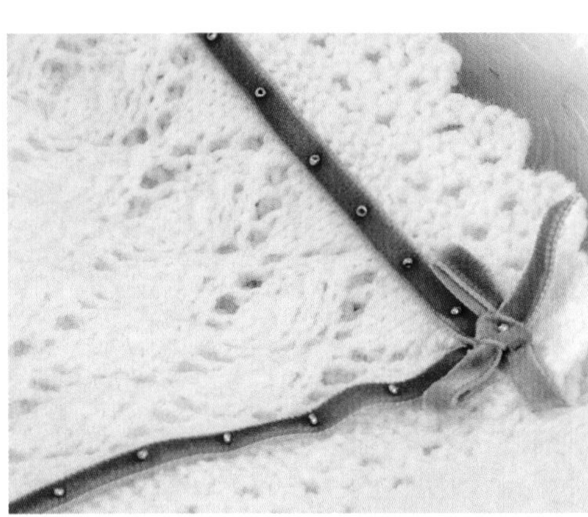

YOU WILL NEED

- 100g (4oz) 3-ply yarn in white
- 3.25mm (size 3) and 4mm (size 6) long knitting needles or circular needle
- 2.5m (2½yd) 7mm- (¼in-) wide velvet ribbon
- Seed beads
- Needle and matching sewing thread

SIZE

46 x 68cm (18 x 27in)

TENSION

2 patt reps (16 sts) to 7.5cm (3in)
2 patt reps (24 rows) to 7cm (2¾in)

TO FINISH

Block knitting to size. Sew in the ends. Sew edging around shawl, easing the fabric at the corners. Join the short ends. Sew on beads to secure a length of ribbon along inner edge of edging, spacing the beads about 2cm (¾in) apart. Make four ribbon bows and sew one to each corner, then trim with a seed bead.

Pattern

MAIN PIECE

Using 4mm (size 6) needles, cast on 131 sts. Work in Fern Leaf patt as follows:

Row 1 (RS) K2, *yfd, K2, sl 1, K2tog, psso, K2, yfd, K1, rep from * to last st, K1.

Row 2 and every alt row P to end.

Row 3 K3, *yfd, K1, sl 1, K2 tog, psso, K1, yfd, K3, rep from * to end.

Row 5 K4, *yfd, sl 1, K2tog, psso, yfd, K5, rep from * to end, finishing last rep K4.

Row 7 K1, K2tog, *K2, yfd, K1, yfd, K2, sl 1, K2tog, psso, rep from * to last 8 sts, K2, yfd, K1, yfd, K2, skpo, K1.

Row 9 K1, K2tog, *K1, yfd, K3, yfd, K1, sl 1, K2tog, psso, rep from * to last 8 sts, K1, yfd, K3, yfd, K1, skpo, K1.

Row 11 K1, K2tog, *yfd, K5, yfd, sl 1, K2tog, psso, rep from * to last 8 sts, yfd, K5, yfd, skpo, K1.

Row 12 P to end.

These 12 rows form the patt.

Rep them 10 times more. Cast off.

EDGING

Using 3.25mm (size 3) needles, cast on 8 sts. Work in Scallops patt as follows:

Row 1 (RS) Sl 1, K to end.

Row 2 K to end.

Row 3 Sl 1, K3, ytrn, K2tog, ytrn, K2. 11 sts.

Row 4 K2, work P1 and K1 into double loop, K1, work K1 and P1 into double loop, K4.

Row 5 Sl 1, K to end.

Row 6 K2, ytrn, skpo, K1, K2tog, ytrn, skpo, K2. 12 sts.

Row 7 Sl 1, K2, work P1 and K1 into double loop, K3, work K1 and P1 into double loop, K2.

Row 8 K to end.

Row 9 Sl 1, K2, K2tog, ytrn, sl 2 as if to K2tog, K1, p2sso, ytrn, (K2tog) twice. 11 sts.

Row 10 K2, work P1 and K1 into double loop, K1, work K1 and P1 into double loop, K4.

Row 11 Sl 1, K to end.

Row 12 Slipping first st, cast off 3, K to end. 8 sts.

These 12 rows form the patt.

Cont in patt until edging, when slightly stretched, fits all round outer edge, ending row 12. Cast off.

project 13: guest towels

Pattern

TO MAKE

Using 3.25mm (size 3) needles, cast on 16 sts.
Work in Wave Edging patt as follows:

Row 1 (RS) Sl 1, (K5, yfd) twice, K2tog, yfd, K3. 18 sts.

Row 2 and every alt row K3, P to last 3 sts, K3.

Row 3 Sl 1, K6, ssk2po, K2, (yfd, K2tog) twice, K2. 16 sts.

Row 5 Sl 1, K5, K2tog, K2, (yfd, K2tog) twice, K2. 15 sts.

Row 7 Sl 1, K4, K2tog, K2, (yfd, K2tog) twice, K2. 14 sts.

Row 9 Sl 1, K3, K2tog, K2, (yfd, K2tog) twice, K2. 13 sts.

Row 11 Sl 1, K2, K2tog, K2, yfd, K1, yfd, K2tog, yfd, K3. 14 sts.

Row 13 Sl 1, K5, yfd, K3, yfd, K2tog, yfd, K3. 16 sts.

Row 14 K3, P to last 3 sts, K3.

These 14 rows form the patt.

Cont in patt until work measures 40cm (16in), ending with a WS row.

Cast off.

designer's tip

Due to the frequent washing of your towels, it is recommended you use a cotton yarn for your edgings. Knit them in a colour to tone with your towels, as here, or be bold and choose a bright contrasting colour.

Add lacy edgings to plain towels for a touch of sophistication. Match the colours to your decor for a totally coordinated look.

YOU WILL NEED

- 50g (1¾oz) 4-ply cotton in brown
- 50g (1¾oz) 4-ply cotton in white
- 3.25mm (size 3) knitting needles
- Guest towels 40cm (16in) wide

SIZE

5.5 x 40cm (2¼ x 16in)

TENSION

33 sts and 38 rows to 10cm (4in) over patt

TO FINISH

Block knitting to size, paying particular attention to the points. Sew in the ends. Pin in position on the towel, then sew across the top and along each end to secure.

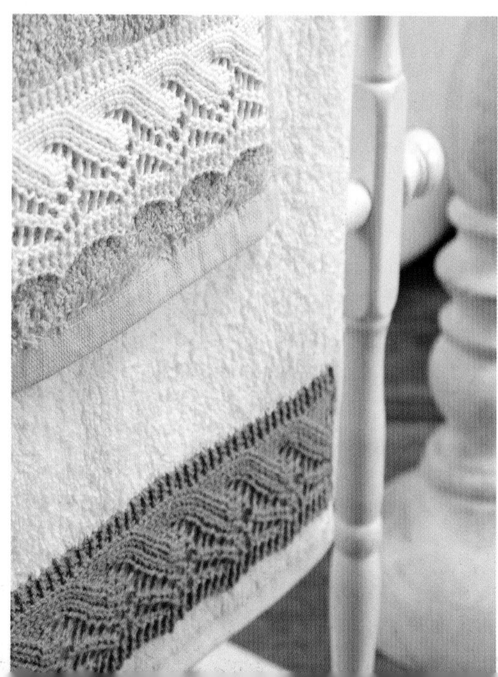

finishing techniques

Blocking and pressing, mattress stitch and backstitch – your handknits deserve a perfect finish. Beads, sequins, plain tassels, beaded tassels, buttons and pompoms – enhance your lacy knits with a touch of texture or surface embellishment.

lesson 16 blocking and pressing

Before you assemble a project it is essential to block and/or press all knitted pieces to size and shape. By using heat, water or steam you can even out any stitch irregularities and help curled edges lie flat, so giving your knitting a professional finish.

Always check your pattern instructions and the yarn label before pressing knitting – a beautiful piece of work can be ruined by using the wrong procedure.

steaming and pressing

Knitting worked in natural fibres, such as wool or cotton, and fairly plain textures can usually be steam pressed – always check your pattern and the yarn label. Pin the knitted pieces out to size on a blocking board using the grid on the fabric as a guide (see Tip, right), then place a clean dry or damp cloth over the fabric and press lightly with an iron set at the recommended temperature – keep the iron moving and don't leave the full weight of the iron on the fabric. Never place an iron directly on a knitted fabric as you may burn the fibres and spoil the knitting.

Bold textures such as bobbles should not be pressed as this will flatten the pattern. Instead, hold a steam iron over the cloth and allow the steam to pass through to the knitted fabric.

After pressing or steaming, remove the cloth and leave the fabric to dry before removing the knitting from the blocking board.

Ribs can lose their elasticity when pressed, so unless they need to match the width of the fabric they are best avoided.

Once the pieces have been joined the seams will need to be pressed. Working on the wrong side, place a dry or damp cloth over the seams and use an iron set at the recommended temperature to lightly press the seams.

Do not press or steam synthetic yarns as the heat and steam will take the 'body' out of the yarn, making it limp – use the wet-spray method instead (see opposite).

Tip

A blocking board is a very useful piece of equipment and is easy to make. Place a sheet of wadding or curtain interlining on a piece of board and cover with gingham fabric. Stretch the fabric, making sure you don't distort the checks, and secure it on the back with tape or staples. Lay the knitting on the blocking board and match the edges to the checks on the fabric to ensure they are straight.

Tip

If you are not sure how to finish your knitting, use your tension piece and the method you think suitable. If you are in any doubt, use the wet-spray method (see opposite).

wet blocking

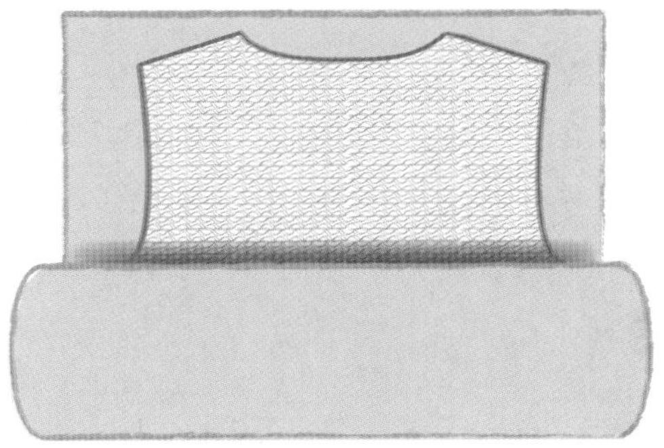

Use this method for yarn that cannot be pressed, textured or fluffy yarns, lace patterns and boldly textured stitch patterns. Wet the knitted sections gently by hand in lukewarm water. Carefully lift the knitting out of the water, gently squeezing out the water as you lift – do not lift it out while it is soaking wet as the weight of the water will stretch the knitting. To remove excess water, lay the knitting on a towel and smooth out flat, then loosely roll up the towel from one end, applying a little pressure.

Unroll the towel and lay the knitting on a blocking board, or for larger pieces, on a towel on a flat surface, such as a worktop or floor. Using long, rustproof glass-headed or knitting pins, pin the knitting out to size and shape, using the grid on the fabric as a guide. Leave to dry thoroughly to 'set' the fabric.

wet-spray blocking

This method is similar to wet blocking and can also be used for yarns that cannot be pressed. Pin the sections of dry knitting out on a blocking board to size and shape, then use a water spray to thoroughly wet the knitting. Press gently with your hands to even out the fabric, then leave to dry before removing the pins.

three-dimensional blocking

For projects worked in the round, use steaming or wet or spray blocking – choose the method most suited to the yarn and stitch pattern. Work on one side at a time, pinning the knitting out to size, taking care not to damage the stitches. Leave to dry, then repeat on the other side.

If you are blocking a small, circular item such as a hat, you can drape the piece over an upturned plastic pot or mixing bowl that is the right size. Wet the knitting, drape it over the form and leave to dry.

blocking all-over lace patterns

When a piece of lace knitting comes off the needles it is invariable crinkly and smaller than it should be. It is essential that lace patterns are blocked and stretched to size – as the knitting is stretched the lace details are opened up, showing each eyelet and intricate detail at its best. Small pieces of lace can be stretched to size and pinned at regular intervals around the outer edge without distorting the edges, but for larger pieces of lace it is advisable to use blocking wires to ensure the edges lie flat and even.

Blocking wires save time and provide an even tension. Thoroughly wet the knitting and remove excess water (see wet blocking, above). Thread a wire through the loops at the edge of the knitting, leaving a few centimetres (inches) at each end free to stretch the lace. Repeat along each edge with more wires. Spread out to size and pin just inside the blocking wires at regular intervals. Let the knitting air dry, then remove the pins and carefully remove the wires.

lesson 17 perfect seams

One of the most important stages of a knitted project is the finishing – a beautifully knitted item can be ruined with poor seams. By following these simple techniques you can be assured of a professional finish every time. Refer to the finishing instructions on your pattern for the order of joining the pieces and, unless otherwise stated, use mattress stitch to join the seams.

mattress stitch

Mattress stitch produces an invisible seam and is worked on the right side of the knitting, making it easy to see how stitches and patterns are aligning.

Tip

If you have used a slubbed or beaded yarn for your project, it may be difficult to join the seams with the same yarn. Try using a plain yarn in a similar weight and matching colour.

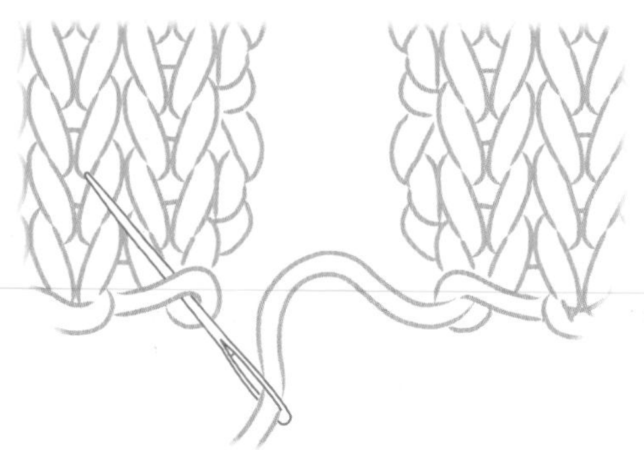

1 Place the two pieces to be joined side by side with the right sides facing and thread the end of yarn from the cast-on onto a tapestry needle. To start the seam, insert the needle from back to front through the corner stitch of the opposite piece.

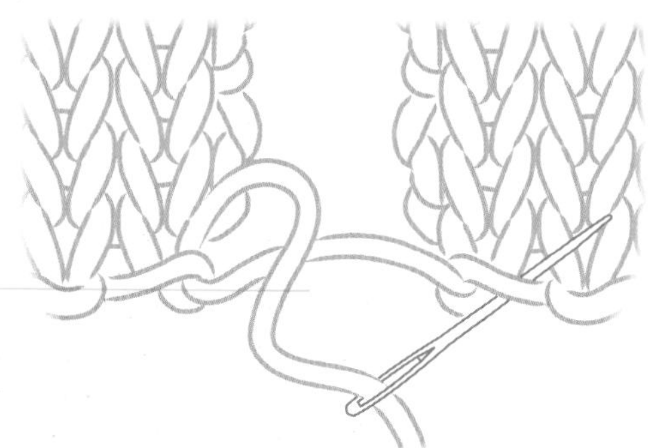

2 Make a figure-of-eight and insert the needle from back to front into the stitch the end of yarn comes from. Pull the yarn through and close the gap between the pieces of knitting.

3 Now insert the needle under the horizontal bar between the first and second stitches on the first piece, then under the horizontal bar between the first and second stitches on the second piece. Continue to work backwards and forwards between the pieces until a few rows have been worked.

4 Draw up the thread to form the seam – do not draw up too tightly or you will distort the fabric. Continue to join the seam in this way. When you reach the end, fasten off neatly by working a few stitches on the wrong side.

backstitch

Backstitch, one of the most commonly used stitches, can also be used to join seams. This is worked with the right sides of the knitting together and the wrong side facing you. To reduce bulk on the seams and to ensure a neat finish, work the stitches near the edge of the knitting.

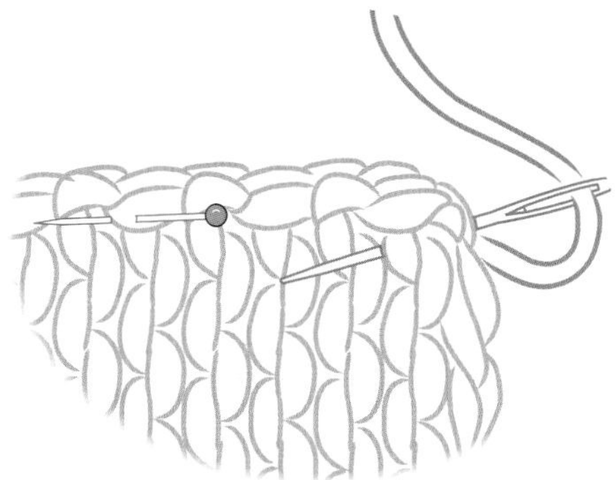

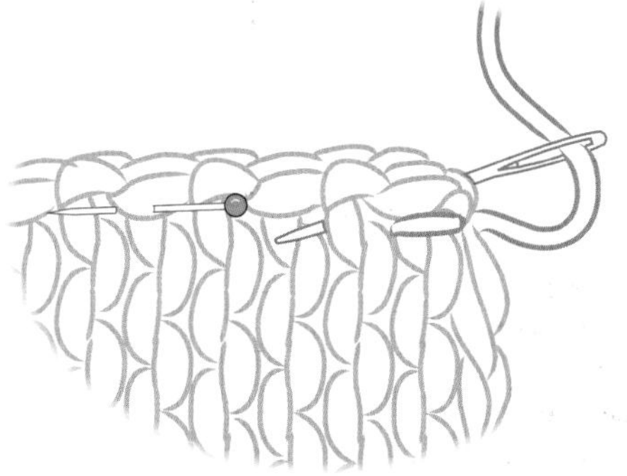

1 Pin the pieces to be joined with the right sides together and the edges level. Thread a tapestry needle with a length of yarn and work two small stitches on the right-hand edge of the back piece of knitting to secure the yarn. Working one stitch in from the edge, insert the needle between the first two rows of knitting from back to front.

2 Take the needle back over the first row and insert it between the first row and the edge and pull the yarn through. Now insert the needle between the second and third rows and bring to the front, drawing the yarn through.

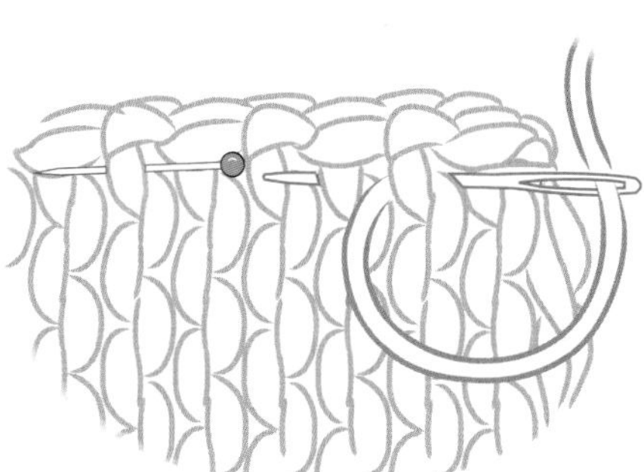

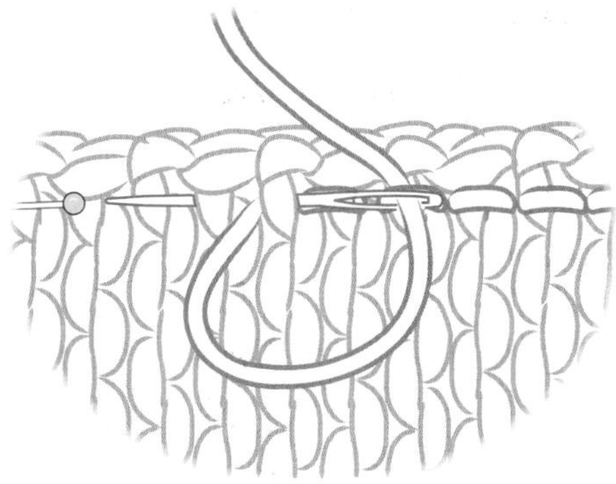

3 Take the needle back over the last row and insert it at the point where the last stitch was worked, then bring it to the front between the next two rows and pull the yarn through.

4 Continue to work in this way, inserting the needle at the point where the last stitch was worked from front to back, then inserting it between the next two rows from back to front. At the end of the seam, work a couple of small stitches to secure the yarn. Cut off the yarn.

lesson 18 adding beads and sequins

Decorative beads and sequins add a new dimension to lacy knits. The embellishments can stand alone, perhaps in a contrasting colour, or be incorporated into the fabric. When using beads, choose carefully, matching them to the weight and type of yarn – too small and they will disappear into the fabric, too heavy and they will make the knitting sag. Depending on your project, you may need to use washable beads.

sewing on beads

Single beads can be scattered over the right side of a knitted piece to add decoration and texture. Using this simple technique, the beads can be added once the design is complete.

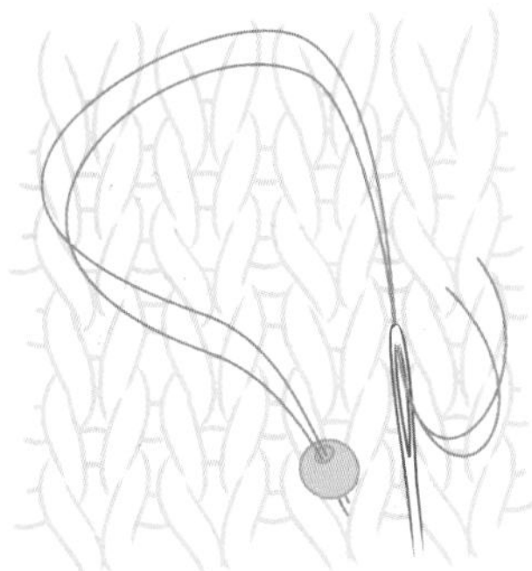

1 Thread a beading needle with a double length of cotton and secure it to the wrong side of the knitting, at the position for the first bead, with a few tiny backstitches. Bring the needle to the right side of the work and thread on a bead.

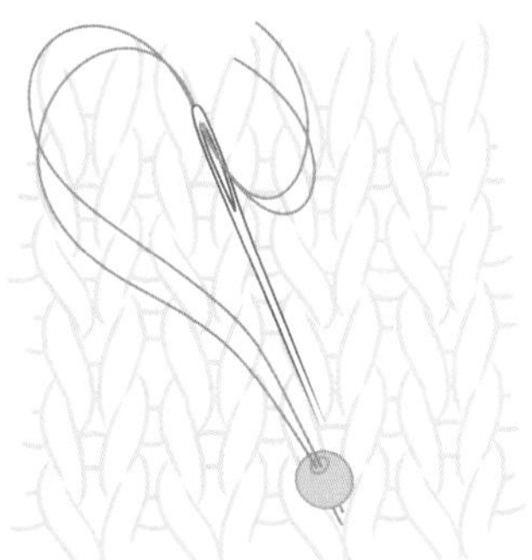

2 Take a small stitch through the knitting, and pull the cotton through until the bead is sitting on the knitted fabric. Bring the needle through to the front again, through the bead, and back through the knitting to secure the bead. Work a few tiny backstitches on the wrong side and fasten off. Continue to sew on beads in this way.

sewing on sequins with a bead

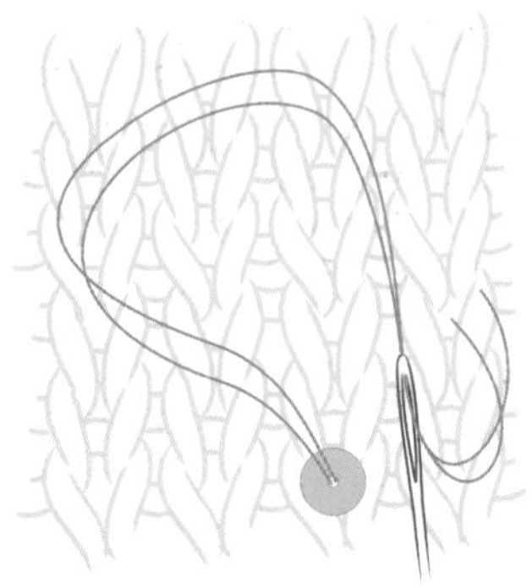

1 Thread a beading needle with a double length of cotton and secure it to the wrong side of the knitting, at the position for the first sequin, with a few tiny backstitches. Bring the needle to the right side of the work and thread on a sequin.

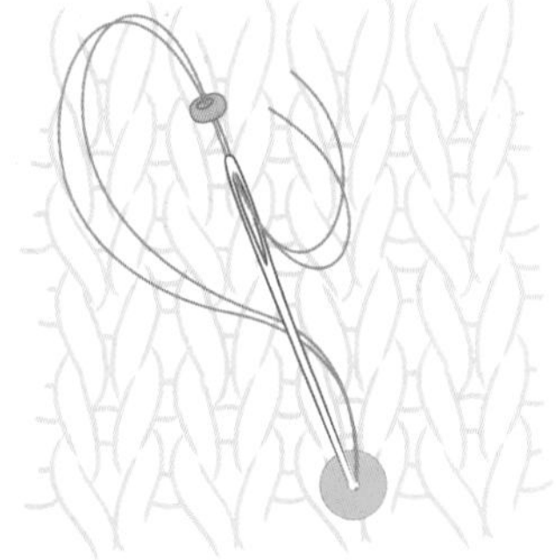

2 Thread a small bead onto the needle, then take the needle back through the hole in the sequin and through the knitting from front to back. Pull the cotton up until the bead is sitting on the sequin. Work a few tiny backstitches on the wrong side and fasten off. Continue to sew on sequins with beads in this way.

threading beads onto yarn

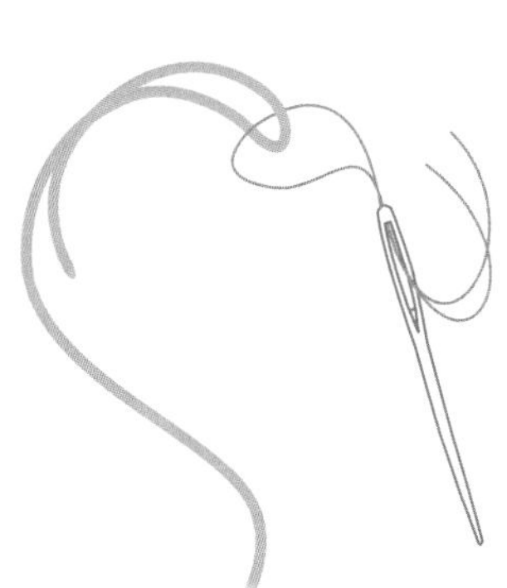

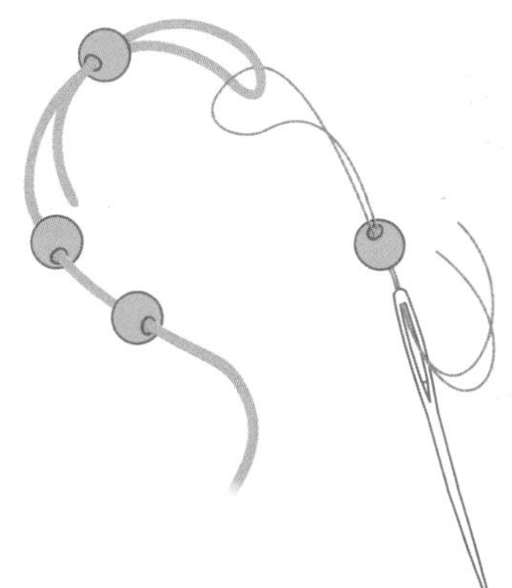

1 Cut a length of sewing cotton and fold it in half. Thread the ends through the eye of a needle. Place the end of the knitting yarn through the loop of the cotton.

2 Thread on a bead, pushing it along the cotton and onto the knitting yarn. Thread on beads in this way until the number of beads required for your project are on the knitting yarn. Remove the yarn from the loop of cotton.

Beads to be threaded onto yarn should have a hole large enough to let the bead move easily along the yarn – if the hole is too small it may fray the yarn. It isn't always possible to thread them directly onto the yarn, as the hole may be too small to take a needle threaded with yarn. If this is the case use a length of sewing cotton – a leader thread – to thread the beads onto the yarn.

knitting in beads

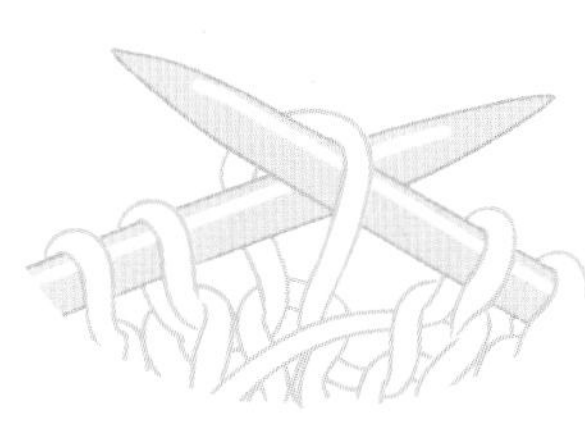

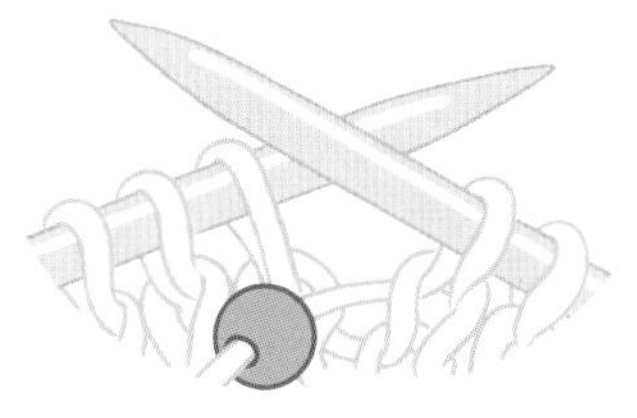

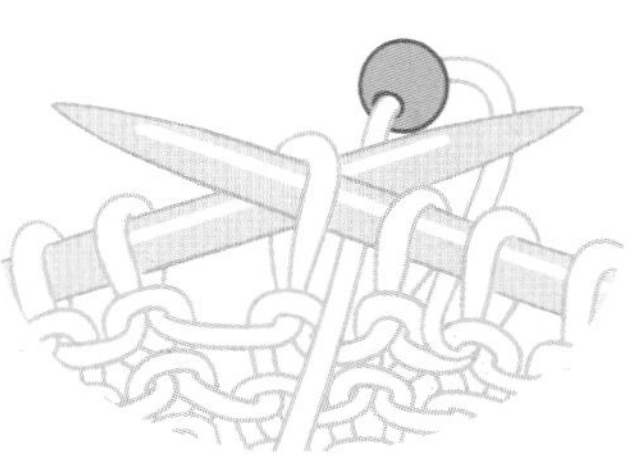

1 On a knit row, knit to the position of the bead, bring the yarn to the front of the work between the needles and slip the next stitch purlwise.

2 Push a bead along the yarn until it is up against the right-hand needle. Take the yarn to the back of the work and knit the next stitch. Continue to place beads in this way as required.

3 On a purl row, purl to the position of the bead, take the yarn to the back between the two needles and slip the next stitch purlwise.

4 Push a bead along the yarn so that it sits behind the slipped stitch. Bring the yarn to the front of the work and purl the next stitch. Continue to place beads in this way as required.

lesson 19 basic tassels

Tassels are an ideal trimming for soft furnishings. Made in beautiful yarns such as wool, cotton, tape or ribbon, they can add a touch of elegance or, in unusual materials such as raffia, leather and torn fabric, a touch of frivolity. Materials can be combined to great effect – to wool or cotton add a silky yarn for a subtle shimmer, or mix lengths of satin or organza ribbon with a ribbon yarn for sheer grandeur.

basic tassel technique

To make a simple tassel you will need yarn or cotton, card, a tapestry needle and sharp scissors.

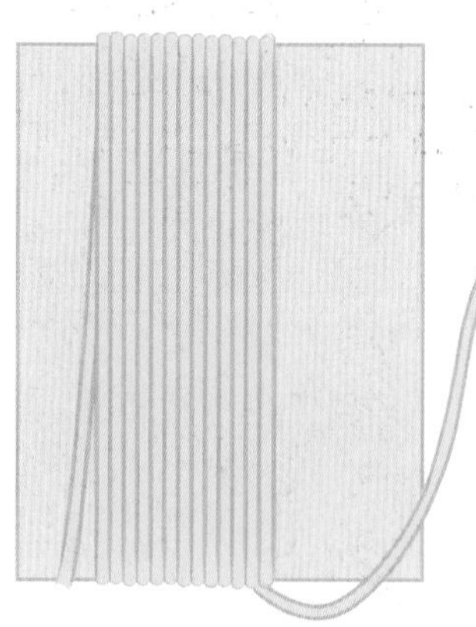

1 Cut a piece of card the required length of the tassel and about 8cm (3in) wide. Hold the card lengthways in one hand and hold the end of the yarn level with the bottom edge. Now wrap the yarn evenly around the card to the thickness required, finishing at the bottom edge. Cut off the yarn.

2 Thread a length of yarn onto the tapestry needle and slip the needle under the loops along the top edge. Remove the needle and tie the ends, gathering the loops on the card loosely together. Do not trim the ends as they can be used to attach the tassel.

3 Cut a long length of yarn. Carefully ease the loops off the card and hold them together. Knot one end of the length of yarn around the tassel about one third down from the top. Then wrap the yarn firmly around the tassel as many times as required to cover the knot.

4 Thread the end of the yarn onto the tapestry needle and take it up through the centre of the tassel. Use sharp scissors to cut through the loops at the bottom of the tassel and to trim the ends.

lesson 20 beaded tassels

Beading can be added to readymade tassels or tassels you have made yourself. For a subtle effect, match the beads to the colour of the tassel, or use clear glass to reflect the light. For a bit of dazzle, use shiny coloured beads or sparkly faceted ones. Choose lightweight beads either all of one kind or mix different types, sizes and colours.

beaded tassel technique

To make a beaded tassel you will need a plain tassel, narrow ribbon, fine sharp needle, beads, tapestry needle and sharp scissors.

1 To make a plain tassel, follow steps 1 and 2 of the basic tassel technique (see left). Tie a short length of yarn around the top to form the tassel shape – the knot will be covered later. Use sharp scissors to cut through the loops at the bottom of the tassel and to trim the ends.

2 Thread a fine sharp needle with a length of thread and knot the end. Bring the needle to the right side of a length of narrow ribbon with the knot against the ribbon. Thread on beads to make a strand about the same length as the tassel fringe.

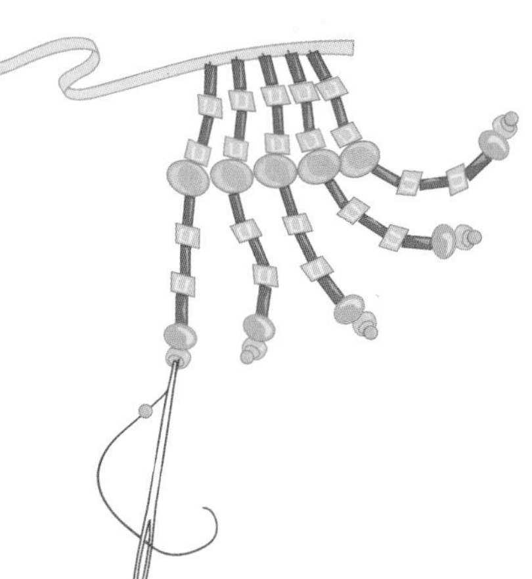

3 Take the thread around the last bead, then back up through the line of beads and secure with a stitch in the ribbon. Repeat until you have enough beaded strands to wrap around the tassel top.

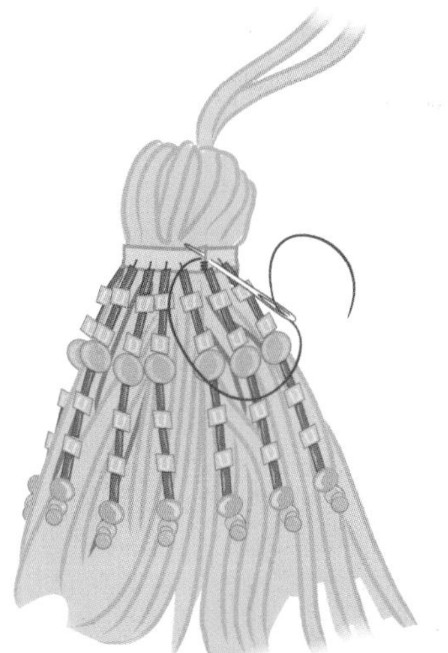

4 Wrap the beaded ribbon around the top of the tassel, covering the length of knotted yarn. Turn in the raw ends and stitch firmly in place with small stitches.

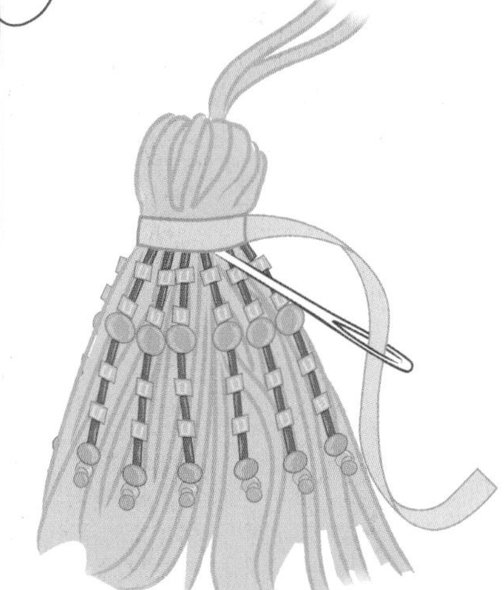

5 To finish, wrap a length of yarn or ribbon around the beaded ribbon to cover the stitching. Secure the end by threading it onto a tapestry needle and passing the needle up through the top. Cut off the end close to the top of the tassel.

lesson

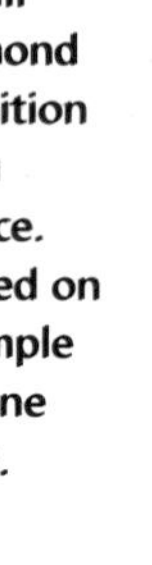

adding buttons

Buttons can be used as simple fastenings or to add a decorative touch. There are so many beautiful buttons available that you will be spoilt for choice. If you are using buttons and buttonholes as a fastening, make sure the button is the right size for the buttonhole – too small and it will keep coming undone; too big and you will stretch the buttonhole. Always start by marking the button positions as stated in the 'Finishing' section of the pattern.

A scattering of buttons will add extra interest to diamond patterns. Plan out the position of the buttons before you start securing them in place. Buttons can be sewn or tied on following one of these simple techniques – choose the one best suited to your design.

buttons with two holes

Straight stitch

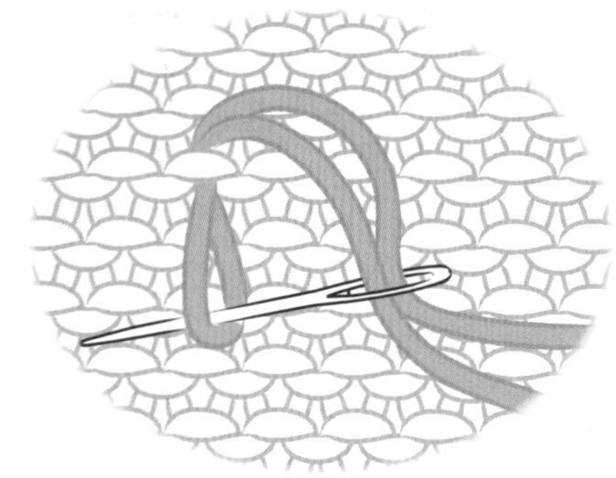

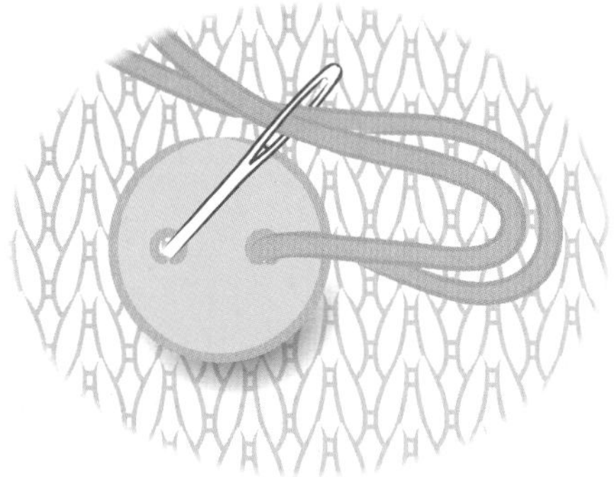

1 Cut a length of yarn or thread, fold it in half and thread the ends through a large-eyed needle. Working on the wrong side of the knitting, insert the needle through the knitting in the marked button position. Pull the ends of the yarn through, then insert the needle through the loop and draw up to secure.

2 Insert the needle from back to front through the knitting, then up through one hole of the button. Take the needle down through the other hole and through the knitting from front to back. Repeat as many times as required, then work a few small stitches on the wrong side to secure.

buttons with two holes

Beaded straight stitch

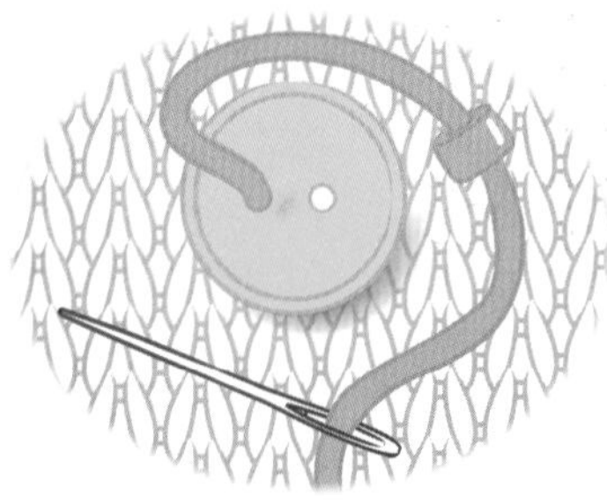

1 Thread a length of yarn or thread through a needle and work a few small stitches on the back of the knitting in the marked button position to secure. Insert the needle from back to front up through the knitting and up through one hole of the button. Now insert the needle through a small bead.

2 Take the needle down through the other hole of the button from front to back. Repeat once more, then work a few small stitches to fasten off.

buttons with two holes

Tied

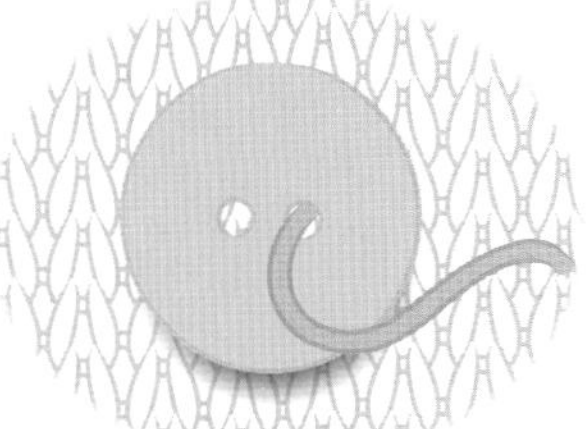

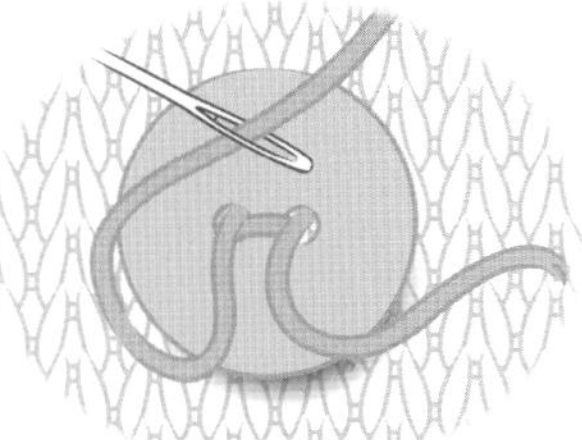

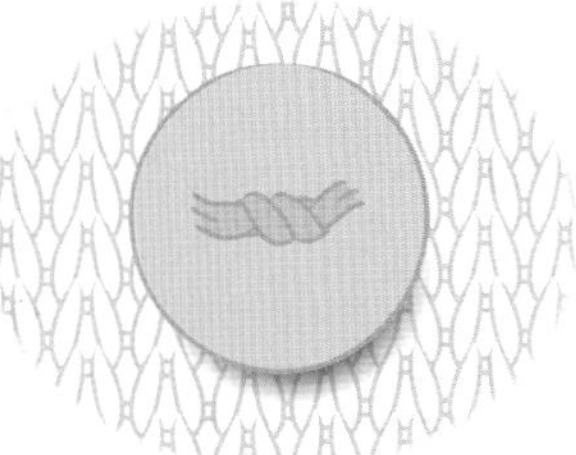

1 Cut a length of yarn and thread one end through a large-eyed needle. Working on the right side, take the needle down through one hole of the button and through the knitting at the marked button position from front to back, leaving a 5cm (2in) end on the right side.

2 Insert the needle up through the knitting and the other hole of the button from back to front, then take the needle down through the first hole and back up through the second hole again.

3 Cut off the yarn, leaving a 5cm (2in) end. Now tie a square knot; take the left end over the right and around, then take the right end over the left and around and pull the ends to secure. Trim the ends as required.

---

buttons with four holes

Cross stitch

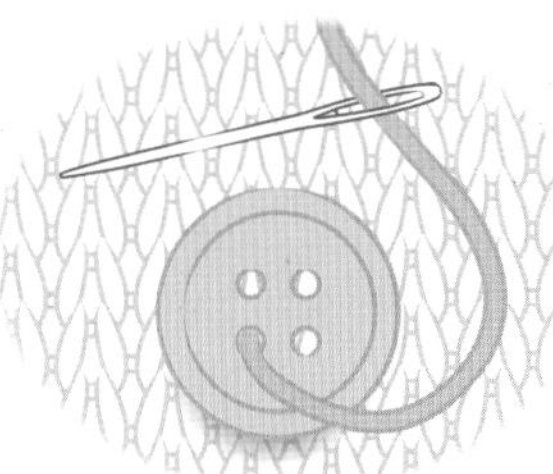

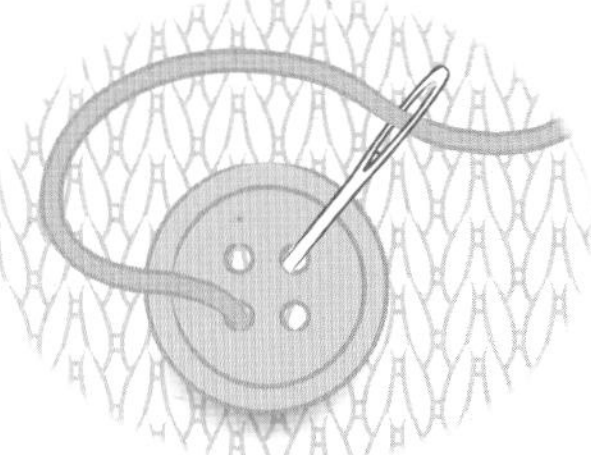

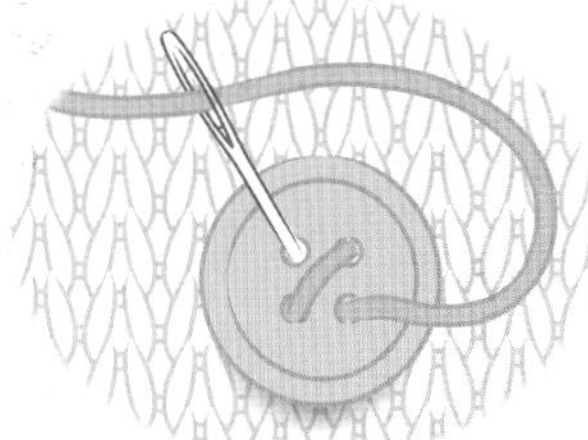

1 Cut a length of yarn and thread one end through a large-eyed needle. Working on the wrong side of the knitting, sew a few small stitches to secure the yarn at the button position. Now take the needle up through the knitting from back to front and through one hole of the button.

2 Lay the button in position on the knitting with the thread at the bottom left, and take the needle down through the hole at top right and through the knitting.

3 Bring the needle up through the knitting and through the hole at bottom right, then down through the hole at top left – this forms the first cross. Work another cross in this way, then fasten off by working a few small stitches on the wrong side of the knitting.

lesson 22 pompoms

Pompoms are so simple to make and are perfect for trimming soft furnishings and garments – see Hat and scarf on page 46. You can add single pompoms to the corners of cushions or dangle them in bunches at just one corner. You can make single-colour pompoms or add in extra yarn colours for multi-coloured variations.

basic pompom technique

To make a pompom you will need yarn, a pair of compasses, a pencil, card and sharp scissors.

1 On the card, use a pencil and a pair of compasses to draw a circle the size of the pompom. Now draw another circle inside it, about a third of the diameter of the first circle. Use the scissors to carefully cut around the pencil lines of the two circles, so forming a ring. Make a second ring in the same way.

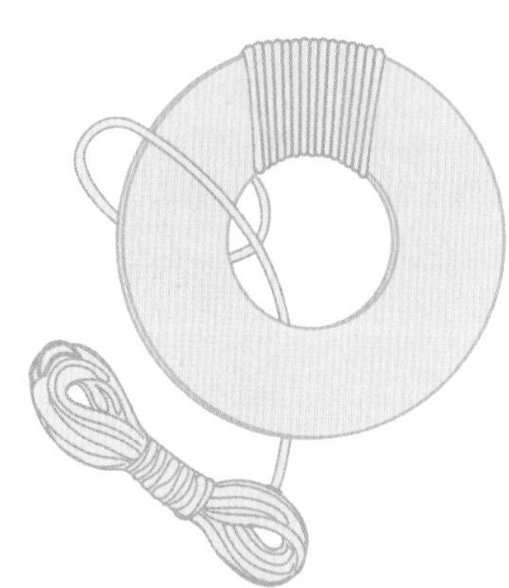

2 With the two rings together, wind yarn evenly around them – don't pull the yarn too tight. Continue to wind yarn until the centre hole is filled.

3 To form the pompom, insert a scissor blade between the card rings and cut the yarn around the outer edges. Slip a length of yarn between the rings and tie it tightly. Pull or tear off the card and fluff out the pompom. Trim any uneven ends, but leave the yarn tie for attaching the pompom to your work.

lesson 23 aftercare essentials

It is important to take care of your finished knits – designs knitted in a quality yarn will last for many years if washed and cared for properly. Follow these simple guidelines to achieve the best results.

machine washing

Before you wash any item check the yarn label for washing instructions. For best results use soapflakes, mild detergent or specially formulated liquids. Many yarns are now machine-washable but do take care to select the correct cycle. To prevent the knitting shrinking or becoming matted or felted, wash on a delicate wool cycle with as little fast-spin action as possible.

hand washing

When washing your knits by hand, use warm water rather than hot and make sure the detergent is completely dissolved before submerging your knits. Handle them gently in the water – do not rub or scrub the knitting or wring it out, as this can felt the fabric. Rinse well to get rid of any soap and squeeze out excess water – never lift a soaking-wet item out of the water or you will stretch the knitting. Gently squeeze the water out as you carefully lift it out of the water. Lay the section out of the water on a surface while you handle the next section.

drying

It is important to remove as much water as possible before laying the knitting out to dry. Lay the item out flat on a towel and roll up from one end, applying a little pressure – the towel will absorb excess water.

Lay the damp item out flat on a dry towel and smooth it gently to size and pat to shape. Let it dry away from direct heat such as sunlight or a radiator and turn it occasionally.

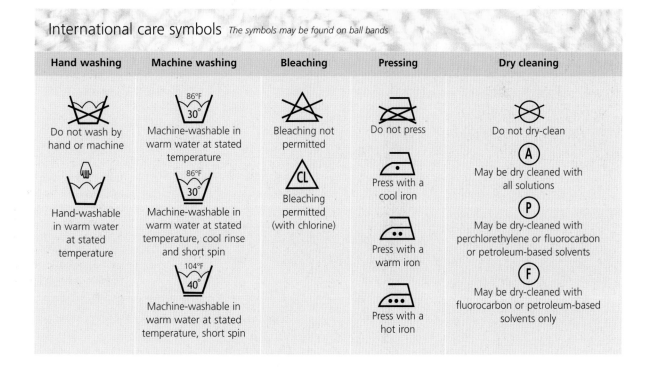

International care symbols *The symbols may be found on ball bands*

Hand washing	Machine washing	Bleaching	Pressing	Dry cleaning
Do not wash by hand or machine	86°F 30° Machine-washable in warm water at stated temperature	Bleaching not permitted	Do not press	Do not dry-clean
Hand-washable in warm water at stated temperature	86°F 30° Machine-washable in warm water at stated temperature, cool rinse and short spin	CL Bleaching permitted (with chlorine)	Press with a cool iron	A May be dry cleaned with all solutions
	104°F 40° Machine-washable in warm water at stated temperature, short spin		Press with a warm iron	P May be dry-cleaned with perchlorethylene or fluorocarbon or petroleum-based solvents
			Press with a hot iron	F May be dry-cleaned with fluorocarbon or petroleum-based solvents only

abbreviations

K
knit

P
purl

st(s)
stitch(es)

st st
stocking stitch

rev st st
reverse stocking stitch

g st
garter stitch

patt
pattern

rep(s)
repeat(s)

cont
continue

beg
beginning

rem
remain(ing)

alt
alternate

foll
following

tog
together

dec
decrease(ing)

inc
increase(ing)

tbl
through back of loop(s)

yfd
yarn forward

yon
yarn over needle

yrn
yarn round needle

yfrn
yarn forward and round needle

ytrn
yarn twice round needle

sl
slip

psso
pass slipped stitch over

p2sso
pass 2 slipped stitches over

skpo
sl 1, K1, pass slipped stitch over

ssk2po
slip 2 sts one at a time knitwise, insert left-hand needle in the front of these sts, K2tog, slip resulting st onto left-hand needle, slip next st over it, then slip it back onto right-hand needle

puk
pick up loop lying between needles and K into back of it

B1 (bead 1)
With yarn at front, slip the next stitch purlwise and push the bead against the right-hand needle, ready to work the next stitch

RS
right side

WS
wrong side

LH
left hand

RH
right hand

in
inch(es)

mm
millimetre(s)

cm
centimetre(s)

yd
yard(s)

m
metre(s)

MB-1 (make bobble 1)
P1, K1, P1, K1 and P1 all into next st, turn and K5; turn and P5; then pass 2nd, 3rd, 4th and 5th sts over first st and off needle – bobble completed

MB-2 (make bobble 2)
P1, K1, P1, K1 and P1 all into next st, take yarn to back, then pass 2nd, 3rd, 4th and 5th sts over first st and off needle – bobble completed

MB-3 (make bobble 3)
K1, P1, K1 and P1 all into next st, turn and K4; turn and P4; then pass 2nd, 3rd and 4th sts over first st and off needle – bobble completed

C4F (Cable 4 front)
slip next 2 sts onto cable needle and leave at front of work, K2, then K sts from cable needle

C4B (Cable 4 back)
slip next 2 sts onto cable needle and leave at back of work, K2, then K sts from cable needle

C6B (Cable 6 back)
slip next 3 sts onto cable needle and leave at back of work, K3, then K sts from cable needle

Chart symbols

□ K on RS rows, P on WS rows

⊡ P on RS rows, K on WS rows

◺ K2tog on RS rows and P2tog on WS rows

◺• K2tog on WS rows and P2tog on RS rows

◹ K2togtbl

△ K3tog

◺ skpo on RS rows and P2togtbl on WS rows

◺• skpo on WS rows

○ yfd, yon, yrn, yfrn

∧ sl 1, K2tog, psso on RS rows

∧• sl 1, K2tog, psso on WS rows

∧| sl 2 as if to K2tog, K1, then p2sso

● **MB-1 (make bobble 1)**
P1, K1, P1, K1 and P1 all into next st, turn and K5; turn and P5; then pass 2nd, 3rd, 4th and 5th sts over first st and off needle – bobble completed

● **MB-2 (make bobble 2)**
P1, K1, P1, K1 and P1 all into next st, take yarn to back, then pass 2nd, 3rd, 4th and 5th sts over first st and off needle – bobble completed

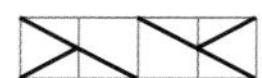

C4F (Cable 4 front)
slip next 2 sts onto cable needle and leave at front of work, K2, then K sts from cable needle

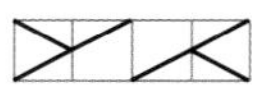

C4B (Cable 4 back)
slip next 2 sts onto cable needle and leave at back of work, K2, then K sts from cable needle

C6B (Cable 6 back)
slip next 3 sts onto cable needle and leave at back of work, K3, then K sts from cable needle

index

Credits

Yarn information

The following Debbie Bliss, Patons, Rowan, Malabrigo and BC Garn yarns have been used for the knitting patterns in this book.

Baby blanket and slippers (Project 1)
Debbie Bliss Cashmerino Aran 55% Merino Wool/33% Microfibre/12% Cashmere 110m/120yd/50g
Debbie Bliss Cashmerino DK 55% Merino Wool/ 33% Microfibre/12% Cashmere 90m/98yd/50g
Debbie Bliss Eco Baby 100% Organic Cotton 125m/136yd/50g

Hat and scarf (Project 2)
Debbie Bliss Rialto DK 100% Merino Wool 105m/114yd/50g

Child's cardi (Project 3)
Debbie Bliss Eco Baby 100% Organic Cotton 125m/136yd/50g

Cushion wraps (Project 4)
Rowan Cotton Glace 100% Cotton 115m/125yd/50g

Jewellery purse (Project 5)
Rowan Siena 100% Mercerised Cotton 140m/153yd/50g

Women's sweaters (Project 6)
Louisa Harding Willow Tweed 40% Alpaca/ 40% Merino Wool/20% Silk 116m/126yd/50g

Scarf (Project 7)
BC Garn Babyalpaca 100% Baby Alpaca 250m/273yd/50g

Wrap (Project 8)
Rowan Kidsilk Aura 75% Kid Mohair/25% Silk 75m/82yd/25g

Evening bag (Project 9)
Rowan Kidsilk Haze 70%Super Kid Mohair/30% Silk 210m/229yd/25g

Pillow cover (Project 10)
Malabrigo Lace 100% Baby Merino Wool 430m/470yd/50g

Shrug (Project 11)
Rowan Kidsilk Haze 70%Super Kid Mohair/30% Silk 210m/229yd/25g

Baby's shawl (Project 12)
Patons Fairytale Dreamtime 3 ply 100% Wool 230m/252yd/50g

Guest towels (Project 13)
BC Garn Allino 50% Cotton/50% Linen 125m/136yd/50g
Patons Cotton 4 ply 100% Cotton 330m/361yd/100g

Go to the websites below to find a mail order stockist or store in your area.
www.patonsyarns.com
www.knitrowan.com
www.debbieblissonline.com
www.louisaharding.co.uk
BC Garn and Malabrigo yarns are available from www.loopknittingshop.com

Acknowledgements

I would to thank the following people for their invaluable contribution in helping me to create this book.

Kate Kirby, Moira Clinch and Katie Crous – it's been a pleasure working with you all again. Jo Bettles for her creative design. Phil Wilkins for the clarity shown in photography of the stitch patterns and the wonderful chapter openers.
Lizzie Orme for photographing the projects so beautifully.
Neal Monk Stevens for the technical illustrations. Marilyn Wilson for her thorough pattern checking. Special thanks to Rowan and Debbie Bliss for their generosity in supplying their gorgeous yarns for some of the projects.